# MORALE
## *Quality of Work Life*

## GEORGE MANNING, 1957–

**Professor of Psychology**
**Northern Kentucky University**

## KENT CURTIS

**Professor of Industrial Technology and Education**
**Northern Kentucky University**

U255

**VistaSystems**
DEVELOPING HUMAN POTENTIAL
*A Division of South-Western Publishing Co.*

62,752

# About
# The
# Authors

Dr. George Manning

Dr. Kent Curtis

George Manning is a professor of psychology and business at Northern Kentucky University. He is a consultant to business, industry, and government; his clients include AT&T, Sun Oil, IBM, Marriott Corporation, United Auto Workers, the Internal Revenue Service, and the National Institutes of Health. He lectures on economic and social issues including quality of work life, work force values, and business ethics. He serves as advisor to such diverse industries and professions as energy, transportation, justice, health, finance, labor, commerce, and the military.

He received graduation honors from George Williams College, the University of Cincinnati, and the University of Vienna. He was selected Professor of the Year at Northern Kentucky University, where his teaching areas include management and organization, organizational psychology, and personal adjustment. He maintains an active program of research and study in organizational psychology. His current studies and interests include the changing meaning of work, leadership development, and coping skills for personal and social change.

Kent Curtis has served as an administrator and faculty member at Northern Kentucky University since its inception in 1970. He is a professor in the departments of industrial technology and education. His teaching areas include supervisory development, human relations in business and industry, techniques of research design, counseling, and group dynamics.

He received a baccalaureate degree in biology from Centre College, a master's in counseling from Xavier University, and a doctorate in adult technical education from the University of Cincinnati. He has designed numerous employee and management training and development programs, which are presented to Fortune 500 companies, small businesses, and federal, state, and local government agencies.

Kent also presents open seminars and on-site programs for the Office Productivity Institute and VistaSystems in the areas of time and stress management, communication skills, and team building. His current studies and interests include developing effective "executive pairs" (secretary/manager teams); the manager as an effective teacher; and improving the quality of work life in organizations using employee involvement groups.

# PREFACE

Each book in *The Human Side of Work* is special in its own way. *Morale* is special because this was the theme that first captured our interest and attracted us to the field of organizational psychology. Quality-of-work-life questions have been the focus of our professional lives for more than 20 years. *Morale* is also special because it is the end objective of all of the other books in the series. The purpose for studying communication, leadership, motivation, stress, and other "human side" topics is to improve the quality of work life.

Our goal is to present the changing meaning of work in Western society; the importance of employee morale in four key areas — the job itself, the work group, management practices, and economic rewards; the importance of organizational climate; and the role of management in determining employee satisfaction and organizational success. Learning exercises are included to personalize the subject. You will evaluate your own level of morale, the climate of your workplace, and your organization's overall effectiveness. Practical answers are provided to maximize learning.

Specific topics, questions, and activities include:

- What does work mean to you? Learn the *changing meaning of work* across cultures and down through the ages. See pages 6–13.

- What is your *level of morale?* How do you compare with the national average? See pages 32–38.

- How do you diagnose *attitude problems?* What should companies do to raise employee morale? See pages 38–65.

- How does *organizational climate* influence employee morale? See pages 74–92.

- What are the *characteristics of successful organizations?* How does your company stack up? See pages 92–102.

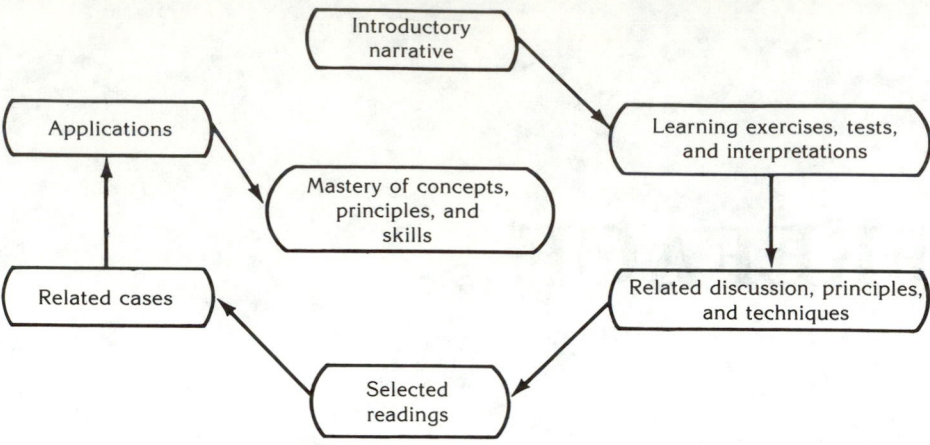

## HOW TO USE THIS BOOK

This is a desk book for ready reference, a handbook for teaching others, and a workbook for personal development in the area of morale and the quality of work life. The material is arranged in a logical sequence for learning.

The best approach is to *interact* with the material. Read the narrative, take the tests and exercises, examine the interpretations, and review the principles and techniques—then ask: "How does this apply to me? How can I use this concept or information to improve?" Then take action. Also, use the related readings, cases, and applications to improve your knowledge and skills.

To increase interest and improve your overall learning, try the following:

1. Use the learning objectives, discussion questions, and study quizzes included in each part of the book. This will focus your reading, improve comprehension, and increase retention of the material.

2. Share the results of your tests and exercises with family, friends, and co-workers. In this way, you can make tangible use of what you learn and may even help others.

3. Write in the book. Use the margins; underline; write your own ideas and thoughts about the material.

Good luck in your learning!

## HOW TO TEACH FROM THIS BOOK

Personalize *Morale*—for yourself and for the learner. Use the information, exercises, questions, activities, and tests to complement your own teaching style and resources; use any or all of the materials provided to suit the needs and goals of the group.

## Steps

First, scan the material for topics and exercises. Second, outline a curriculum and lesson plan based on time frames and learning goals. Third, arrange learning aids, media, and other resources for smooth instruction. For assistance in this area, refer to the suggested readings, cases, applications, and films that accompany each part of the text. Also, see Appendix A for suggestions on teaching, testing, and grading as well as for information about other books in *The Human Side of Work* series.

## Instruction

Multimedia, multimethod instruction usually works best. Each class period ideally would include a lecture to set the stage, learning exercises to personalize the subject, a discussion to interpret results, and use of related activities such as cases and readings to enhance knowledge and skills. A film, followed by group discussion and panel debate, is an ideal learning enhancer. See Appendix C for an annotated list of excellent films.

## Final Note

Because this book is easy to read and covers the factual information needed by the learner, class periods should be used primarily for group involvement. Learning activities and group discussion will promote maximum enjoyment and learning.

*Morale* is intrinsically interesting. People relate naturally to such topics as the changing meaning of work, job satisfaction, organizational climate, and management practices. But they won't learn the material unless they get involved with it. As the instructor, the more practical you can make it for them, the better; the more personalized it is, the more helpful it will be. In this spirit, we conclude with a favorite proverb:

> I listen and I hear;
> I see and I remember;
> I do and I understand.

*Confucius* (551–479 B.C.)

Good luck in your teaching!

*Request:* We want your suggestions. If you have questions or see a way to improve this book, please write. Thank you.

George Manning
Kent Curtis
Northern Kentucky University
Highland Heights, Ky. 41076

# ACKNOWLEDGMENTS

*The Human Side of Work* is written by many people. It is the result of countless hours and endless effort from colleagues, students, and others who have helped in some important way. From initial draft to final form, many hands bring these books to life. To each we are grateful.

For this book, recognition is given to the following scientists and authors whose ideas and findings provide theoretical framework and important factual data:

| | | |
|---|---|---|
| Saul Gellerman | Elton Mayo | R. A. Stringer |
| Frederick Herzberg | Douglas McGregor | Adriano Tilgher |
| Rensis Likert | Nancy Morse | Robert H. Waterman, Jr. |
| G. H. Litwin | Thomas Peters | |

Appreciation goes to the following colleagues and supporters for substantive help in research, manuscript review, preparation, and advice:

| | | |
|---|---|---|
| Jim Alford | Bill Holloway | Vince Schulte |
| Terry Almond | Ron Kelley | Louise Schwarber |
| Tim Baker | Lonnie Lewis | Bill Stewart |
| Ken Carter | Steve Martin | Cliff Stone |
| Don Dover | Steve McMillen | Ralph Tesseneer |
| Gordon Duke | Herb Pence | Sam Vinci |
| Charlotte Galloway | Joseph Podota | Teresa Waterman |
| Judy Gamm | Robert Quirk | Susan Wehrmeyer |
| Leonard Goodstein | Scott Rich | Linda Williams |
| Judy Hahn | Gene Scholes | Robert Wooding |

We want to thank J. Ellen Gerken for many of the figures, illustrations, and photographs.

George Manning
Kent Curtis

# CONTENTS

# READINGS 111

# CASES 225

# APPLICATIONS 243

# Morale

**Mo•rale** (mə-ral′, mô-räl′), noun [Fr., fem. of moral], 1. the moral or mental condition of a person or group with respect to courage, discipline, and willingness to endure hardship. 2. a state of confidence, cheerfulness, and enthusiasm: team morale was high after winning the contest. 4. a sense of well-being and satisfaction. 5. a positive attitude by an individual or group as shown by a willingness to perform tasks.

*An army's success depends on its size, equipment, experience, and morale . . . and morale is worth more than all of the other elements combined.*

*— Napoleon*

# PART ONE

## The Changing Meaning of Work

*Learning Objectives*

After completing Part One, you will better understand:

1. the changing meaning of work in Western society;
2. the economic, social, and psychological importance of work in America today;
3. how much time is spent at work, and the changing composition of the work force;
4. the relationship between employee morale and job performance;
5. the psychological and economic costs of employee turnover;
6. the eight critical symptoms of low morale.

# INTRODUCTION

The following is a discussion of the changing meaning of work in Western society, the relationship between morale and job performance, the importance of organizational climate, and the role of management in determining employee satisfaction and organizational success. The subject is personalized so you can discover your own level of morale and evaluate the organizational climate in which you work. Management practices are presented to maximize the quality of work and the quality of work life.

If you are a supervisor, manager, or labor leader and are concerned with the human side of work, then the concepts, principles, and techniques discussed here should be of interest to you. The success of any work group or organization depends on its size, equipment, experience, and morale . . . and morale is worth more than all of the other elements combined.

# THE CHANGING MEANING OF WORK

History has witnessed an evolving definition of the meaning of work. To the ancient Greeks, work was a curse. Their name for work was *ponos*, having the same root as the Latin *poeno*, meaning sorrow. Homer wrote that the gods hated mankind and, out of malice, condemned human beings to work. As such, the Hellenes developed a slave-based economy and relegated labor to "inferior people." In general, the Greeks, and later the Romans, viewed work as a painful necessity.[1]

The Hebrews constitute the second pillar of Western culture, and they too viewed work as punishment. The Hebrews saw work as man's burden to pay for original sin. "If man," says the Talmud, "does not find his food like the animals and birds, but must earn it, that is due to sin." To the Hebrews, work was atonement and a way to regain lost spirituality. So any work, no matter how lowly, was preferred over idleness.[2]

Early Christians shared the Hebraic attitude toward work. Although they believed that it was better to work than to be idle, they placed relatively low value on productive enterprise and the accumulation of wealth. Consider the words of Jesus (Matthew 6:24, 19:24):

> No man can serve two masters. . . .Ye cannot serve God and Mammon.
> . . .It is easier for a camel to go through the eye of a needle, than for a rich man to enter into the kingdom of God.

Essentially, early Christianity taught that the best work is that which least fills men's minds with desire for profit and which least distracts them from God. Work at its best would be pure spirituality — a loving gaze fixed on a better world after death. The only admission of virtue in work was that it could be a means of charity in providing for the needs of others. This view of work remained virtually unchanged for the first one thousand years A.D. The dominant attitude toward work during this period was one of disregard and disdain.[3]

Between the eleventh and fourteenth centuries, Christianity came closer to the mainstream of society, assigning to work a more important role in life. The teachings of Thomas Aquinas, the church philosopher, speak for this era:

> Work is natural and a duty, an important basis of society, and it is the legitimate foundation of property and gain, and of guilds and crafts; but all of this to a higher spiritual end; and all of this according to a divine plan.[4]

The next five hundred years included the Renaissance, the Reformation, and the Industrial Revolution, and Western society's attitude toward work changed significantly during this period. At the beginning of the sixteenth century, Martin Luther proclaimed that all forms of labor have equal value in the eyes of God and that to carry out God's will was to perform one's vocational duties to the best of one's ability. Luther taught that idleness is an unnatural and evil aberration, and to maintain oneself by work is a way of serving God. With this, the historical split between religious piety and worldly activity was resolved as work came to be defined as a "calling" and a religious duty for all men.[5] In 1536, John Calvin taught a doctrine of predestination that placed only the industrious among the chosen for Heaven's grace. Under Calvin, work during this life and for this life was endowed with religious dignity. Calvin wrote:

> Work alone suffices, and to please God, work must not be casual — now this, now that, now prolonged for the whole day, tomorrow laid down after an hour. Intermittent, occasional work will not do. It must be methodical, disciplined, rational, uniform, and hence specialized, work. To select a calling, and follow it with all one's conscience, is a religious duty.[6]

With Luther and Calvin, Protestant theology gave sanction to worldly achievements, and the Protestant work ethic was born. Other doctrines of the period joined this new religious ethic to help establish work as a central tenet of Western society. The Renaissance mission to build, create, and so realize one's potential; the mercantilistic disregard for unproductive citizens; the Age of Enlightenment and the emergence of science; the survival-of-the-fittest beliefs of social Darwinists; and the primacy of work in socialist societies — all served to elevate man's attitude toward work.

By the twentieth century, Protestant ethics, freewheeling capitalism, and humanistic socialism had meshed to form an essentially multidisciplinary religion of work. Each of these major currents of thought embraced the idea that it was every man's right and duty to perform work that would bring the greatest good to himself and society. The good man was the one who did good work.[7] Consider the words of Karl Marx, father of socialism, who believed work to be the sum total of human rights and duties and who viewed work as the moral ideal:

> Production for the purpose of meeting men's needs (as opposed to our present production for the purpose of making a profit) will free labor from egotism, avarice and fraud. In such a regime, work will no longer be a painful expiation or an abstract moral duty: it will be seen as the normal human way of living. The model man will no longer be the wise man, the ascetic, or the citizen, but the worker, understood as producer. An immense society of free workers, freely associated, administering in common the instruments of work and endlessly transforming the matter of the world for the greater good of the community — such is the Socialist ideal.[8]

Capitalism, too, taught the importance of productive labor as a moral duty. This can be seen in a letter Abraham Lincoln wrote to his brother, who had asked for a loan:

Dec. 24, 1848

Dear Johnston:

> Your request for eighty dollars, I do not think it best to comply with now. At the various times when I have helped you a little, you have said to me, "We can get along very well now," but in a very short time I find you in the same difficulty again. Now this can only happen by some defect in your conduct. What that defect is, I think I know. You are not lazy, and still you are an idler. I doubt whether since I saw you, you have done a good whole day's work, in any one day. You do not very much dislike to work, and still you do not work much, merely because it does not seem to you that you could get much for it.
> This habit of uselessly wasting time is the whole difficulty. It is vastly important to you, and still more so to your children, that you should break this habit. It is more important to them, because they have longer to live, and can keep out of an idle habit before they are in it, easier than they can get out after they are in.
> You are now in need of some ready money; and what I propose is that you shall go to work, "tooth and nail," for somebody who will give you money for it.
> Let Father and your boys take charge of your things at home — prepare for a crop, and make the crop, and you go to work for the best money wages, or in discharge of any debt you owe, that you can get. And to secure you a fair reward for your labor, I now promise you that for every dollar you will, between this and the first of May, get for your own labor either in money or in your own indebtedness, I will then give you one other dollar.
> By this, if you hire yourself at ten dollars a month, from me you will get ten more, making twenty dollars a month for your work. In this, I do not mean you shall go off to St. Louis, or the lead mines, or the gold mines in California, but I mean for you to go at it for the best wages you can get close to home — in Coles County.
> Now if you will do this, you will soon be out of debt, and what is better, you will have a habit that will keep you from getting in debt again. But if I should now clear you out, next year you will be just as deep in as ever. You say you would almost give your place in Heaven for seventy

or eighty dollars. Then you value your place in Heaven very cheaply, for I am sure you can, with the offer I make you, get the seventy or eighty dollars for four or five months' work. You say if I furnish you the money you will deed me the land, and if you don't pay the money back, you will deliver possession —

Nonsense! If you can't now live with the land, how will you then live without it? You have always been kind to me, and I do not now mean to be unkind to you. On the contrary, if you will but follow my advice, you will find it worth more than eight times eighty dollars to you.

Affectionately,

Your brother,

A. Lincoln[9]

## THE MEANING OF WORK IN AMERICA TODAY

We have seen dramatic changes in the meaning of work in Western culture — from Greek scorn for labor, to Hebraic atonement for sin, to early Christianity's disregard and disdain, to later Christianity's calling to work, to socialist doctrines of work for joy, to the present day, when work represents for many a search for meaning and self-expression. The following passage reflects this attitude toward work.

Then a ploughman said, Speak to us of Work.
And he answered, saying:
You work that you may keep pace with the earth and the soul of the earth.
For to be idle is to become a stranger unto the seasons, and to step out of life's procession, that marches in majesty and proud submission towards the infinite.
When you work you are a flute through whose heart the whispering of the hours turns to music.
Which of you would be a reed, dumb and silent, when all else sings together in unison?
Always you have been told that work is a curse and labour a misfortune.
But I say to you that when you work you fulfill a part of earth's furthest dream, assigned to you when that dream was born,
And in keeping yourself with labour you are in truth loving life,
And to love life through labour is to be intimate with life's inmost secret. . . .
You have been told also that life is darkness, and in your weariness you echo what was said by the weary.
And I say that life is indeed darkness save when there is urge,
And all urge is blind save when there is knowledge,
And all knowledge is vain save when there is work,
And all work is empty save when there is love;
And when you work with love you bind yourself to yourself, and to one another, and to God.
And what is it to work with love?
It is to weave the cloth with threads drawn from your heart, even as if your beloved were to wear that cloth.
It is to build a house with affection, even as if your beloved were to dwell in that house.

It is to sow seeds with tenderness and reap the harvest with joy, even as if your beloved were to eat the fruit.

It is to charge all things you fashion with a breath of your own spirit,

And to know that all the blessed dead are standing about you and watching.

Often have I heard you say, as if speaking in sleep, "He who works in marble, and finds the shape of his own soul in the stone, is nobler than he who ploughs the soil.

And he who seizes the rainbow to lay it on a cloth in the likeness of man, is more than he who makes the sandals for our feet."

But I say, not in sleep but in the over-wakefulness of noontide, that the wind speaks not more sweetly to the giant oaks than to the least of all the blades of grass;

And he alone is great who turns the voice of the wind into a song made sweeter by his own loving.

Work is love made visible.[10]

The value the individual attaches to the work experience is an important factor. It makes an enormous difference whether work is viewed as punishment or as an opportunity for growth and self-expression. Primarily because of the influence of culture, work has a positive value for large numbers of people in American society, who seek personal meaning and a sense of self-worth in the work experience. Consider the alcoholic who endures all loss until he loses his job, or the individual whose loss of status at work results in the afflictions of self-doubt and depression. The following passage reflects a sentiment that would have been foreign to the mainstream of Western thought a mere five hundred years ago:

**ILLUS. 1.1**

An ideal job has personal meaning and instills a sense of self-worth.

Three laborers were laying bricks. The first was asked, "What are you doing?"

The reply: "I am laying bricks."

The second was asked, "Why are you working?"

The answer: "For five dollars a day."

The third worker was asked, "What are you doing, sir?"

The response: "I am a bricklayer, and I am building a great cathedral."[11]

Figure 1.1 shows that the majority of American workers attach a high degree of importance to the work experience. The data represent the responses of a cross section of people representing all levels of responsibility and all classifications of work. Figure 1.2 shows that work is an important source of happiness for the majority of workers in America today.

To personalize the subject of the meaning of work, consider: What does work mean to you? What value do you attach to your job or your career? Are you one who lives to work, or are you one who works to live? Discuss this in the space provided below and on page 12.

_____

_____

_____

_____

_____

## FIGURE 1.1

### The Importance of Work

*If you had enough money to live as comfortably as you would like for the rest of your life, would you continue to work?*

| Attraction to Work | Percentages for Three Years | | |
|---|---|---|---|
| | 1969 (N = 1522) | 1973 (N = 2083) | 1977 (N = 2273) |
| Worker would continue to work | 67.4% | 67.2% | 71.5% |
| Worker would not continue to work | 32.6% | 32.8% | 28.5% |

71.5% of American workers would continue to work, even if they did not need the money.

*Source:* *Robert P. Quinn and Graham L. Staines*, Quality of Employment Survey: Descriptive Statistics, with Comparison Data from the 1969–70 and 1972–73 Surveys *(Ann Arbor, Mich.: The University of Michigan, Institute for Social Research, 1979)*, 241.

## FIGURE 1.2

**Work and Personal Happiness**

*"I'd be happier if I did not have to work at all."*

| Responses | Percentages |
|---|---|
| Strongly agree | 10.9% |
| Agree | 12.8% |
| Disagree | 45.8% |
| Strongly disagree | 30.5% |

76.3% of American workers view work as a source of personal happiness.

*Source:* Robert P. Quinn and Graham L. Staines, Quality of Employment Survey: Descriptive Statistics, with Comparison Data from the 1969–70 and 1972–73 Surveys *(Ann Arbor, Mich.: The University of Michigan, Institute for Social Research, 1979), 240.*

## Work and the Human Condition

Work influences nearly every aspect of life in America today: economic well-being, social identity, and psychological health.

**Economic Well-Being.** Work is vital to the solvency of individuals and societies. Our culture values self-sufficiency and views work as the primary path to independence and material well-being. Indeed, American society defines social maturity largely as the ability to earn an independent living—the ability to provide for oneself through one's vocation. Work also constitutes the major means for achieving other important goals, such as raising a family, buying a home, obtaining an education, and participating in leisure-time activities.

**Social Identity.** Work provides an important vehicle for relating to others, as identifications and allegiances are formed and acted out. Social man fights alienation, and such potentially satisfying roles as leader, colleague, and expert find their expression in the work setting. A person's position in economic enterprise has become so associated with social identity in

American society that when people ask, "Who is she?" they often mean, "What kind of work does she do?" Whereas individual and family identities were once determined primarily by birth and geography (They are the McIntosh family from Scotland), identities today stem largely from the occupation of the primary breadwinner (Her husband is a lawyer).[12]

**Psychological Health.**  A satisfying work experience is important for emotional well-being. People have always searched for meaning in life, and purpose and self-expression are increasingly pursued on the job. The philosopher Thomas Carlyle expressed this when he wrote, "It is the first of all problems for a man to find out what kind of work he is to do in this Universe." The German writer Goethe describes the importance of work in defining life's purpose and providing personal satisfaction:

> Blessed is he who has found his work; let him ask no other blessedness. He has a work, a life-purpose; he has found it and will follow it.

Finally, Sigmund Freud once said that to be mentally healthy, a person must be able to love and to work. He saw these as the central tasks of adulthood. Work, he pointed out, was a consistent and fundamental way of staying in touch with the world and of mastering it.[13]

Because of the psychological importance of work in American society, loss of one's job, regardless of the cause, usually results in a severe emotional setback. If joblessness continues for long, self-confidence and self-esteem deteriorate. People who are unemployed for a prolonged period normally pass through four stages — denial, anger, depression, and finally, a sense of worthlessness. The words of one who lost her job summarize this feeling: "My job was my whole life. That's all I did. It's unbearable now . . . I can't go on like this."[14]

The emotional and physical consequences of job loss can be significant. A mere 1 percent increase in the national unemployment rate is associated with a 4.1 percent increase in suicides, a 3.4 percent increase in admissions to mental hospitals, a 4 percent increase in admissions to prisons, and a 5.7 percent increase in homicides.[15]

Consider your own case: What role does work play in your economic well-being, social identity, and psychological health? Discuss.

## How Much Time Is Spent Working?

Are you working more or less than your ancestors did? A comparison of annual work and leisure patterns shows that the average worker today spends roughly the same amount of time at work as did the average worker in the thirteenth century. Although innovations such as electricity, improved communications, and mass production have combined to allow a shorter workday, the average number of hours people work each year now, as then, remains around 1,900 to 2,500.[16] However, because people often live longer, retire later, and enter postretirement careers, modern workers may spend significantly more hours on the job over their lifetimes.

Figure 1.3 on page 16 shows how much time American workers actually spend on their main jobs each week.

People in the upper strata of position and responsibility do not fit the norm, and the number of hours they spend at work can be extremely high. The following describes the dedication to work displayed by many of these individuals:

> But the elite . . . the managing class, have made work their God, their duty, their reward, a joy in itself, and this is so much like their attitude toward sport that it is easy for them to pass from one to the other. Often they hardly know whether they are playing or working; often they seem to play at their work and to work at their games. Naturally enough. Once the result of the work is forgotten, once it is pursued as an end in itself, the difference between it and sport grows dim, and shrinks to a mere question of degree.[17]

Working evenings and weekends, people in higher levels of responsibility often amass enormous totals of time spent on the job. The top leaders of our economic, political, social, aesthetic, and religious institutions show a clear preference for work over leisure and appear truly absorbed by their work. The writer W. H. Whyte, Jr., states:

> It seems clear that most executives work far more hours than they are required or asked to, not because of any compulsion, either internal or external, but simply because they are totally absorbed in their work. . . . It is of interest to note that, despite a work week of from 67 to 112 hours, most executives do not complain.[18]

Mark Twain helps to explain some people's commitment to work and the long hours they spend on the job: "Work and play are words that can be used to describe the same thing under differing conditions."

As for people in the lower economic strata, many must work long hours, and even at two jobs, to carve out a living and maintain self-sufficiency. Figure 1.4 on page 17 shows data on the total hours worked by American workers each week, including main and secondary jobs.

## Who Is Working Today?

The American work force has changed. A mere generation ago the typical worker was a male employed full-time on one job, providing full support for his wife and children. Today, fewer than one out of every five people who work for pay meet this description.[19]

Changes in the work force are still occurring. By the late 1970s, the majority of American women were working outside the home. By 1980, for the first time in history, almost three out of five mothers of children aged six or younger were working for pay. And today, the majority of families earning over $25,000 annually depend on the incomes of both the husband and the wife.[20] Management consultant Peter Drucker writes:

> We are busily unmaking one of the proudest social achievements of the 19th century, which was to take married women out of the work force so they could devote themselves to family and children.[21]

The entry of more women into the work force has occurred simultaneously with an exodus of men from the ranks of the working. During the years 1947 through 1977, the number of males in their prime working years (sixteen to sixty-five) who dropped out of employment either permanently or temporarily almost doubled, increasing from 13 percent to 22 percent.[22]

---

**FIGURE 1.3**

**Hours Worked Each Week on
Main Job**

"The 40-hour work week" is a common term. When people give the hours they work a second thought, however, and begin counting the time, they sometimes find that they work somewhat more or less than 40 hours.

*During the average week, how many
hours do you work, not counting
the time you take off for meals?*

| Hours Actually Worked | Percentages for three years | | |
|---|---|---|---|
| | **1969** | **1973** | **1977** |
| 20–39 hours | 21.7% | 23.7% | 28.2% |
| 20–24 hours | 3.6 | 3.6 | 5.2 |
| 25–29 hours | 2.4 | 3.2 | 2.3 |
| 30–34 hours | 4.2 | 5.8 | 6.2 |
| 35–39 hours | 11.5 | 11.1 | 14.5 |
| 40 hours | 39.2% | 32.4% | 29.5% |
| More than 40 hours | 39.2% | 43.8% | 42.2% |
| 41–44 hours | 6.2 | 6.1 | 7.2 |
| 45–49 hours | 11.0 | 13.7 | 11.5 |
| 50–54 hours | 7.8 | 9.3 | 8.8 |
| 55–59 hours | 4.0 | 4.5 | 3.9 |
| 60–64 hours | 5.3 | 4.1 | 5.4 |
| 65 or more hours | 4.9 | 6.1 | 5.4 |

71.7% of American workers spend 40 or more hours per week "on the job."

---

*Source:* *Robert P. Quinn and Graham L. Staines,* Quality of Employment Survey: Descriptive Statistics, with Comparison Data from the 1969–70 and 1972–73 Surveys *(Ann Arbor, Mich.: The University of Michigan, Institute for Social Research, 1979),* 78.

# THE IMPORTANCE OF MORALE

If meaning is the helmsman of work, morale is the wind that fills the sails. Morale energizes people, bringing out the best in their job performance. In essence, morale is a person's attitude toward the work experience in four important areas — the job itself, the work group, management practices, and economic rewards.

---

**FIGURE 1.4**

**Hours Worked Each Week on Main and Secondary Jobs**

| Total Hours Worked Each Week | Percentages for three years | | |
|---|---|---|---|
| | 1969 | 1973 | 1977 |
| 20–39 hours | 20.7% | 22.3% | 27.0% |
| 20–24 hours | 3.4 | 3.1 | 4.4 |
| 25–29 hours | 2.6 | 3.3 | 2.8 |
| 30–34 hours | 3.8 | 5.5 | 5.8 |
| 35–39 hours | 10.9 | 10.4 | 14.0 |
| 40 hours | 36.4% | 30.7% | 26.5% |
| More than 40 hours | 42.8% | 46.9% | 46.6% |
| 41–44 hours | 6.7 | 5.7 | 7.6 |
| 45–49 hours | 11.5 | 14.3 | 12.0 |
| 50–54 hours | 8.6 | 10.5 | 9.6 |
| 55–59 hours | 4.5 | 5.1 | 4.5 |
| 60–64 hours | 6.3 | 4.8 | 6.6 |
| 65–69 hours | 1.9 | 1.8 | 2.6 |
| 70–74 hours | 1.9 | 3.0 | 2.0 |
| 75–79 hours | 0.8 | 0.5 | 0.8 |
| 80 or more hours | 0.6% | 1.2% | 0.9% |

73.1% of American workers spend 40 or more hours each week on their main and secondary employment.

---

*Source:* Robert P. Quinn and Graham L. Staines, Quality of Employment Survey: Descriptive Statistics, with Comparison Data from the 1969–70 and 1972–73 Surveys *(Ann Arbor, Mich.: The University of Michigan, Institute for Social Research, 1979)*, 79.

## ILLUS. 1.3

A majority of women are now working outside the home.

## The Relationship Between Morale and Performance

Job performance equals ability plus morale. This is true regardless of the nature of the work or the level of responsibility. Assuming that the worker has the ability to perform the job, high morale usually results in high job performance; low morale results in low job performance. Two less common relationships between morale and performance are as follows.

**High Morale, Low Job Performance.** When morale is high, but job performance is low, the usual causes are lack of employee knowledge or skill; insufficient equipment and resources; poor or absent leadership; and poor work habits. Each of these causes of poor performance can be corrected. Respectively, the solutions are employee training; proper use of equipment, tools, and supplies; effective supervisory practices; and employee counseling.

**Low Morale, High Job Performance.** When morale is low, but job performance is high, the most likely cause is the dedication of the worker to do a job well, regardless of environmental support. "A job worth doing is worth doing right" is the belief of such workers. Experience shows that this attitude does not last indefinitely; most employees must experience personal satisfaction if they are to remain productive over a sustained period of time. Without positive morale, the commitment of the individual, the work group, and the organization deteriorate, and job performance ultimately declines.

### Job Turnover—Mental and Physical

When job performance declines as a result of low morale, employees usually are asked to leave, or choose to leave, the job. Sometimes employees remain on the job physically, but leave mentally. They are present in body, but commitment and productivity are absent. Such mental turnover can be just as harmful as physical turnover for both the individual and the organization.

The problem of physical turnover in our country is significant. Because of either dropout or discharge, during each month in 1980, 4 percent of the work force changed jobs.[23] The consequences of such turnover can be great. It is difficult to develop teamwork, loyalty, and a common commitment to productivity when nearly half of the work force will be gone within a year (4 percent $\times$ 12 months = 48 percent turnover). Employees and managers do not have enough time together to develop an interest in each other's success, and both morale and performance are reduced.

With a high rate of turnover, employees (including management personnel) typically are unwilling to expend the energy or make personal sacrifices to help build the future of the organization, since they know that they will probably not be around to share in the long-term rewards. Similarly, the company often is unwilling to invest in the future of the individual through training or other development activities, since that person will probably be gone before the investment pays off.[24] The following summarizes the problem:

> Employee turnover is expensive, costing American industry billions of dollars every year. It strikes operations of all sizes, and is not any less devastating in the public sector than it is in the private sector. These financial costs can be classified as both direct (additional fees for recruitment,

steeper assessments for unemployment taxes, and the rising expenses of payroll administration for people who are rapidly moving in and out of the organization) and indirect (the marked decrease in productivity, as replacements require training time to reach adequate levels of job performance).

If the monetary costs of employee turnover are not staggering enough, the human costs can be even more aggravating. Those who do not fit into an organization spend a large amount of their time upsetting the morale of more contented employees. Before they leave, many unsatisfactory workers can antagonize customer, client, and community relations. While these human costs may be less tangible, their expense is equally significant.[25]

## Signs of Low Morale

The signs of low morale are unmistakable. They are the same in every organization, trade, or profession, and they indicate a reduced quality of work life. The following are the major symptoms of low morale:

- *high turnover* — employees who can leave, do leave;
- *high absenteeism* — people dislike coming to work or are genuinely made ill by their jobs;
- *numerous grievances* — employee complaints reflect misunderstanding and dissatisfaction;
- *lack of loyalty* — employees are not dependable and demand compensation for everything they do;
- *poor work habits* — shoddy workmanship results from lack of concern and lack of effort;
- *loss of materials, tools, and equipment* — supplies are wasted or stolen because of an attitude that says, "I don't care";
- *lack of pride* — performance standards decline as inferior products and poor services become the norm;
- *resistance* — strikes and sabotage represent psychic and physical breakdown of the organization.

Use the following exercise to evaluate conditions in your work group or organization.

If conditions are good in your work group or organization, take satisfaction; yours is an environment that will attract good people and bring out the best in job performance. Also, continue to use the policies and practices that are meeting employee needs and resulting in low turnover, low absenteeism, few grievances, high loyalty, good work habits, minimum waste, high pride, and low resistance.

If your organization's scores are not satisfactory, take heart. Part Two provides an in-depth look at employee morale and offers practical steps that employees and managers can take to raise morale and achieve a high quality of work life.

## SYMPTOMS OF LOW MORALE

### Directions

Consider your present work environment, and evaluate each of the following factors. Circle the number on the scale that best represents conditions as they are now (sometimes 1 is high; sometimes 1 is low).

| Turnover | low | 10 9 8 7 6 5 4 3 2 1 | high |
|---|---|---|---|
| Absenteeism | low | 10 9 8 7 6 5 4 3 2 1 | high |
| Grievances | low | 10 9 8 7 6 5 4 3 2 1 | high |
| Loyalty | low | 1 2 3 4 5 6 7 8 9 10 | high |
| Work habits | low | 1 2 3 4 5 6 7 8 9 10 | high |
| Waste | low | 10 9 8 7 6 5 4 3 2 1 | high |
| Pride | low | 1 2 3 4 5 6 7 8 9 10 | high |
| Resistance | low | 10 9 8 7 6 5 4 3 2 1 | high |

## DISCUSSION

How did your work group or organization score on the symptoms of Low Morale test? Add up the circled numbers and find the total on the following chart.

| If Scores Total: | Conditions Are: |
|---|---|
| 72–80 | Excellent; outstanding |
| 56–71 | Very good; solid |
| 40–55 | Just OK; not great |
| 24–39 | Poor; much work needed |
| 8–12 | Very poor; failing |

# RECOMMENDED RESOURCES

The following readings, case, and films are suggested for greater insight into the material in Part One:

**Readings** — Work
The Shoeshine Boy
Who Will Do the Dirty Work Tomorrow?

**Case** — Making Eight Is a Hassle

**Films** — Understanding Human Behavior in the Organization
The People Factor: The Hawthorne Studies
Understanding Motivation
Wilmar Eight
The Life and Times of Rosie the Riveter
With Babies and Banners

# REFERENCE NOTES

1 Adriano Tilgher, *Work: What It Has Meant to Men Through the Ages* (New York: Harcourt Brace Jovanovich, Inc., 1930), 3.

2 Tilgher, *Work*, 11–12, 29–37.

3 Tilgher, *Work*, 29–27.

4 Tilgher, *Work*, 38–46.

5 C. Wright Mills, "The Meaning of Work Throughout History," in Fred Best, ed., *The Future of Work* (Englewood Cliffs, N.J.: Prentice-Hall, Inc., 1973), 7.

6 Tilgher, *Work*, 59–60.

7 Tilgher, *Work*, 137.

8 Tilgher, *Work*, 111.

9 Abraham Lincoln, Letter to John D. Johnston, 24 December 1848.

10 Reprinted from *The Prophet*, by Kahlil Gibran, by permission of Alfred A. Knopf, Inc. Copyright © 1923 by Kahlil Gibran and renewed 1951 by Administrators C.T.A. of the Kahlil Gibran Estate and Mary G. Gibran.

11 Charles M. Schwab, in Will Forpe and John C. McCollister, *The Sunshine Book: Expressions of Love, Hope and Inspiration* (Middle Village, N. Y.: Jonathan David Publishers, Inc., 1979), 8.

12 Harry Levinson, *Executive* (Cambridge, Mass.: Harvard University Press, 1981), 26.

13 Levinson, *Executive,* 28.

14 Frank Trippett, "The Anguish of the Jobless," *Time* (18 January 1982), 90.

15 Trippett, "The Anguish of the Jobless," 90.

16 Robert P. Quinn and Graham L. Staines, *Quality of Employment Survey: Descriptive Statistics, with Comparison Data from the 1969–70 and 1972–73 Surveys* (Ann Arbor, Mich.: The University of Michigan, Institute for Social Research, 1979), 78–79.

17 Tilgher, *Work,* 189–90.

18 William H. Whyte, Jr., *The Organization Man* (New York: Simon & Schuster, Inc., 1956), 142–50.

19 Daniel Yankelovich, "New Rules in American Life: Searching for Self-Fulfillment in a World Turned Upside Down," *Psychology Today* 15, no. 4 (April 1981), 78.

20 Yankelovich, "New Rules in American Life," 78.

21 Cullen Murphy, "Men and Women: How Different Are They?" *The Saturday Evening Post* 255, no. 7 (October 1983), 51.

22 Yankelovich, "New Rules in American Life," 78.

23 Lester C. Thurow, "A Plague of Job Hoppers," *Time,* 117 (22 June 1981), 66.

24 Thurow, "A Plague of Job Hoppers," 66.

25 Stephen Laser, "Dealing with the Problem of Employee Turnover," *Human Resource Management* 19, no. 4, (Winter 1980), 17.

# STUDY QUIZ

As a test of your understanding and the extent to which you have achieved the objectives in Part One, complete the following questions. See Appendix D for the answer key.

1. Which of the following best describes high morale in the workplace?

   a. Poor job performance and high turnover
   b. Average work habits and numerous grievances
   c. Poor attitudes and low productivity
   d. High productivity and low turnover

2. Which answer best illustrates the response of American workers when given a choice to work or not to work?

   a. The majority prefer not to work
   b. The majority prefer to work
   c. Half prefer to work; half prefer not to work
   d. Those who prefer to work are in the minority

3. High morale usually results in _____ performance.

   a. low
   b. no
   c. high
   d. average

4. The shift in attitude toward work in Western civilization has been:

   a. negative to positive
   b. positive to negative
   c. right to left
   d. negative to right

5. Symptoms of low morale include all of the following except:

   a. high turnover
   b. high absenteeism
   c. lack of loyalty
   d. numerous grievances
   e. poor work habits
   f. loss of materials, tools, and equipment
   g. lack of pride
   h. resistance
   i. upward mobility

6. Workers seek dignity:

   a. regardless of consequence
   b. whether earned or not
   c. in the work experience
   d. at the expense of others

7. Which of the following best describes low morale in the workplace?

   a. Poor job performance and high turnover
   b. Good work habits and numerous grievances
   c. Poor attitudes and high productivity
   d. Lack of loyalty and low absenteeism

8. Napoleon wrote that the success of an army depends on its:

   a. supervision, size, equipment, and morale
   b. supervision, size, leadership, and morale
   c. size, equipment, experience, and morale
   d. equipment, experience, management, and morale

9. What percentage of American workers would continue to work even if they did not need the money?

   a. 71.5
   b. 55.5
   c. 85
   d. 32

10. What percentage of American workers view work as a source of personal happiness?

    a. 60
    b. 90
    c. 76.3
    d. 50.2

11. Work influences _____ aspect of life in America today.

    a. the economic
    b. the social
    c. the psychological
    d. all of the above

12. The relationship between job performance and morale is:

    a. positive
    b. negative
    c. neutral
    d. unknown

13. Through what stages does a person pass if unemployment persists for a long period of time?

    a. Depression, anger, denial, acceptance
    b. Anxiety, repression, confusion, depression
    c. Anger, sadness, self-blaming, suppression
    d. Denial, anger, depression, worthlessness

14. An important factor affecting the quality of work life is the meaning the _____ attaches to the work experience.

    a. government
    b. union
    c. individual
    d. customer

15. All of the following are signs of high morale except:

    a. low turnover
    b. low absenteeism
    c. good work habits
    d. low productivity

16. Regardless of the type of work or the level of responsibility, job performance equals:

    a. need + reward
    b. luck + chance
    c. ability + morale
    d. energy + time

17. We spend _____ time working per year than (as) our ancestors.

    a. more
    b. less
    c. the same

18. Today the typical worker is a male employed full-time on one job, providing full support for his wife and children.

    a. True
    b. False

19. Increased unemployment can contribute to an increase in suicide and homicide rates.

    a. True
    b. False

**20.** According to Sigmund Freud, to be mentally healthy, a person must be able to love and to work.

a. True
b. False

**21.** About 71% of American workers spend 40 or more hours per week "on the job."

a. True
b. False

———

# DISCUSSION QUESTIONS AND ACTIVITIES

1. What does work mean to you? What influence have family, education, and work experience had on your attitude toward work? How important is your job in your life?

   _____

   _____

   _____

2. Do you work long hours? Is this by choice? Explain.

   _____

   _____

   _____

3. Have you ever experienced low job satisfaction? If so, describe the symptoms.

   _____

   _____

   _____

4. In small groups, discuss the importance of morale. Have you seen the influence of morale in a work group or organization? Does employee morale affect the quality of work? Quality of work life?

5. Do you know a family member, friend, or co-worker with high job satisfaction? What are the psychological, social, and economic benefits?

6. Discuss the changing composition of the work force in American society. Are you in favor of the increasing numbers of women working outside the home? What are the effects on men, women, relationships, and families?

# PART TWO

## Employee Morale

*Learning Objectives*

After completing Part Two, you will better understand:

1. the importance of morale in four key areas — the job itself, the work group, management practices, and economic rewards; and your own level of satisfaction with your job;

2. the status of worker satisfaction in America today;

3. how to help employees develop positive attitudes toward the job, the work group, management, and the economic aspects of the work experience;

4. the role of management in creating the best morale possible.

# WHAT IS YOUR MORALE AT WORK?

The English philosopher-scientist Francis Bacon wrote, "Knowledge is power," and Socrates, the Greek teacher-philosopher, said, "Know thyself." It follows that knowledge of self results in greatest power. One of the best ways to understand the nature and importance of morale is to study your own attitudes toward your own work.

---

## MORALE SURVEY— HOW SATISFIED ARE YOU?

### Directions

The following survey addresses a number of work-related issues. Answer each question as it relates to your own experience. Circle the appropriate response.

### Job

1. At this point in my job, I am doing the things I feel are important.

| Strongly disagree | Disagree | Undecided | Agree | Strongly agree |
|---|---|---|---|---|

2. When it comes to challenge, the job I am doing is demanding.

| Strongly disagree | Disagree | Undecided | Agree | Strongly agree |
|---|---|---|---|---|

3. As things are now, I have a sense of accomplishment in the work I am doing.

| Strongly disagree | Disagree | Undecided | Agree | Strongly agree |
|---|---|---|---|---|

**4.** When it comes to pride in the work of my co-workers, it is high.

| Strongly disagree | Disagree | Undecided | Agree | Strongly agree |
|---|---|---|---|---|
| | | | | |

**5.** I like the people with whom I work.

| Strongly disagree | Disagree | Undecided | Agree | Strongly agree |
|---|---|---|---|---|
| | | | | |

**6.** There is teamwork between my co-workers and me.

| Strongly disagree | Disagree | Undecided | Agree | Strongly agree |
|---|---|---|---|---|
| | | | | |

## Management

**7.** Management strives to be fair.

| Strongly disagree | Disagree | Undecided | Agree | Strongly agree |
|---|---|---|---|---|
| | | | | |

**8.** I understand and agree with the goals of management.

| Strongly disagree | Disagree | Undecided | Agree | Strongly agree |
|---|---|---|---|---|
| | | | | |

**9.** Management shows concern for employees.

| Strongly disagree | Disagree | Undecided | Agree | Strongly agree |
|---|---|---|---|---|
| | | | | |

## Economics

**10.** My wages are satisfactory.

| Strongly disagree | Disagree | Undecided | Agree | Strongly agree |
|---|---|---|---|---|
| | | | | |

**11.** My fringe benefits are satisfactory.

| Strongly disagree | Disagree | Undecided | Agree | Strongly agree |
|---|---|---|---|---|
| | | | | |

**12.** The opportunity for advancement is satisfactory—if I desire to pursue it.

| Strongly disagree | Disagree | Undecided | Agree | Strongly agree |
|---|---|---|---|---|

## SCORING

What does the Morale Survey tell you about your own work situation? To find your level of satisfaction in four important areas—the job itself, relations with co-workers, practices of management, and economic rewards—complete the following three steps.

### Step One

For each question, score 1 for Strongly disagree, 2 for Disagree, 3 for Undecided, 4 for Agree, and 5 for Strongly agree.

### Step Two

Add the total scores for each section of the questionnaire, divide by 3, and enter the averages in the spaces below.

| **Job** | **Group** | **Management** | **Economics** |
|---|---|---|---|
| _____ | _____ | _____ | _____ |
| Average for items 1, 2, and 3 | Average for items 4, 5, and 6 | Average for items 7, 8, and 9 | Average for items 10, 11, and 12 |

### Step Three

Make a three-dimensional picture of your morale at work, using Figure 2.2. Circle the appropriate number on each edge of the box, and connect the circles with straight and dotted lines as shown in the example (Figure 2.1).

## INTERPRETATION

This exercise shows the importance of morale, both for personal satisfaction and for job performance. Assuming that a person has the basic skills and knowledge to perform a job, the quality of work and the quality of work life depend on commitment to do a good job. Regardless of the field—transportation, manufacturing, or medicine—and regardless of the level of responsibility—front-line employee, manager, or president—commitment results from positive attitudes (high morale) in four key areas:

## FIGURE 2.1

Example

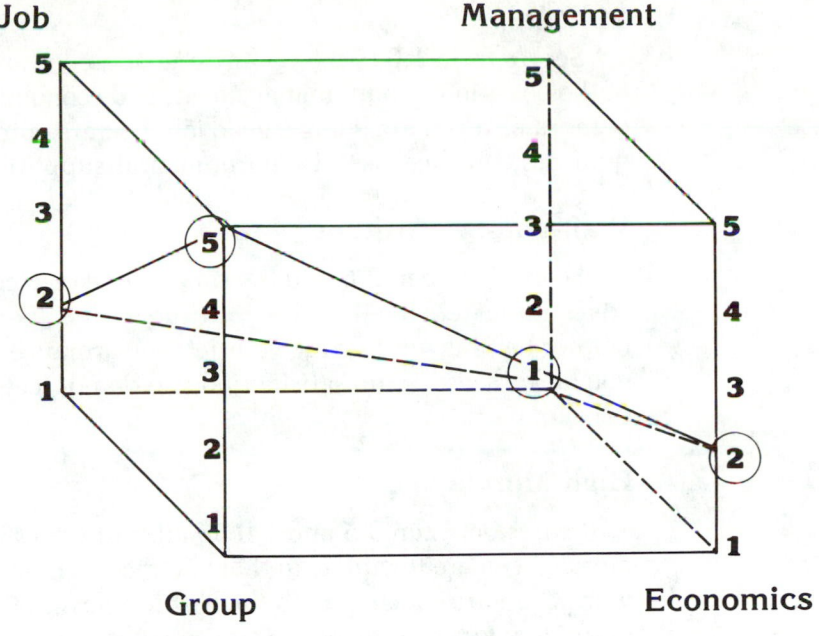

## FIGURE 2.2

Your Levels of Morale

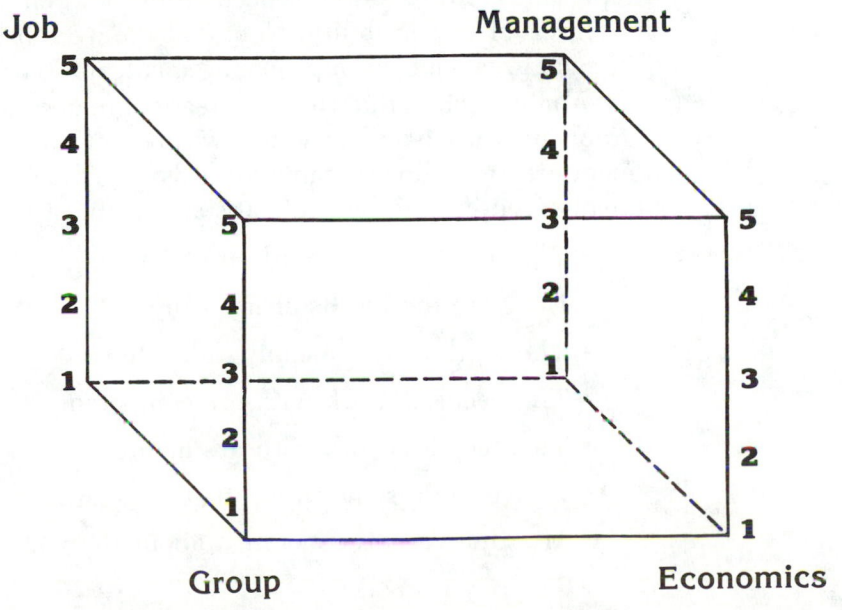

the job itself, the work group, management practices, and economic rewards.

The following is a description of what your scores mean.

### Low Morale

Scores from 1.0 to 2.5 on any one or a combination of the four edges of the box — job, group, management, and economics — indicate a low level of morale. If you are doing a good job, you are doing it because of personal qualities, not because of environmental support.

### Wait-and-See Attitude

Scores between 2.6 and 3.4 on any one or a combination of the four edges indicate a wait-and-see attitude. It is likely that your morale is neither helping nor hurting your job performance at this point. However, you lack a sense of full satisfaction and do not feel complete commitment to your work.

### High Morale

Scores between 3.5 and 5.0 on all four edges indicate a high level of morale. You are fortunate in that you receive much satisfaction from your work. You are striving to do the best job possible, and with training and practice your level of performance could be expected to be high.

## THE NATIONAL MORALE PICTURE

It is interesting to know how your own morale compares with that of others. Figure 2.3 shows the level of morale in our country. These data represent a cross section of occupations and employees and encompass all levels of responsibility. Note that the overall level of morale is high in each area — job, group, management, and economics.

Analysis shows that the two areas of greatest satisfaction are the work group and the job itself, and the two areas of least satisfaction are management practices and economic rewards. The exact ranking of morale statements according to level of satisfaction (most to least) is as follows:

- The people I work with are friendly.
- I can see the results of my work.
- The work I do is meaningful.
- The people I work with are competent.
- The people I work with are helpful.
- I have to do some things that go against my conscience.
- My supervisor is concerned about the welfare of subordinates.
- The pay is good.
- The fringe benefits are good.

## FIGURE 2.3

**Employee Morale in America**

### JOB

| Statements | Responses | | | |
|---|---|---|---|---|
| The work I do is meaningful | *Strongly disagree* 3.4% | *Disagree* 12.2% | *Agree* 59.9% | *Strongly agree* 24.5% |
| The problems I am expected to solve are challenging | *Not at all true* 15.1% | *Not too true* 26.3% | *Somewhat true* 36.2% | *Very true* 22.4% |
| I can see the results of my work | *Not at all true* 2.8% | *Not too true* 11.5% | *Somewhat true* 29.2% | *Very true* 56.5% |

### GROUP

| | | | | |
|---|---|---|---|---|
| The people I work with are competent | *Not at all true* 2.6% | *Not too true* 13.9% | *Somewhat true* 44.3% | *Very true* 39.2% |
| The people I work with are friendly | *Not at all true* 1.3% | *Not too true* 6.6% | *Somewhat true* 35.1% | *Very true* 57.0% |
| The people I work with are helpful | *Not at all true* 4.0% | *Not too true* 14.3% | *Somewhat true* 38.6% | *Very true* 43.1% |

### MANAGEMENT

| | | | | |
|---|---|---|---|---|
| My supervisor treats some subordinates better than others* | *Not at all true* 38.1% | *Not too true* 22.0% | *Somewhat true* 21.0% | *Very true* 18.9% |
| I have to do some things that go against my conscience* | *Strongly disagree* 25.3% | *Disagree* 46.5% | *Agree* 22.2% | *Strongly agree* 6.0% |
| My supervisor is concerned about the welfare of subordinates | *Not at all true* 11.2% | *Not too true* 19.3% | *Somewhat true* 35.4% | *Very true* 34.1% |

FIGURE 2.3—*continued*

## ECONOMICS

| | Not at all true | Not too true | Somewhat true | Very true |
|---|---|---|---|---|
| The pay is good | 14.6% | 20.2% | 38.0% | 27.2% |
| The fringe benefits are good | 20.3% | 15.0% | 32.2% | 32.5% |
| The chances for promotion are good | 29.8% | 28.2% | 26.2% | 15.8% |

*Direction of responses reversed for these items.

*Source:* Robert P. Quinn and Graham L. Staines, Quality of Employment Survey: Descriptive Statistics, with Comparison Data from the 1969–70 and 1972–73 Surveys *(Ann Arbor, Mich.: The University of Michigan, Institute for Social Research, 1979), 177, 178, 195, 199, 217–19.*

• My supervisor treats some subordinates better than others.

• The problems I am expected to solve are challenging.

• The chances for promotion are good.

This shows that the three areas employees are most satisfied with are good relations with co-workers, a feeling of accomplishment, and a sense of meaning in the job. The three areas of most concern are opportunity for advancement, increased job challenge, and fair treatment from supervisors.

Figure 2.4 shows that although morale levels are generally high in America, they have been declining in recent years.

Analysis of the data shows that the rate of decline has been roughly the same for attitudes toward the job, management practices, and economic rewards and that attitudes toward relations with co-workers have remained nearly the same.

## HOW CAN EMPLOYEE MORALE BE DEVELOPED?

The following is a discussion of each area of morale, including recommendations (Rx) for developing the best possible attitudes in employees.

### Attitudes Toward the Job

Included in this area are a sense of meaning in the job, the amount of challenge in the work, and a feeling of accomplishment.

**FIGURE 2.4**

**How Satisfied Are American Workers?**

| Questions | Response Categories | Percentages for Three Years | | |
|---|---|---|---|---|
| | | **1969** | **1973** | **1977** |
| 1. All in all, how satisfied would you say you are with your job—very satisfied, somewhat satisfied, not too satisfied, or not at all satisfied? | Very satisfied | 46.4% | 52.0% | 46.7% |
| | Somewhat satisfied | 39.1% | 38.0% | 41.7% |
| | Not too satisfied | 11.3% | 7.6% | 8.9% |
| | Not at all satisfied | 3.2% | 2.4% | 2.7% |
| | | (*N* = 1528) | (*N* = 2088) | (*N* = 2281) |
| 2. Knowing what you know now, if you had to decide all over again whether to take the job you now have, what would you decide? Would you decide without hesitation to take the same job; would you have some second throughts; or would you decide definitely not to take the same job? | Would decide without hesitation to take the same job | 64.0% | 70.5% | 63.9% |
| | Would have some second thoughts | 26.9% | 23.7% | 28.3% |
| | Would decide definitely not to take the job | 9.1% | 5.8% | 7.8% |
| | | (*N* = 1527) | (*N* = 2078) | (*N* = 2282) |
| 3. If a good friend of yours told you he was interested in working in a job like yours (for your employer)*, what would you tell him? Would you strongly recommend this job; would you have doubts about recommending it; or would you strongly advise him against this sort of job? | Would strongly recommend it | 63.2% | 64.4% | 61.8% |
| | Would have doubts about recommending it | 24.7% | 26.4% | 29.7% |
| | Would advise friend against it | 12.1% | 9.2% | 8.6% |
| | | (*N* = 1498) | (*N* = 2042) | (*N* = 2242) |

*This phrase was omitted for self-employed workers.

**FIGURE 2.4**—*continued*

88.4% of American workers are satisfied with their jobs, all in all.
63.9% of American workers would decide without hesitation to take the same job.
61.8% of American Workers would strongly recommend their job to a good friend.

*Source:   Robert P. Quinn and Graham L. Staines, Quality of Employment Survey: Descriptive Statistics, with Comparison Data from the 1969–70 and 1972–73 Surveys (Ann Arbor, Mich.: The University of Michigan, Institute for Social Research, 1979), 210–11.*

**Job Importance.**  It has been said that people do not fear extinction; what people fear is extinction without meaning. The chance to leave one's mark, to do something of value, is a powerful motive that is often expressed on the job. Psychologist Carl Rogers writes: "It seems to me that at bottom each person is asking, 'Who am I, really? How can I get in touch with this real self underlying all my surface behavior? How can I become myself?' "[1] Many people answer this question by the work they do.

Because work is an important source of meaning and identity in our society, the right person should be matched with the right job whenever possible. Those who want to farm and are good at farming should be society's farmers; those who want to build and are good at building should be builders; those who want to manage and are good at managing should be managers; and so on, through all walks of life and all levels of occupations, from cook to cashier and from secretary to soldier. The fact that there are 20,000 separate jobs listed in the *Dictionary of Occupational*

**ILLUS. 2.1**

It is important to find the right job for personal satisfaction.

*The Greyhound Corporation*

*Titles* and 97 million workers in America today shows the magnitude of the task.[2]

**Rx:** One solution to the problem of matching the right person with the right job is vocational counseling. This can be done in the home, school, and work setting. Available occupations should be discussed, personal aptitudes and interests should be considered, and appropriate steps should be taken to match the requirements of the job with the attributes of the individual. The rewards to the person, to the organization, and to society are worth the effort of good vocational guidance.

Another solution is for supervisors to consider the interests, skills, and goals of each employee when making day-to-day work assignments. Success at any level of management depends on being able to choose the right person for the right job. In doing this, first-line supervisors face essentially the same problems as do company presidents. They must determine the interests and abilities required for a job, then assign the job to the person most qualified to do it. When managers do this effectively, both the individual and the organization benefit.

**Job Challenge.** If a job is too easy, morale goes down, and ultimately, so does performance, for both the individual employee and the work group. The best assignments are those that are challenging without being overwhelming. Assigning reasonably demanding work is one of the best ways to maintain employee interest, keep job skills current, and increase productivity.

**Rx:** Goal setting is an effective tool for creating job challenge. By meeting challenging goals, the employee can learn important skills, which can provide personal satisfaction and improve job performance. Imagine an employee whose interest is stimulated, whose skills are improved, and whose productivity is increased by tackling new and challenging tasks.

Another means of creating job challenge is to provide opportunities for employees to become involved in the decision-making process. This is the purpose of employee committees, task forces, and quality circles. The following shows the value of employee participation:

> . . . In one firm . . . computer operations were running $100,000 over budget, and management sought ways to reduce this drain on resources. In the beginning, management discussed the problem in several meetings, but the managers could not agree on any major cost-saving changes. Then management sought the advice of a consultant. Although the consultant recommended some changes, they produced minor savings.
>
> Finally, one manager suggested that management should ask employees for ideas. Some managers doubted that this approach would help, but after discussion they decided to bring the employees in the computer department into full participation on the problem. Within 30 days the employees suggested cost-saving ideas that eventually provided about double the savings needed.[3]

**Job Progress.** A reasonable sense of accomplishment must be experienced if commitment and effort are to be sustained. Consider the following:

Workers were hired to cut trees in the Adirondack Mountains. The wages were high, and many applied. On the first day, 40 workers were bused to the mountains, given axes, and instructed to chop as many trees as they could—but they were to use the wrong end of the axe. The workers didn't see the purpose of this, but since the pay was good, they proceeded with vigor.

By the end of the day, both enthusiasm and effort had decreased, and there was little work accomplished. The next morning, only one-half of the workers showed up. The following day, only one-fourth reported to work. Even though the researchers raised the wages several times to encourage participation, by the end of the week, only a few hungry workers were willing to work without making any progress.[4]

The same principle is found in all types of occupations and at all levels of responsibility: progress builds morale; morale builds commitment; commitment builds performance; performance builds progress; and so on, as both morale and productivity are improved.

*Rx:*   The task of management is to ensure employee productivity. This can be accomplished by providing the following:

- *Planning.* Plans should be developed and communicated to employees. Elements include a statement of the organization's mission, based on shared values; organization-wide goals to support the mission; specific and measurable objectives for accomplishing each goal; and specific plans of action to achieve each objective.

- *Organization of resources.* Sufficient personnel, tools, materials, and other human and nonhuman resources must be made available to accomplish the plan. These must be allocated and coordinated effectively.

**ILLUS. 2.2**

The standard is often set by the work group.

*Courtesy of International Paper Company*

- *Leadership practices.* The role of leadership is to facilitate worker productivity. As such, leaders should be coaches and coordinators rather than bottlenecks and enforcers.
- *Systems for control.* Effective records should be kept in order to gather information, maintain order, make sound decisions, and accomplish the plan.[5]

## WHAT ARE YOUR JOB ATTITUDES?

### Directions

Analyze your own attitudes toward the job. Discuss the following:

1. What does your job mean to you?

2. If your job lacks meaning, what should you do?

3. Are you sufficiently challenged by your work?

4. If your job is too easy, what should you do?

5. Do you have a sense of accomplishment in the work that you do?

**6.** If you are not making progress, what should you do?

_____

_____

_____

### Attitudes Toward Co-Workers

This area includes a sense of group pride, good relations with co-workers, and a spirit of teamwork among employees.

**Group Pride.** The work group often determines the standards for job performance. Groups can either resist or encourage the productivity of individual members. The power of group pressure is described in Figure 2.5.

Team pride will usually bring out the best in work group performance. With team pride, members believe in the group's capability, and this results in increased enthusiasm and energy to perform. High standards of performance are set by the group, and the overall quality of work is improved.

*Rx:* The following are proven techniques to build work group pride:

- *Set standards of behavior and dress.* People tend to become what they think they are, and this is based to a great degree on personal conduct and appearance. Establish and enforce standards of behavior and, where appropriate, standards of dress for a work group. Consider the experience of successful organizations and their standards of behavior and dress—Oxford University, the U.S. Supreme Court, and the Roman Legion.

- *Provide group honors and awards.* Work groups should receive recognition for team performance. Group honors such as team championships raise pride and reinforce high performance. Consider the Super Bowl championship and the American and National League pennants.

- *Assign complete tasks to work groups.* The father of capitalism, Adam Smith, wrote about the virtues of the pin factory with its efficiencies due to division of labor and economies of scale. Yet, overdoing this can rob employees of a sense of ownership in their jobs, weakening their commitment to do the best quality of work. A solution is to enrich the work experience by assigning complete jobs to teams of workers, providing immediate feedback on job performance, and rewarding high-quality work. Consider the following:

## FIGURE 2.5

### The Power of Group Pressure

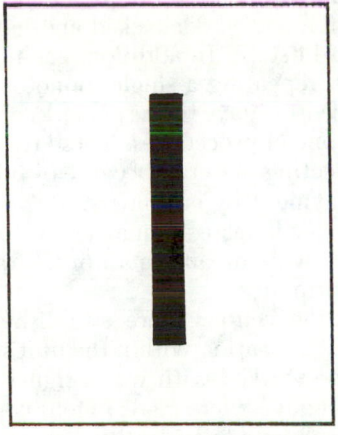 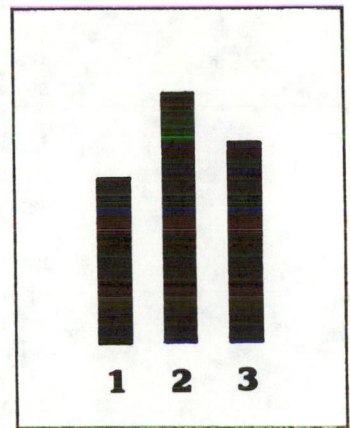

Solomon Asch conducted an experiment that dramatically illustrated the power of group pressure. Asch assembled groups of eight subjects to participate in a study of visual judgment. The subjects sat around a table and judged the lengths of various lines. But only one member of each group was a genuine subject. All the others were Asch confederates, and on prearranged trials they reported ridiculously incorrect judgments.

In the case above, the confederates each reported confidently that line 1 was most similar in length to the comparison line on the left. These events put the real subject, who was one of the last to call out his decision, in a difficult situation. Should he report his real judgment, even though it would make him look different in the eyes of other group members, or should he go along with the crowd? The situation was an extremely uncomfortable one for many of Asch's subjects, and different subjects resolved the dilemma in different ways: some of the subjects never conformed, while others conformed almost all of the time. Overall, subjects conformed to the false group consensus on about 35 percent of the trials.

In some cases, the subject's confidence was genuinely shaken by the reports of the unanimous majority. One subject who went along with the group on almost every trial explained afterward, "If they had been doubtful, I probably would have changed, but they answered with such confidence." Most of the subjects who went along with the majority admitted later that they really didn't believe that the majority was correct, but they were afraid of seeming foolish in the eyes of their fellow students.

*Source:* Solomon E. Asch, *Social Psychology (Englewood Cliffs, N.J.: Prentice-Hall, Inc., 1952); Solomon E. Asch, "Opinions and Social Pressures,"* Scientific American 193, no. 5 *(November 1955); 31–35; and Henry Gleitman,* Psychology *(New York: W. W. Norton & Co., Inc., 1981), 530–33.*

In the 1960s, AT&T was experiencing a high turnover rate among clerical workers who were responsible for compiling telephone directories. This high turnover rate resulted in increased employment and training costs. A job enrichment program involved the implementation of four concepts.

First, instead of 21 separate steps, including a lengthy verification procedure in which one clerk checked another clerk's work, the routine was decreased to 14 steps. In addition, each clerk could perform all 14 steps rather than repeating a single monotonous task.

Second, supervisors gave teams of clerks additional responsibility for handling work-control procedures. These responsibilities included such procedures as rejecting material because of poor quality and cutting off service for nonpayment by customers.

Third, direct feedback of employee performance was provided by having each clerk evaluate and monitor the quality and quantity of his or her own performance.

Finally, decision centers were established that involved physical relocations. At each location within the unit's building, a particular set of customers to be worked with was assigned to a specific work team.

Work design changes were made in four core job dimensions: variety, autonomy, feedback, and task identity. The results revealed not only cost savings, but also improvement in efficiency, worker attitudes, and turnover.[6]

**Social Needs.** People are social by nature, and whether extroverted or introverted, every person needs some degree of human interaction. The average employee spends one-third of the day in the company of co-workers, and it is natural to experience social needs on the job.

### ILLUS. 2.3

Being included in the peer group is important on and off the job.

Management has not always recognized employee social needs, and the growth of unionism is due in part to this insensitivity. During the era of the "company store" and sweatshops in American industry, many companies actively suppressed attempts of workers to socialize. Group discussions on the job were "busted up," and union busters even followed workers into their homes to bust *them* up. Where no central purpose for gathering together had existed previously, a dominant goal developed: to fight management. The resulting conflict that has marked the American work scene has been costly for labor, management, and society.

*Rx:*   Constructive ways to meet employee social needs include orientation training for new employees; periodic staff meetings; company picnics; holiday parties for employees' families; informal discussions; athletic teams and leagues (bowling, softball, etc.); ride sharing to and from work; lounge areas; quality circles; and, most important, a willingness to help employees with job-related problems.

Participation in social activities may be minimum for some employees. If these individuals are criticized or otherwise singled out, the organization will fail to meet another important need, the need for social tolerance.

Closely related to social needs are communication needs. Communication problems result in frustration, low morale, and reduced productivity. Research on where employees want to get information, as opposed to where they actually do get information, shows the following.

The sources from which employees want to get information (in rank order) include:

1. immediate supervisor;

2. small-group meetings;

3. top executives;

4. employee handbook;

5. orientation programs;

6. regular general employee publications;

7. annual business report to employees;

8. regular local employee publications;

9. bulletin boards;

10. upward communication programs;

11. mass meetings;

12. audiovisual programs;

13. unions;

14. mass media;

15. grapevine.

Where employees actually get information, however, is as follows (in rank order):

1. immediate supervisor;
2. grapevine;
3. employee handbook;
4. bulletin boards;
5. small-group meetings;
6. regular general employee publications;
7. annual business report to employees;
8. regular local employee publications;
9. mass meetings;
10. unions;
11. orientation programs;
12. top executives;
13. audiovisual programs;
14. mass media;
15. upward communication programs.

The most important conclusion derived from this study is that management should increase supervisor-subordinate communications, small-group meetings, and top executive involvement and should decrease dependency on the grapevine.[7]

**Teamwork.** The small boy in the following story believes in the power of teamwork. He thinks that he can accomplish anything with a little help from his friends.

> A young boy called at a neighbor's home and offered to mow the lawn.
> "What are you going to do with the money?" he was asked.
> "I am raising one million dollars for the earthquake relief fund," he answered gravely. He was so small, and the sum he named was so large, that the neighbor laughed.
> "One million dollars! Do you expect to raise it all by yourself?"
> "No," he replied. "Two other boys are helping me."[8]

The English poet John Donne wrote, "No man is an island," and this reflects today's world of work as never before. Few employees are islands unto themselves, untouched and not affecting other people. The solitary artist who creates alone is the exception. More typical is the office worker or industrial employee whose success depends on the support of others.

When a halfback races for a touchdown, he and his blockers know he didn't do it alone; and when a company succeeds, everyone involved knows that no single person is solely responsible. The contribution and cooperation of loyal laborers, office personnel, supervisors, and top management are all necessary.

*Rx:* Management has the power to shape the behavior of employees, and its best tools are example and reward. If teamwork is desired, leaders should act cooperatively and should reward employees who help co-workers. If managers protect their own interests to the disadvantage of others and seek personal rewards over the good of the group or the mission of the organization, they discourage teamwork and reduce employee morale and productivity.

A second way to encourage teamwork is to involve employees in the success of the organization. Keeping them informed of activities generates enthusiasm. Ex-chief of U.S. naval operations Elmo (Bud) Zumwalt tells a story about one of his first commands that illustrates the importance of teamwork:

> . . . What I tried hardest to do was ensure that every officer and man on the ship not only knew what we were about, not only why we were doing each tactical execution, however onerous, but that he also managed to understand enough about how it all fitted together that he could begin to experience some of the fun and challenge that those of us in the top slots were having.
>
> Our techniques were not unusual. We made frequent announcements over the loudspeaker about the specific event that was going on. At the beginning and end of the day, I discussed with the officers, who, in turn, discussed with their men, what was about to happen and what had just happened, what the competition was doing and what we should do to meet it.
>
> We published written notes . . . that would give the crew some of the color or human interest of what the ship was doing. I had bull sessions in the chief petty officers' quarters, where I often stopped for a cup of coffee. More important than any of these details, of course, was the basic effort to communicate a sense of excitement, fun, and zest in all that we were doing.[9]

Within a short 18 months, practices like these vaulted Zumwalt's ship from last to first in efficiency within his squadron.

# WORK GROUP MORALE

### Directions

To see how attitudes toward co-workers influence your own morale, discuss the following:

1. Does your work group have a strong sense of pride?

   _____

   _____

   _____

   _____

2. If not, what should be done to raise team pride?

   _____

   _____

   _____

3. Do you like the people you work with?

   _____

   _____

   _____

   _____

4. If friendliness is low, what should the group do?

   _____

   _____

   _____

   _____

5. Do people in your work group cooperate and help each other?

   _____

   _____

   _____

   _____

6. If teamwork is low, what should the group do?

_____

_____

_____

_____

### Attitudes Toward Management

This area includes management fairness, agreement with organizational goals, and management's concern for employee welfare.

**Management Fairness.** Most employees have a sense of justice, which, if violated, results in reduced morale and decreased performance. The task of management is to establish policies and procedures that are as fair as possible and to administer these in an even-handed way. The following reflects resentment for the perceived injustice of management:

> We the willing,
> Led by the unknowing,
> Are doing the impossible
> For the ungrateful.
> We have done so much, for so long,
> With so little,
> We are now qualified to do anything,
> With nothing, in no time at all.[10]

**ILLUS. 2.4**

Fair management practices attract and keep good employees.

In contrast, consider the sense of fairness shown by New York's famous mayor Fiorello LaGuardia in the following story:

> Mayor LaGuardia was presiding over Night Court when a man was brought before him. He had been charged with stealing a loaf of bread. The accused pleaded guilty, but explained that his family was hungry. The Mayor responded that, since he was guilty, he would have to be fined ten dollars. LaGuardia himself then took a ten-dollar bill from his own pocket and said, "Here is the ten dollars for you to pay your fine. And now, I am going to fine everybody in this courtroom fifty cents for living in a town where a man has to steal bread in order to feed his family. Mister Bailiff, collect the fines and give them to the defendant." The poor man left the courtroom with $47.50 in his pocket.[11]

*Rx:*   To achieve maximum fairness at work, managers should:

- Have communication sessions with employees to share information and air complaints. An open-door policy brings issues into the open, dispels rumors, and results in the feeling that management is trying to be fair.

- Establish an appeal process. Not all decisions are good ones, and an established procedure for review or appeal can meet employee needs for fair play.

- Involve workers in developing policies and making decisions that affect them. Such participation meets important needs for democracy and dignity. When employees participate in the formulation of rules and procedures, they are more likely to adhere to them. From participation comes involvement; from involvement comes ownership; and from ownership comes commitment. Figure 2.6 shows the levels of participation in decision making experienced by American workers for several types of decisions.

**Organizational Goals.**  A priest rejects the rules of the church; a politician rejects the goals of the party; a businessperson rejects the policies of the company. In each of these examples, the individual is out of step with the institution. Neither the priest, the politician, nor the businessperson believes in the goals of management.

When the goals of the organization and the goals of the worker collide, morale and performance are twin casualties. Sometimes the goals of management are not clearly stated; sometimes employees fail to listen. In any case, the result is a sense of frustration over real or imagined differences.

*Rx:*   Two effective ways to communicate organizational goals are (1) the employee handbook, detailing the mission of the organization, the roles of managers and employees, terms of employment, conditions of work, and policies and procedures that guide behavior; and (2) the annual report, describing the previous year's performance and projecting the outlook for the coming year.

**FIGURE 2.6**

**Employee Participation in Decision Making**

| Types of Decisions | Complete Say | A Lot of Say | Some Say | No Say At All |
|---|---|---|---|---|
| Safety equipment and practices | 13.3% | 62.6% | 22.8% | 1.3% |
| How the work is done | 4.8% | 36.0% | 55.1% | 4.1% |
| Wages and salaries paid | 3.6% | 26.8% | 58.9% | 10.7% |
| Particular days and hours people work | 2.7% | 16.7% | 58.2% | 22.4% |
| Hiring or layoffs | 2.5% | 13.0% | 45.1% | 39.4% |

*Source:* *Robert P. Quinn and Graham L. Staines*, Quality of Employment Survey: Descriptive Statistics, with Comparison Data from the 1969–70 and 1972–73 Surveys *(Ann Arbor, Mich.: The University of Michigan, Institute for Social Research, 1979), 178.*

**Management Concern.** If management fails to show concern for the welfare of employees, dissatisfaction develops and job performance declines. Employees think, "If management does not care about us, why should we care about management?" Lack of trust, respect, and loyalty erodes the relationship. Distrust is evidenced as people avoid talking to each other for fear that what they say will be used against them. Disrespect is seen as people fail to listen to each other. Lack of loyalty shows as employees protect their self-interest with little regard for the success of the organization.

*Rx:* Managers should conduct periodic employee meetings (annual, semiannual, or quarterly) during which they share information about past successes; current issues; financial status (including how much is being spent for materials, tools, and equipment, employee wages and benefits, recruitment and training, investments, and ownership); and goals of the organization for the road ahead. The trust and respect managers show by having such meetings will be appreciated by most employees and will be returned in the form of company loyalty and increased productivity.

Another way to show concern for employees is to take note of their personal activities and problems. Almost everyone responds favorably to a word of recognition regarding a personal achievement or a card or visit to show concern for a health problem.

The least expensive and most effective way to create a feeling of concern between managers and employees is to cooperate meaningfully in the many day-to-day contacts, whether they involve work or off-the-job problems. Willingness to listen, talk, and show responsiveness to each other increases the morale and job performance of both managers and employees. A model of concerned, involved management is Sam Walton, owner of Wal-Mart Stores, Inc., the fourth largest retail chain in the United States, and employer of over 26,000 workers:

> "Mr. Walton couldn't sleep a few weeks back. He got up and bought four dozen doughnuts at an all-night bakery. At 2:30 a.m., he took them to a distribution center and chatted for a while with workers from the shipping dock. As a result, he discovered that two more shower stalls were needed at that location." The astonishing point is not the story per se: any small-business person could relate a host of similar tales. The surprising news is that a top executive still exhibits such a bone-deep form of concern for his people in a $2 billion enterprise.
>
> The message that down-the-line people count is mirrored in every activity at Wal-Mart. The executive offices are virtually empty. Headquarters resembles a warehouse. The reason is that Walton's managers spend most of their time out in the field in Wal-Mart's eleven state service areas. And what are they doing? "Leading local cheerleading squads at new store openings, scouting out competing K-mart stores, and conducting soul-searching sessions with the employees." Walton himself visits every store every year (330 now, remember), as he has done since 1962.[12]

## MANAGEMENT AND MORALE

### Directions

To see how attitudes toward management affect your own morale, discuss the following questions:

1. Do you think management is fair with employees?

   _____

   _____

   _____

2. If not, what should be done to correct this?

   _____

   _____

   _____

**3.** Do you know and agree with the goals of your organization?

_____

_____

_____

**4.** If not, what should you do?

_____

_____

_____

**5.** Do you think management is concerned about the needs of employees?

_____

_____

_____

**6.** If not, what should be done?

_____

_____

_____

## Attitudes Toward Economic Rewards

The three subareas of economic rewards include wages, benefits, and opportunity for advancement.

**Wages.** Although some people may enjoy their jobs so much that they would pay for the opportunity to perform them, work is effort for pay, and pay is important to anyone who must earn a living. The two dimensions of pay that affect morale are how much is earned and how fairly wages are distributed.

Some people value material wealth more than others. For these, more income is needed to sustain morale. Consider the contrast between the legendary King Midas and the folk hero Johnny Appleseed. Gold drove the first, while the second had almost no interest in material wealth. The following story makes the point:

> A hardworking mailman once met a millionaire who worked relentlessly and became wealthier every year. The civil service employee, on the other hand, made just enough to support his family.
> One day, while delivering mail to the millionaire, the postman remarked, "I'm richer than you are!"

The rich man looked puzzled. "How can that be?" he asked.

The mailman smiled. "Why," he said, "I have all the money I want, and you don't."[13]

No matter what value an employee places on material wealth, the basic requirements for food, shelter, health care, and other economic needs must be satisfied. If these needs are not met, both morale and job performance suffer. Usually, the employee will seek work elsewhere.

Regarding fairness of wages, both the million-dollar salesman in the insurance industry and the social worker in a human service agency will be equally upset if the employer does not pay fairly, or if another employee with less responsibility or less ability, or who expends less effort, earns more than they do.

*Rx:* Management must pay sufficient wages to attract and keep qualified workers and must pay fairly for work performed; otherwise, morale deteriorates and productivity declines. Figure 2.7 on page 58 provides a summary of new pay practices.

In general, the best pay plan is to provide base wages according to job classification and rank. Then, provide across-the-board cost-of-living adjustments on a systematic basis. Finally, provide additional income based on performance periods (bonuses) and projects (commissions). These bonuses and commissions are one-time-only, after-the-fact rewards for effective job performance. As such, these amounts are not added to base wages.

This pay system accomplishes three important goals: (1) it rewards advancement in job classification and rank, reinforcing employee development; (2) it provides economic stability through cost-of-living adjustments, strengthening the relationship between the employee and the organization; and (3) it provides timely bonuses and commissions for effective performance, reinforcing the relationship between pay and performance.

**Fringe Benefits.** Fringe benefits may be added to wages to constitute an economic reward package for employees. If fringe benefits are used, managers should try to meet the needs and preferences of each employee.

The cost of a retirement program for teenage workers would probably be wasted. Spending the same amount of money to provide a paid birthday holiday may be better; free time is a reward young employees usually appreciate much more.

*Rx:* Given the diversity of interests among employees, managers should work with each individual to develop a personal compensation package within the prescribed amount of money available. Because the needs and goals of people change, this should be reviewed at two- to five-year intervals.

With such a system, one employee may choose straight wages, another may prefer stock in the company, and another may defer a percentage of income for use at retirement. In any case, both the worker and the organization should receive maximum benefit from the financial rewards available.

Figure 2.8 on page 60 presents the fringe benefits American workers typically receive.

**Job Advancement.** Job advancement may or may not present a morale problem. Some employees do not want to change their jobs. Imagine a skilled artist, tradesman, or professional who enjoys the job and wants only to continue with present activities. However, many employees are dissatisfied unless there is opportunity for advancement.

There are many reasons why a worker who wants to advance may fail to do so—inappropriate credentials, restrictive traditions, enemies at the top, and personal shortcomings are a few. Another is a low job ceiling. Consider the following:

> An able and ambitious thirty-two-year-old manager recently transferred to his company's plant in Topeka. He is second in command, reporting to the plant manager, who is thirty-six years old. The average age of the plant managers in the other four plants owned by the company is forty, with none older than forty-four. The five plant managers report to the vice president for manufacturing, who is forty-two years old. The vice president reports to the owner and president, who is fifty-two years old. All plant managers, the vice president, and the president are doing good work, and no one plans to make a career change. The average age of the company vice presidents for finance, marketing, and personnel is forty-eight, and each has trained an heir apparent. The company has no plans to expand its products or markets.

This thirty-two-year-old manager has little opportunity to advance beyond his present post in the company. In time, such a low job ceiling may undermine his morale and even the quality of his work.

*Rx:* Solutions to job advancement problems include promotion from within the company; job postings that cross functional specialities, such as accounting, sales, and production; and human resources planning. Such enlightened personnel policies can help prevent many morale and performance problems.

## FIGURE 2.7

## Summary of New Pay Practices

| Type of Pay Plan | Description | Major Advantages | Major Disadvantages | Favorable Situational Factors |
|---|---|---|---|---|
| Cafeteria-style income | This allows employees some degree of choice in the total package of pay and fringe benefits they receive. For example, older employees may prefer a greater retirement contribution, while younger ones may prefer less in retirement contribution and more in straight wages | Increased satisfaction with pay and benefits | Cost of administration | Well-educated, heterogeneous work force |
| Lump-sum salary increases | These allow employees to choose how they would like to receive their pay increase for the coming year—in the usual equal increments to their monthly check, or in one lump sum at the beginning of the year. The lump sum is treated by the company as an advance to the employee, the unearned portion of which must be paid back if the employee leaves the organization before the end of the year | Increased satisfaction with pay; greater visibility of pay increases | Cost of administration | Fair pay rates |

| Practice | Description | Advantages | Disadvantages | Conditions |
|---|---|---|---|---|
| Skill-based evaluation | This practice, unlike the traditional compensation system based on job analysis and job evaluation, pays employees according to the skill level they have to perform various tasks. This approach encourages employees to develop skills and stimulates managers not to underutilize employees. It can increase intrinsic as well as extrinsic rewards because it can result in assignment of more challenging work | More flexible and skilled work force; increased satisfaction | Cost of training and higher salaries | Employees who want to develop themselves; jobs that are interdependent |
| Open salary information | Making pay rates known gives management added reason to maintain defensible and motivating pay-performance relationships. Public disclosure tends to reduce wage inequities and reinforce the relationship between pay and performance | Increased satisfaction with pay; greater trust and motivation; better salary administration | Pressure to pay all employees the same; complaints about pay rates | Open climate; fair pay rates; pay based on performance |
| Participative pay decisions | Participation and information sharing in pay decisions permits taking employee preferences into account to a greater extent | Better pay decisions; increased satisfaction; motivation; and trust | Time consumed | Democratic management climate; work force that wants to participate and that is concerned about organization goals |

*Source:*  *E. E. Lawler, "New Approaches to Pay: Innovations That Work,"* Personnel 53, *no. 5 (September–October 1976), 11–23, and David R. Hampton, Charles E. Summer, and Ross A. Webber,* Organizational Behavior and the Practice of Management, *4th ed. (Glenview, Ill.: Scott, Foresman & Company, 1982), 447-49.*

## FIGURE 2.8

### Fringe Benefits Available to, and Received by, Workers

| Fringe Benefits | Percentage of Workers Reporting the Availability of the Benefit for Three Years* | | |
|---|---|---|---|
| | 1969 | 1973 | 1977 |
| Paid vacation | 73.7% | 70.3% | 80.8% |
| Medical, surgical, or hospital insurance that covers any illness or injury that might occur while *off* the job | 71.9% | 79.4% | 78.1% |
| Maternity leave with full re-employment rights** | 59.4% | 73.5% | 74.5% |
| A retirement program | 60.7% | 66.6% | 67.4% |
| Life insurance that would cover a death occurring for reasons *not* connected with the job | 62.2% | 69.0% | 64.1% |
| Sick leave with full pay | 59.0% | 63.8% | 62.8% |
| A training (or educational) program to improve skills*** | 39.0% | 43.2% | 49.0% |
| Thrift or savings plan | **** | **** | 39.8% |
| Free or discounted merchandise | 35.9% | 34.7% | 34.3% |
| Dental benefits | **** | **** | 29.4% |
| Maternity leave with pay** | 14.1% | 26.0% | 29.4% |
| Eyeglass or eye-care benefits | **** | **** | 21.8% |
| Profit sharing | 19.0% | 18.8% | 19.8% |
| Stock options | 16.9% | 17.1% | 17.6% |
| Work clothing allowance | **** | **** | 16.8% |
| Free or discounted meals | 16.7% | 17.4% | 16.3% |

FIGURE 2.8—*continued*

| Fringe Benefits | Percentage of Workers Reporting the Availability of the Benefit for Three Years* | | |
|---|---|---|---|
| | 1969 | 1973 | 1977 |
| Legal aid or services | **** | **** | 10.3% |
| Child care facilities | 1.8% | 2.5% | 2.2% |

*Includes only wage-and-salaried workers.
**Women only were asked about this benefit.
***This phrase was not used in 1969 and 1973.
****Not asked in 1969 and 1973.

*Source:* *Robert P. Quinn and Graham L. Staines,* Quality of Employment Survey: Descriptive Statistics, with Comparison Data from the 1969–70 and 1972–73 Surveys *(Ann Arbor, Mich.: The University of Michigan, Institute for Social Research, 1979), 58–59.*

# MORALE AND ECONOMIC REWARDS

## Directions

To personalize the subject of economic rewards, discuss the following questions:

1. How do you feel about the wages you receive?

_____

_____

_____

2. If your pay is unsatisfactory, what should you do?

_____

_____

_____

3. Are your fringe benefits satisfactory? If not, what should be done?

_____

_____

_____

4. Does your job provide opportunity for advancement? If not, what should you do?

_____

_____

_____

## EMPLOYEE MORALE AND THE ROLE OF MANAGEMENT

People become dissatisfied with their jobs for many reasons. Managing employee morale is the task of management. Meeting this responsibility requires a willingness to listen to employees and an ability to "read between the lines" of what they say and do. In this process, the morale of each person should be considered individually. Although the elements of morale are the same for all employees—job, group, management, and economic rewards—each element may be more or less important to different people at different times or in different circumstances:[14]

- The nature of the job itself may not be as important to the individual who views work as a temporary source of income while going to school as it is to the person in mid-career who foresees 25 more years in the same line of work.

- Typically, wages and the opportunity for advancement are of primary importance to younger workers, while older employees are more interested in fringe benefits for their retirement years. All three—wages, benefits, and advancement—are usually important to workers in their middle years, when the financial demands of raising a family must be met, security for sickness and retirement must be considered, and psychic needs for status and responsibility can be great.

- Relations with co-workers and practices of management probably would be less important to the inventor, who works alone, than to factory and office employees, who spend a significant amount of time in the company of co-workers and who are subject to a supervisor's orders.

Some policies and techniques for maximizing morale seem to work with the majority of employees in most cases. A review of 550 studies published since 1959 shows nine areas in which management can take

**ILLUS. 2.6**

Trying to satisfy
employee needs
fosters good morale.

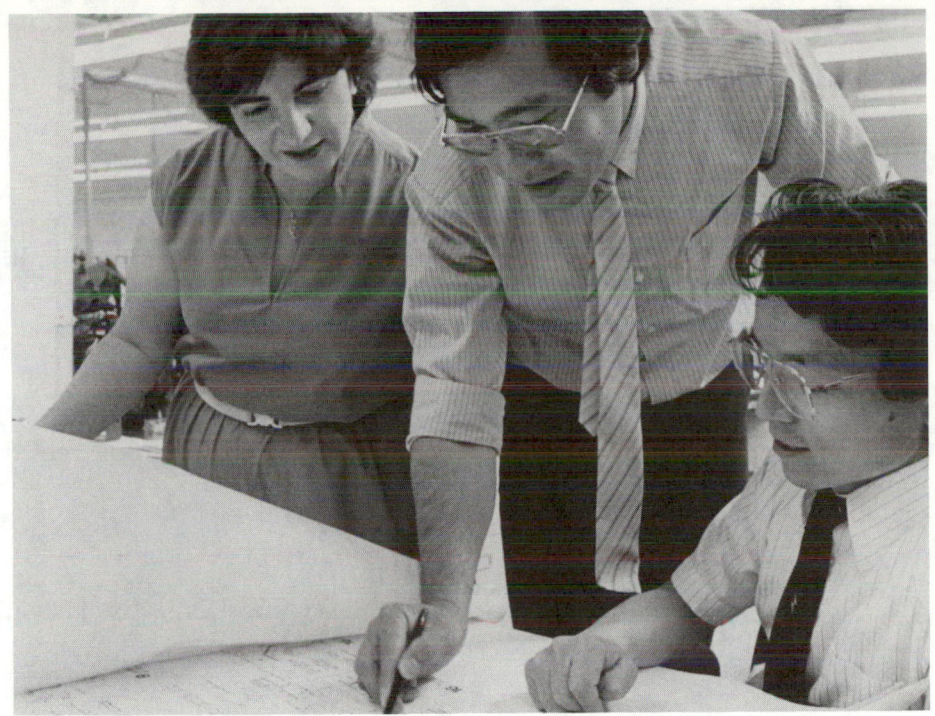

action that will have positive effects on employee satisfaction and job performance. These are:

- *Pay and reward systems.* Introduce a group bonus.

- *Job autonomy and discretion.* Allow workers to determine their own work methods.

- *Support services.* Provide service on demand from technical support groups.

- *Training.* Provide training and development for all employees.

- *Organizational structure.* Reduce the number of hierarchical levels.

- *Technical and physical aspects.* Break long production and assembly lines into smaller work units.

- *Task assignments.* Assign whole tasks, including preparatory and finishing work.

- *Information and feedback.* Provide direct feedback from users—clients, customers, other departments.

- *Interpersonal and group processes.* Increase the amount and kind of group interaction.

Research shows that positive results can be obtained by using one or more of these techniques. Costs go down, and the quality of work and quality of work life improve.[15]

Use the following exercise to evaluate the use of these nine techniques in your work group or organization.

# EFFECTIVE MEASURES FOR RAISING MORALE

## Directions

Consider the policies of your organization in the nine areas listed. Rate each factor on a scale of 1 to 5 (1 is low; 5 is high).

*Pay and reward.*    A group bonus system is used.

| 1 | 2 | 3 | 4 | 5 |

*Job autonomy and discretion.*    Employees determine their own work methods.

| 1 | 2 | 3 | 4 | 5 |

*Support services.*    Technical expertise is available when needed.

| 1 | 2 | 3 | 4 | 5 |

*Training.*    Training is provided for new employees, experienced employees, and managers.

| 1 | 2 | 3 | 4 | 5 |

*Organizational structure.*    The presence of few hierarchical levels allows freedom to operate.

| 1 | 2 | 3 | 4 | 5 |

*Technical and physical aspects.*    Small work units are the norm.

| 1 | 2 | 3 | 4 | 5 |

*Task assignments.*    Whole tasks are assigned, rather than monotonous repetition for one or a few steps.

| 1 | 2 | 3 | 4 | 5 |

*Information and feedback.*    Direct feedback on the quality of work is provided on a timely basis.

| 1 | 2 | 3 | 4 | 5 |

*Interpersonal and group processes.*    Employee involvement in group activities is encouraged.

| 1 | 2 | 3 | 4 | 5 |

# INTERPRETATION

How does your organization rate on the Effective Measures for Raising Morale test? Add up your scores, and look up the total in the following chart.

| If Scores Total: | Conditions Are: |
|---|---|
| 36–45 | Very good; morale can be expected to be high |
| 27–35 | Good; morale can be expected to be favorable |
| 18–26 | Unsatisfactory; morale problems can be expected |
| 9–17 | Poor; morale can be expected to be low |

In summary, when an employee has an attitude problem that is work related, management should study the situation and try to help. It may be discovered that management is part of the problem. Sometimes, the problem will be caused by other employees. Often, the problem is self-caused by the individual employee. In any case, management's potential to help is enormous.

If you are a manager and have an employee attitude problem, you should be concerned for the sake of the individual and the good of the organization. If the problem is work related, it has its origin in one or a combination of the following areas—problems with the job; problems with the work group; problems with management; problems with economic rewards—and you can help to solve it if you try.

## RECOMMENDED RESOURCES

The following readings, cases, application, and films are suggested for greater insight into the material in Part Two:

| | |
|---|---|
| **Readings** | — What Job Attitudes Tell About Motivation |
| | Personnel Directors Are the New Corporate Heroes |
| **Cases** | — The Coffee Break |
| | The Disappointed OD Practitioner |
| **Application** | — The Joe Bailey Problem |
| **Films** | — Staffing for Strength |
| | Motivation: It's Not Just the Money |
| | Pay for Performance |
| | Working with Troubled Employees |
| | Controlling Absenteeism |

# REFERENCE NOTES

1 Carl Rogers, *On Becoming a Person* (Boston: Houghton Mifflin Company, 1961), 108.

2 U.S. Department of Labor, *Dictionary of Occupational Titles*, 4th ed. (Washington, D.C.: U.S. Government Printing Office, 1977), xiv, v.

3 Keith Davis, *Human Behavior at Work: Organizational Behavior*, 6th ed. (New York: McGraw-Hill, Inc., 1981), 160.

4 James Coleman, *Personality Dynamics and Effective Behavior* (Chicago: Scott, Foresman & Company, 1960).

5 Peter Drucker, *Management: Tasks and Responsibilities* (New York: Harper & Row, Publishers, Inc., 1974).

6 John M. Ivancevich, Andrew D. Szilagyi, Jr., and Marc Wallace, Jr., *Organizational Behavior and Performance* (Santa Monica, Calif.: Goodyear Publishing Company, Inc., 1977), 162; and Robert N. Ford, "Job Enrichment Lessons from AT&T," *Harvard Business Review* 51 (January/February 1973), 97–106.

7 Selma Friedman, "Where Employees Go for Information (Some Surprises!)," *Administrative Management* (September 1981), 72–73.

8 Will Forpe and John McCollister, *The Sunshine Book: Expressions of Love, Hope and Inspiration* (Middle Village, N. Y.: Jonathan David Publishers, Inc., 1979), 112.

9 Thomas J. Peters and Robert H. Waterman, Jr., *In Search of Excellence: Lessons from America's Best-Run Companies* (New York: Harper & Row, Publishers, Inc., 1982), 236–37.

10 Source unknown.

11 Forpe and McCollister, *The Sunshine Book*, 125.

12 Peters and Waterman, *In Search of Excellence*, 247.

13 Forpe and McCollister, *The Sunshine Book*, 37.

14 See Chapter 7 of Harry Levinson, *Executive* (Cambridge, Mass.: Harvard University Press, 1981), and Chapter 5 of Ivancevich, et al, *Organizational Behavior and Performance*.

15 Based on T. G. Cummings' analysis of job satisfaction studies, Case Western Reserve University, Cleveland, Ohio.

# STUDY QUIZ

As a test of your understanding and the extent to which you have achieved the objectives in Part Two, complete the following questions. See Appendix D for the answer key.

1. Approximately what percentage of American workers would decide without hesitation to take the same job again?

   a. 64%
   b. 54%
   c. 44%

2. There are _____ separate job titles listed in the *Dictionary of Occupational Titles*.

   a. 5,000
   b. 10,000
   c. 15,000
   d. 20,000

3. Solomon Asch conducted experiments dramatically illustrating:

   a. the role of stress
   b. the power of group pressure
   c. the need for leadership
   d. the importance of organizational climate

4. The four most important sources from which employees want to receive information are:

   a. the grapevine, mass media, unions, regular employee publications
   b. bulletin boards, mass meetings, orientation programs, annual business report
   c. immediate supervisor, small-group meetings, top executives, employee handbook

5. To achieve maximum fairness, management should do all of the following except:

   a. conduct regular communication sessions with employees
   b. establish an appeal process
   c. appoint an impartial judge to make rules
   d. involve workers in developing policies and making decisions

6. Approximately what percentage of American workers receive paid vacations?

   a. 81%
   b. 71%
   c. 61%
   d. 51%

7. The least expensive and most effective way to create a feeling of concern between management and employees is to have meaningful:

   a. parties
   b. computers
   c. seminars
   d. cooperation

8. Jobs should be challenging, but not overwhelming, if positive attitudes and good morale are to be maintained.

   a. True
   b. False

9. When an employee has an attitude problem, it can be the fault of the employee, other employees, management, or a combination of all of these.

   a. True
   b. False

10. According to the results of approximately 550 studies published since 1959, there are nine actions management can take to raise employee morale. Two of the nine are:

    a. provide training to all employees; assign complete tasks, rather than portions of a task
    b. limit group interaction; pay well rather than give a bonus
    c. determine specific work methods and communicate these to workers; increase the number of promotional levels
    d. provide feedback to poor performers; increase the number of workers on an assembly line

11. There are several effective ways to meet the socialization needs of employees. Two of these are:

    a. picnics; mandatory attendance at parties
    b. staff meetings; quality circles
    c. longer breaks; longer vacations
    d. generous pay; job security

12. Poor employee relations result in:

    a. loyal employees
    b. lack of trust

c. financial solvency
d. repeat business

13. When an employee has an attitude problem that is work related, management should study the situation and:

a. report to upper management
b. do everything possible to help
c. call in a consultant
d. terminate the employee

14. If a job is too easy:

a. morale declines and performance increases
b. morale declines and ultimately so does performance
c. morale increases and so does performance
d. morale increases but performance decreases

15. It is management's task to ensure employee productivity, and this can be best accomplished by providing:

a. planning, honors and rewards, leadership practices, contests
b. feedback, planning, contests, systems for emergencies
c. planning, organization of resources, leadership practices, systems for control
d. organization of resources, employee benefits, planning, honors and rewards

16. All of the following are proven techniques that help build work group pride except:

a. high standards for behavior and dress
b. honors and rewards
c. assignment of complete tasks
d. vacation and relief time

17. Two effective ways to communicate organizational goals are:

a. the employee handbook and *Business Today*
b. the employee handbook and the annual report
c. *Business Today* and the annual report
d. the annual report and *The Wall Street Journal*

18. In order to achieve maximum fairness at work, management should consider:

a. hiring an outside arbitrator
b. conducting regular communication sessions with employees
c. installing a suggestion box
d. holding regular meetings with the N.L.R.B.

19. People must experience _____ on the job if commitment and performance are to be sustained.

   a. anger
   b. disappointment
   c. meaning
   d. criticism

20. Job progress must be experienced if morale is to remain high.

   a. True
   b. False

21. Areas in which management can take action that will have positive effects on employee satisfaction and productivity were identified in a review of approximately 550 studies. These include all except:

   a. job autonomy and discretion
   b. training
   c. information and feedback
   d. related readings and assignments
   e. pay and rewards

22. If fringe benefits are to be added, management should be sure they meet the needs and preferences of:

   a. individual employees
   b. members of management
   c. the work force negotiators
   d. labor union leaders

23. Approximately what percentage of American workers are satisfied with their jobs?

   a. 88%
   b. 72%
   c. 65%
   d. 53%

24. All but one of the following is an essential area affecting morale; which is it?

   a. The job
   b. The work group
   c. Management practices
   d. Economic rewards
   e. Education level

# DISCUSSION QUESTIONS AND ACTIVITIES

1. How is your morale affected by your job, your work group, the economic rewards you receive, and management practices in your organization? How does your morale influence your level of performance?

_____

_____

_____

_____

2. Is employee morale in America higher or lower than you would have expected? Discuss.

_____

_____

_____

_____

3. Divide into groups to discuss ways to keep employee morale high and to bring out the best in job performance. How can the right person be matched to the right job? How can employees be kept challenged and interested? How can teamwork and employee pride be developed? How can managers gain the trust and respect of their employees? What pay plans and benefits work best? What methods have you seen to be effective in practice? What would you recommend?

4. What can individual employees do to maximize their own morale? What techniques work for various group members?

5. What should be the role of management in the question of morale? Describe a case in which management practices lowered morale; describe a case in which management practices raised morale.

# PART THREE

## Organizational Climate

*Learning Objectives*

After completing Part Three, you will better understand:

1. the importance of organizational climate in such areas as reward systems, standards of performance, organizational clarity, warmth and support, leadership, and physical working conditions;

2. how management practices create the climate of an organization;

3. the climate of your organization. You should know if it is exploitive, impoverished, supportive, or enlightened, and how this influences the quality of work life;

4. how to develop an enlightened, System IV organization;

5. the eight essential attributes common to excellent organizations.

## ORGANIZATIONAL CLIMATE

In addition to the changing meaning of work and the level of employee morale, the human side of work depends on the climate of an organization. Important dimensions of organizational climate include the reward system, standards of performance, warmth and support, leadership, organizational clarity, communications, creativity, job stress, ethics, tolerance, feedback and controls, resources, employee growth, physical working conditions, teamwork, employee pride, and employee involvement. By completing the following questionnaire, you can evaluate the climate of your organization.

## CLIMATE MAKES A DIFFERENCE — TYPES OF ORGANIZATIONS

### Directions

Read the description of each dimension of organizational climate. Consider the statements at each end of the scale. Then, circle the number on the scale that reflects your evaluation of conditions in your organization (1 is the lowest evaluation; 20 is the highest).

1. *Reward system* — The degree to which employees feel they are being recognized and rewarded for good work rather than being ignored, criticized, or punished when something goes wrong.

| Rewards are not in line with effort and performance | 1 2 3 4 5 | 6 7 8 9 10 | 11 12 13 14 15 | 16 17 18 19 20 | Employees' efforts are recognized and rewarded positively |
|---|---|---|---|---|---|

2. *Standards of performance* — The emphasis placed on quality performance and achieving results, including the degree to which employees feel that meaningful and challenging goals are being set at every level of the organization.

| Performance standards are low | 1 2 3 4 5 | 6 7 8 9 10 | 11 12 13 14 15 | 16 17 18 19 20 | Performance standards are high |
|---|---|---|---|---|---|

3. *Warmth and support* — The feeling that friendliness is valued and that employees trust, respect, and support one another. The feeling that good human relationships prevail in the day-to-day work of the organization.

| There is little warmth and support in the organization | 1 2 3 4 5 | 6 7 8 9 10 | 11 12 13 14 15 | 16 17 18 19 20 | Warmth and support are characteristic of the organization |
|---|---|---|---|---|---|

4. *Leadership* — The willingness of employees to accept leadership and direction from others who are more qualified. The extent to which people feel free to take leadership roles as the need arises and are rewarded for successful leadership. The organization is not dominated by or dependent on just one or two individuals.

| Leadership is not respected or rewarded; the organization is dominated by or dependent on one or two individuals | 1 2 3 4 5 | 6 7 8 9 10 | 11 12 13 14 15 | 16 17 18 19 20 | Leadership is accepted and rewarded based on expertise |
|---|---|---|---|---|---|

5. *Organizational clarity* — The feeling among employees that things are well organized and that goals and responsibilities are clearly defined rather than disorderly, confused, or chaotic.

| The organization is disorderly, confused, and chaotic | 1 2 3 4 5 | 6 7 8 9 10 | 11 12 13 14 15 | 16 17 18 19 20 | The organization is well organized, with clearly defined goals and responsibilities |
|---|---|---|---|---|---|

6. *Communications* — The degree to which important information is shared quickly and accurately — up, down, and sideways — in the organization.

| Information is wrong, censored, or unavailable | 1 2 3 4 5 | 6 7 8 9 10 | 11 12 13 14 15 | 16 17 18 19 20 | Information is accurate, open, and available |
|---|---|---|---|---|---|

7. *Creativity* — The extent to which new ideas are sought and used in all areas of the organization. Creativity is encouraged at every level of responsibility.

| The organization is closed and unresponsive to change | 1 2 3 4 5 | 6 7 8 9 10 | 11 12 13 14 15 | 16 17 18 19 20 | The organization is innovative and open to new ideas |
|---|---|---|---|---|---|

8. *Job stress* — The presence of appropriate stress levels for the job: employees are neither overworked nor underworked.

| Stress levels are harmful | 1 2 3 4 5 | 6 7 8 9 10 | 11 12 13 14 15 | 16 17 18 19 20 | Stress levels are optimal |
|---|---|---|---|---|---|

9. *Ethics* — The emphasis the organization places on high standards of conduct at all levels of responsibility.

| Double standards exist; ethics are low | 1 2 3 4 5 | 6 7 8 9 10 | 11 12 13 14 15 | 16 17 18 19 20 | High standards of conduct are expected at all levels |
| --- | --- | --- | --- | --- | --- |

10. *Tolerance* — The degree of open-mindedness that exists toward different people, ideas, and customs in the organization.

| Discrimination is the norm | 1 2 3 4 5 | 6 7 8 9 10 | 11 12 13 14 15 | 16 17 18 19 20 | Nondiscrimination is the norm |
| --- | --- | --- | --- | --- | --- |

11. *Feedback and controls* — The use of reporting, comparing, and correcting procedures such as employee evaluations and financial audits.

| Controls are used for policing and punishment | 1 2 3 4 5 | 6 7 8 9 10 | 11 12 13 14 15 | 16 17 18 19 20 | Controls are used to provide guidance and solve problems |
| --- | --- | --- | --- | --- | --- |

12. *Resources* — The financial and physical resources available to accomplish the job (funds, equipment, and supplies).

| Funds, equipment, and supplies are insufficient | 1 2 3 4 5 | 6 7 8 9 10 | 11 12 13 14 15 | 16 17 18 19 20 | There are sufficient supplies, equipment, and funds |
| --- | --- | --- | --- | --- | --- |

13. *Employee growth* — The degree to which personal and professional development is emphasized at all levels and in all job classifications in the organization.

| Employee growth is a low priority in the organization | 1 2 3 4 5 | 6 7 8 9 10 | 11 12 13 14 15 | 16 17 18 19 20 | Employee growth is a high priority in the organization |
| --- | --- | --- | --- | --- | --- |

14. *Physical working conditions* — The presence of safe and comfortable working conditions; adequate lighting, space, heat, washroom facilities, and so on.

| Working conditions are poor | 1 2 3 4 5 | 6 7 8 9 10 | 11 12 13 14 15 | 16 17 18 19 20 | Working conditions are good |
| --- | --- | --- | --- | --- | --- |

15. *Teamwork* — The amount of understanding and cooperation between different levels and work groups in the organization.

| Teamwork is low | 1 2 3 4 5 | 6 7 8 9 10 | 11 12 13 14 15 | 16 17 18 19 20 | Teamwork is high |
| --- | --- | --- | --- | --- | --- |

16. *Employee pride* — The degree of pride that exists — pride in individual workmanship and pride in organizational goals and accomplishments.

Pride is low

| 1 2 3 4 5 | 6 7 8 9 10 | 11 12 13 14 15 | 16 17 18 19 20 |

Pride is high

17. *Employee involvement* — The extent to which responsibility for decision making is broadly shared in the organization and employees are involved in decisions that affect them.

There is little employee participation in decision making

| 1 2 3 4 5 | 6 7 8 9 10 | 11 12 13 14 15 | 16 17 18 19 20 |

Employee participation in decision making is high

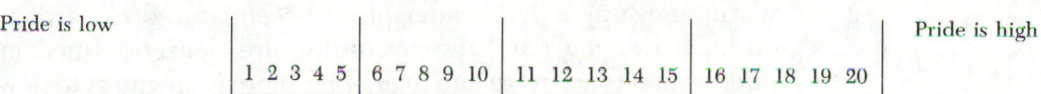

*Source:* *Steve Martin and Terry Almond, Northern Kentucky University, based on Rensis Likert,* The Human Organization *(New York: McGraw-Hill, Inc., 1967); also George H. Litwin and Robert A. Stringer, Jr.,* Motivation and Organizational Climate *(Boston: Harvard University, Graduate School of Business Administration, Division of Research, 1968), 66–88.*

## SCORING

To see how your organization rates on the Climate Makes a Difference test, total all the scores you gave to all the dimensions of organizational climate; divide by 17. Place this number on the scale below.

### TYPES OF ORGANIZATIONS

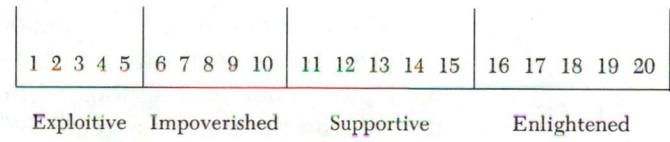

| 1 2 3 4 5 | 6 7 8 9 10 | 11 12 13 14 15 | 16 17 18 19 20 |

Exploitive Impoverished     Supportive     Enlightened

## INTERPRETATION

You now have an evaluation of your organization based on 17 important dimensions. Results may be used to reinforce strengths and improve weaknesses. High scores represent enlightened and supportive organizations. Low scores reflect exploitive and impoverished organizations. Six points should be remembered:

- Characteristics of the best organizations include the following: employees' efforts and accomplishments are recognized and rewarded positively; performance standards are high; human relations are warm and supportive; leadership is accepted and rewarded based on expertise; goals and responsibilities are clearly defined; needed information is accurate and available; there is openness to new ideas and innovations; stress levels are balanced; high standards of conduct are expected from all levels of personnel; nondiscrimination is the norm; feedback and controls are used to provide guidance and solve problems; sufficient supplies, equipment, and funds are available to do the job; employee growth is a high priority in the organization; working conditions are good; teamwork and cooperation between employees is high; employee pride is high; and employees are involved in decisions that affect them.

- An organization is as strong as its weakest link. An individual may have an excellent nervous system, a sound muscular system, and a good respiratory system, but if the liver is bad, ultimately the whole organism will fail. Similarly, an organization may be strong in performance standards, organizational clarity, and communication, but if the employee reward system is poor, the entire organization will ultimately suffer.

- The climate of an organization is important because it influences both the quality of work and the quality of work life. Depending on the mission of the organization, even life-and-death consequences can result.

  Consider an exploitive or impoverished hospital: employees who can find employment elsewhere will probably leave, and these may be some of the best workers. Employees who remain may spend more time complaining about working conditions and management practices than actually doing the work, with the result of poor housekeeping, unattended patients, and medical and clerical errors. Exploitive and impoverished hospitals experience unnecessary mistakes due to human factors (untrained, unqualified, or uncommitted workers).

  Now consider an enlightened or supportive hospital where communications are good, standards of performance are high, leadership is effective, goals and responsibilities are clear, warmth and support prevail, and the reward system reinforces good work. Given a choice, where would you want to be treated, and where would you want to work? Which type of organization provides the best quality of health care and the best quality of employment?

- Enlightened and supportive organizations represent good business investments. Because of their superior organizational climate, these organizations attract excellent personnel, who usually outperform their demoralized counterparts in exploitive and impoverished organizations.

- Organizations are composed of interdependent work groups. The success of the total organization depends on conditions in each of its subgroups. As such, every division and work group should develop an enlightened or supportive climate.

- Management and employees may have different views about the climate of a work group or organization. People in upper levels of responsibility often evaluate conditions more favorably than do people in lower levels. See the example in Figure 3.1.

## SYSTEMS OF MANAGEMENT

How do organizations become what they are? Who decides whether an organization will be enlightened, supportive, impoverished, or exploitive? Although workers may have considerable influence, management

**FIGURE 3.1**

**Extent to Which Supervisors and Subordinates Agree as to Whether Supervisors Tell Subordinates in Advance About Changes**

| Behavior | Top Staff Say as To Own Behavior* | First-Line Supervisors Say About Top Staff's Behavior | First-Line Supervisors Say as to Own Behavior** | Employees Say About First-line Supervisor's Behavior |
|---|---|---|---|---|
| Always tell subordinates in advance about changes that will affect them or their work | 70% ⎫ | 27% ⎫ | 40% ⎫ | 22% ⎫ |
| Nearly always tell subordinates | 30% ⎭ 100% | 36% ⎭ 63% | 52% ⎭ 92% | 25% ⎭ 47% |
| More often than not tell | — | 18% | 2% | 13% |
| Occasionally tell | — | 15% | 5% | 28% |
| Seldom tell | — | 4% | 1% | 12% |

*Top staff rated themselves 37% higher than they were rated by their subordinates.
**First-line supervisors rated themselves 45% higher than they were rated by their subordinates.

*Source:* New Patterns of Management *by Rensis Likert, copyright © 1961, McGraw-Hill, Inc. Reprinted with permission.*

is the primary determinant of organizational climate. Those in charge reflect the character of and determine the climate of the organization.

Management consultant Rensis Likert identifies four systems of management that correspond with the four types of organizational climate. His conclusions are based on studies of over twenty thousand managers in widely different kinds of organizations, both inside and outside the United States. A description of each of the four systems of management follows.[1]

### System I Management (Exploitive)

System I management is autocratic and hierarchical, with virtually no participation by subordinates. Managers make decisions, and subordinates are expected to comply without question. Managers show little confidence or trust in employees, and subordinates do not feel free to discuss job-related problems with their supervisors. In a free social and economic order, System I managements rarely survive because workers avoid them as much as possible. Where they do exist, they are characterized by a lack of employee loyalty and recurrent financial crises.

### System II Management (Impoverished)

System II management makes some attempt to avoid being completely autocratic. Power remains at the top, but subordinates are given occasional opportunities for participation in the decision-making process. System II managements fall into two categories that determine their relative success. Successful System II managements are benevolent autocracies in which those at the top of the organization have genuine concern for the welfare of their employees. Failing System II managements are autocracies that do not consider the interests or ideas of subordinate workers. Some organizations are founded by autocratic, but benevolent, System II managers, who achieve good results. Then, as time passes and new managers assume power, the autocratic style of management is maintained, but benevolence is not, and the organization fails.

### System III Management (Supportive)

In System III management, superiors are still superiors, but they show a great deal of interest and confidence in subordinates. Power resides in superiors, but there is good communication and participation throughout the organization. Employees understand the goals of the organization, and commitment to achieve them is widespread. Employees feel fairly free to discuss job-related problems with managers. This management system involves employee participation and involvement in decision making.

### System IV Management (Enlightened)

In System IV management, energy and power reside in the logical focus of interest and concern for a problem. Employees have a high degree of freedom to initiate, coordinate, and execute plans to accomplish goals.

Communication between subordinates and superiors is open, honest, and uncensored. Employees are treated with trust rather than suspicion. Managers ask employees for ideas and try to use their suggestions. System IV management results in high employee satisfaction and productivity. Absenteeism and turnover are low, strikes are nonexistent, and efficiency is high. Likert describes System IV management as follows:

> . . .The human organization of a System IV firm is made up of interlocking work groups with a high degree of group loyalty among the members and favorable attitudes and trust among peers, superiors and subordinates.
>
> Consideration for others and relatively high levels of skill in personal interaction, group problem solving, and other group functions also are present. These skills permit effective participation in decisions on common problems. Participation is used, for example, to establish organizational objectives that are a satisfactory integration of the needs and desires of all the members of the organization and of persons functionally related to it.
>
> Members of the System IV organization are highly motivated to achieve the organization's goals. High levels of reciprocal influence occur, and high levels of total coordinated influence are achieved in the organization.
>
> Communication is efficient and effective. There is a flow from one part of the organization to another of all the relevant information important for each decision and action.
>
> The leadership in the System IV organization has developed a highly effective social system for interaction, problem solving, mutual influence, and organizational achievement. This leadership is technically competent and holds high performance goals.[2]

Four principles should be followed in order to develop System IV management: (1) view human resources as the organization's greatest asset; (2) treat every individual with understanding, dignity, warmth, and support; (3) tap the constructive rather than the destructive power of groups; and (4) set high performance goals at every level of the organization.[3]

Likert recommends that all organizations adopt the enlightened principles of System IV management. He estimates that U.S. organizations, as a whole, are between a System II and a System III and that a shift to System IV would improve employee morale and productivity by 20 to 40 percent, or more.[4]

Research has supported Likert's ideas. Study after study shows that when an organization moves to System IV management, employee performance improves, costs decrease, and improvements occur in the overall satisfaction and health of the members of the organization. In addition, research findings show that System IV management is applicable to every size and type of organization, including private businesses and government agencies.[5]

The following evaluation instrument is used to identify Likert's management systems. It is a classic in organizational psychology. Note that this exercise measures employee opinions about management practices in seven key areas—leadership, motivation, communications, teamwork, decision making, goal setting, and controls.

# CHARACTERISTICS OF DIFFERENT MANAGEMENT SYSTEMS

## Directions

Evaluate each organizational variable on a scale of 1 to 20 (1 is low; 20 is high).

## SYSTEMS OF MANAGEMENT

| Organizational Variable | System I | System II | System III | System IV |
|---|---|---|---|---|
| **1.** Leadership processes used: | | | | |
| Extent to which superiors have confidence and trust in subordinates | Have no confidence and trust in subordinates | Have condescending confidence and trust, such as master has to servant | Substantial but not complete confidence and trust; still wish to keep control of decisions | Complete confidence and trust in all matters |

|  1  2  3  4  5 | 6  7  8  9  10 | 11  12  13  14  15 | 16  17  18  19  20 |
|---|---|---|---|

| Organizational Variable | System I | System II | System III | System IV |
|---|---|---|---|---|
| Extent to which superiors behave so that subordinates feel free to discuss important things about their jobs with their immediate superior | Subordinates do not feel at all free to discuss things about the job with their superior | Subordinates do not feel very free to discuss things about the job with their superior | Subordinates feel free to discuss things about the job with their superior | Subordinates feel completely free to discuss things about the job with their superior |

|  1  2  3  4  5 | 6  7  8  9  10 | 11  12  13  14  15 | 16  17  18  19  20 |
|---|---|---|---|

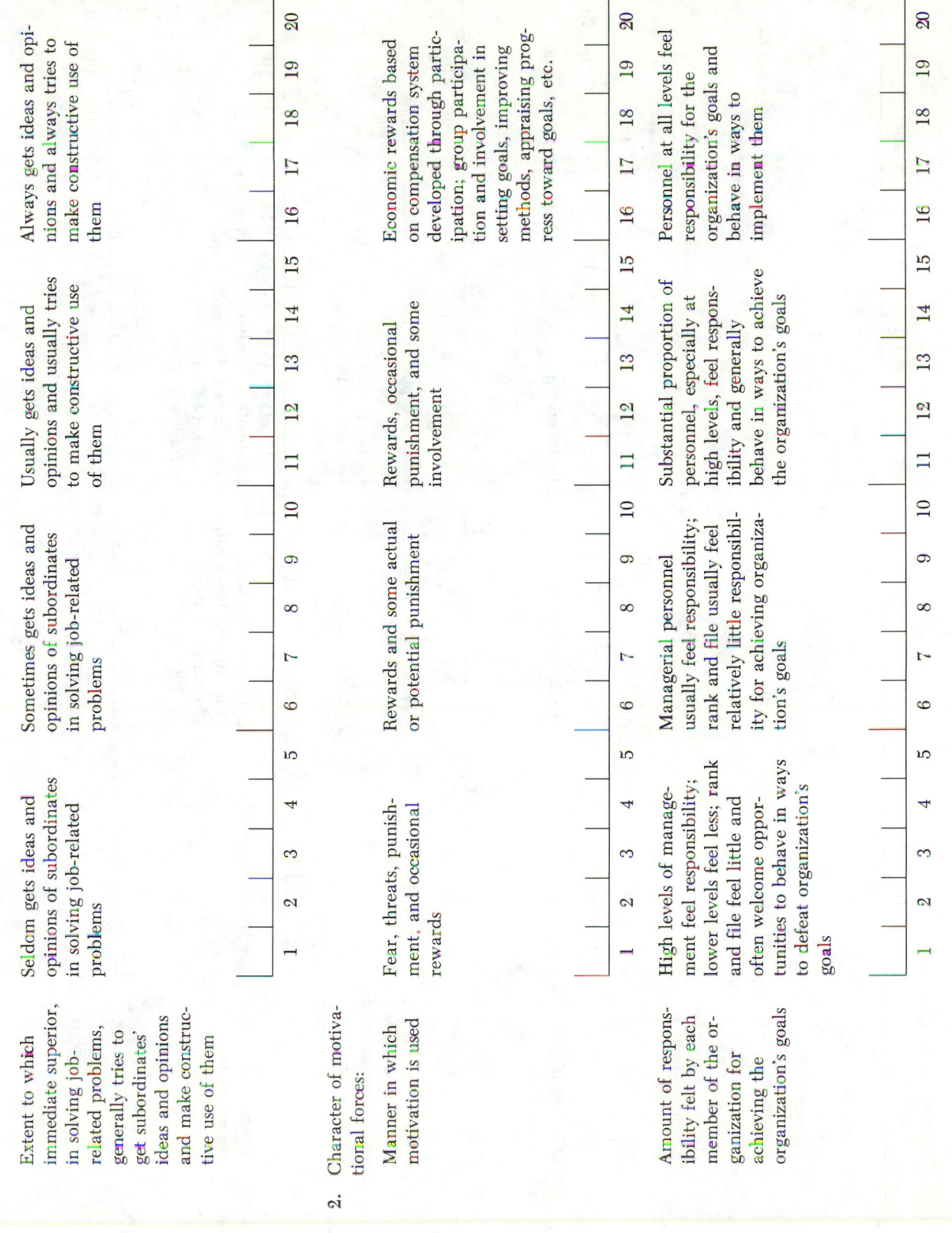

Extent to which immediate superior, in solving job-related problems, generally tries to get subordinates' ideas and opinions and make constructive use of them

| 1 2 3 4 | 5 6 7 8 9 | 10 11 12 13 14 15 | 16 17 18 19 20 |
|---|---|---|---|
| Seldom gets ideas and opinions of subordinates in solving job-related problems | Sometimes gets ideas and opinions of subordinates in solving job-related problems | Usually gets ideas and opinions and usually tries to make constructive use of them | Always gets ideas and opinions and always tries to make constructive use of them |

2. Character of motivational forces:

Manner in which motivation is used

| 1 2 3 4 | 5 6 7 8 9 | 10 11 12 13 14 15 | 16 17 18 19 20 |
|---|---|---|---|
| Fear, threats, punishment, and occasional rewards | Rewards and some actual or potential punishment | Rewards, occasional punishment, and some involvement | Economic rewards based on compensation system developed through participation; group participation and involvement in setting goals, improving methods, appraising progress toward goals, etc. |

Amount of responsibility felt by each member of the organization for achieving the organization's goals

| 1 2 3 4 | 5 6 7 8 9 | 10 11 12 13 14 15 | 16 17 18 19 20 |
|---|---|---|---|
| High levels of management feel responsibility; lower levels feel less; rank and file feel little and often welcome opportunities to behave in ways to defeat organization's goals | Managerial personnel usually feel responsibility; rank and file usually feel relatively little responsibility for achieving organization's goals | Substantial proportion of personnel, especially at high levels, feel responsibility and generally behave in ways to achieve the organization's goals | Personnel at all levels feel responsibility for the organization's goals and behave in ways to implement them |

| Organizational Variable | System I | System II | System III | System IV |
|---|---|---|---|---|
| 3. Character of communication processes: | | | | |
| Amount of interaction and communication aimed at achieving organization's objectives | Very little | Little | Quite a bit | Much with both individuals and group |

| 1 | 2 | 3 | 4 | 5 | 6 | 7 | 8 | 9 | 10 | 11 | 12 | 13 | 14 | 15 | 16 | 17 | 18 | 19 | 20 |
|---|---|---|---|---|---|---|---|---|---|---|---|---|---|---|---|---|---|---|---|

| Organizational Variable | System I | System II | System III | System IV |
|---|---|---|---|---|
| Direction of information flow | Downward | Mostly downward | Down and up | Down, up, and among peers |

| 1 | 2 | 3 | 4 | 5 | 6 | 7 | 8 | 9 | 10 | 11 | 12 | 13 | 14 | 15 | 16 | 17 | 18 | 19 | 20 |
|---|---|---|---|---|---|---|---|---|---|---|---|---|---|---|---|---|---|---|---|

| Organizational Variable | System I | System II | System III | System IV |
|---|---|---|---|---|
| Extent to which downward communications are accepted by subordinates | Viewed with great suspicion | May or may not be viewed with suspicion | Often accepted, but at times viewed with suspicion; may or may not be openly questioned | Generally accepted, but if not, openly and candidly questioned |

| 1 | 2 | 3 | 4 | 5 | 6 | 7 | 8 | 9 | 10 | 11 | 12 | 13 | 14 | 15 | 16 | 17 | 18 | 19 | 20 |
|---|---|---|---|---|---|---|---|---|---|---|---|---|---|---|---|---|---|---|---|

| Organizational Variable | System I | System II | System III | System IV |
|---|---|---|---|---|
| Accuracy of upward communication | Tends to be inaccurate | Information that boss wants to hear flows; other information is restricted and filtered | Information that boss wants to hear flows; other information may be limited or cautiously given | Accurate |

| 1 | 2 | 3 | 4 | 5 | 6 | 7 | 8 | 9 | 10 | 11 | 12 | 13 | 14 | 15 | 16 | 17 | 18 | 19 | 20 |
|---|---|---|---|---|---|---|---|---|---|---|---|---|---|---|---|---|---|---|---|

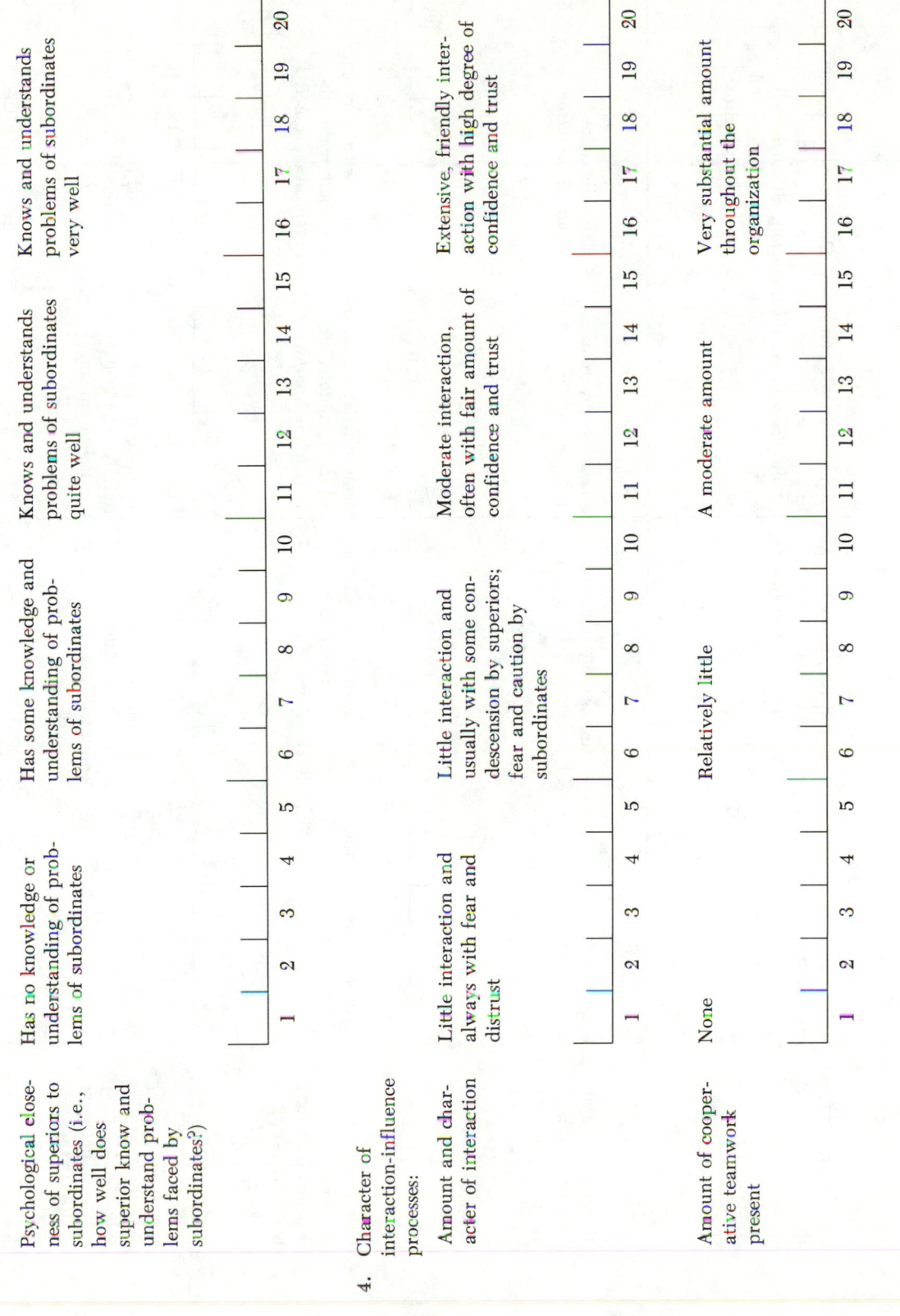

Psychological closeness of superiors to subordinates (i.e., how well does superior know and understand problems faced by subordinates?)

| Has no knowledge or understanding of problems of subordinates | Has some knowledge and understanding of problems of subordinates | Knows and understands problems of subordinates quite well | Knows and understands problems of subordinates very well |
| --- | --- | --- | --- |

1  2  3  4  5  6  7  8  9  10  11  12  13  14  15  16  17  18  19  20

4. Character of interaction-influence processes:

Amount and character of interaction

| Little interaction and always with fear and distrust | Little interaction and usually with some condescension by superiors; fear and caution by subordinates | Moderate interaction, often with fair amount of confidence and trust | Extensive, friendly interaction with high degree of confidence and trust |
| --- | --- | --- | --- |

1  2  3  4  5  6  7  8  9  10  11  12  13  14  15  16  17  18  19  20

Amount of cooperative teamwork present

| None | Relatively little | A moderate amount | Very substantial amount throughout the organization |
| --- | --- | --- | --- |

1  2  3  4  5  6  7  8  9  10  11  12  13  14  15  16  17  18  19  20

| Organizational Variable | System I | System II | System III | System IV |
|---|---|---|---|---|
| **5.** Character of decision-making processes: | | | | |
| At what level in the organization are decisions formally made? | Bulk of decisions at top of organization | Policy at top; many decisions within prescribed framework made at lower levels | Broad policy and general decisions at top; more specific decisions at lower levels | Decision making widely done throughout organization, although well integrated through linking process provided by overlapping groups |

1 2 3 4 5 6 7 8 9 10 11 12 13 14 15 16 17 18 19 20

| | | | | |
|---|---|---|---|---|
| To what extent are decision makers aware of problems, particularly those at lower levels in the organization? | Often unaware or only partially aware | Aware of some, unaware of others | Moderately aware of problems | Generally quite well aware of problems |

1 2 3 4 5 6 7 8 9 10 11 12 13 14 15 16 17 18 19 20

| | | | | |
|---|---|---|---|---|
| Extent to which technical and professional knowledge is used in decision making | Used only if possessed at higher levels | Much of what is available in higher and middle levels is used | Much of what is available in higher, middle, and lower levels is used | Most of what is available anywhere within the organization is used |

1 2 3 4 5 6 7 8 9 10 11 12 13 14 15 16 17 18 19 20

| | | | | |
|---|---|---|---|---|
| To what extent are subordinates involved in decisions related to their work? | Not at all | Never involved in decisions; occasionally consulted | Usually consulted, but ordinarily not involved in the decision making | Involved fully in all decisions related to their work |

1 2 3 4 5 6 7 8 9 10 11 12 13 14 15 16 17 18 19 20

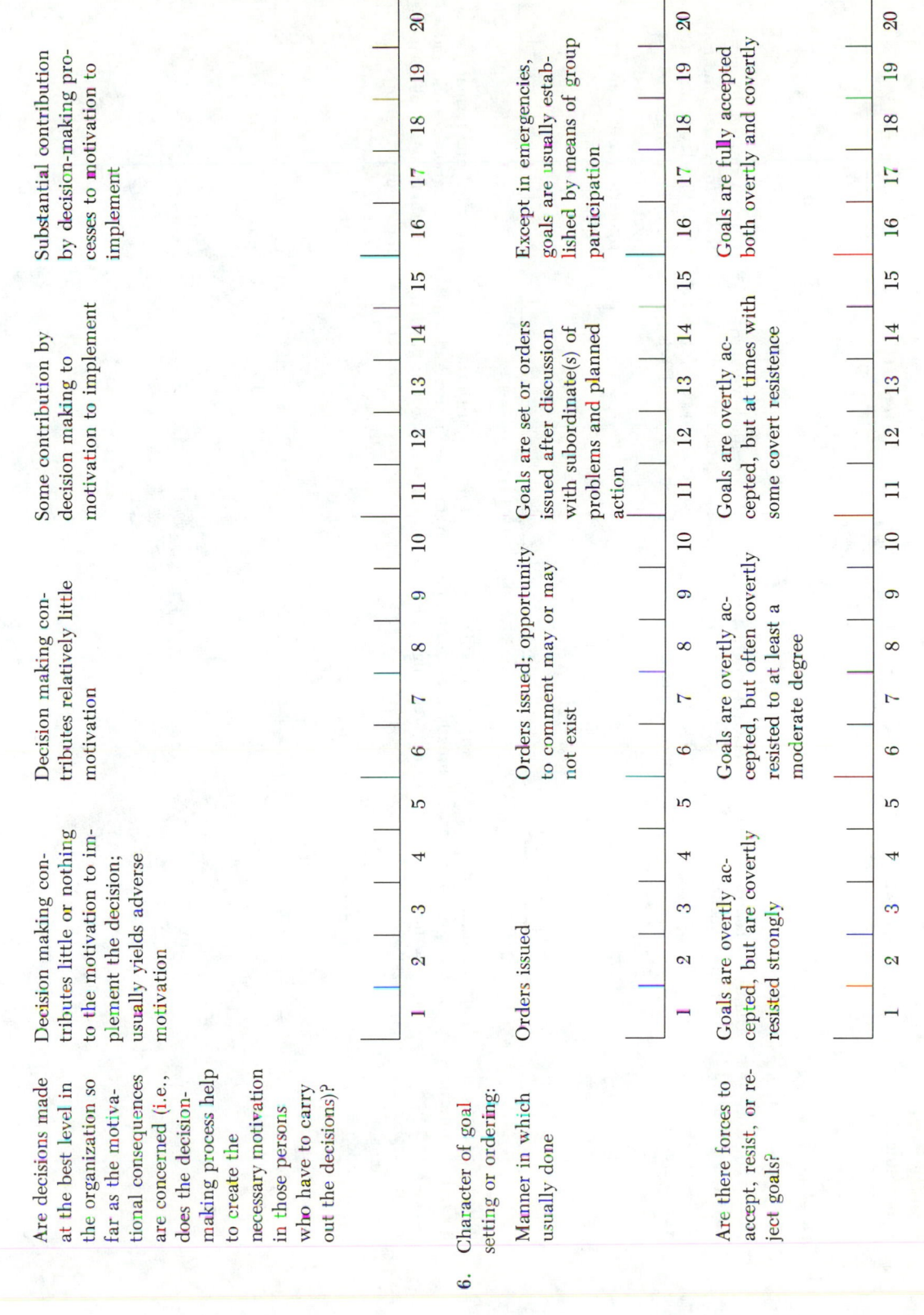

Are decisions made at the best level in the organization so far as the motivational consequences are concerned (i.e., does the decision-making process help to create the necessary motivation in those persons who have to carry out the decisions)?

| 1 2 3 4 | 5 6 7 8 9 10 | 11 12 13 14 15 | 16 17 18 19 20 |
|---|---|---|---|
| Decision making contributes little or nothing to the motivation to implement the decision; usually yields adverse motivation | Decision making contributes relatively little motivation | Some contribution by decision making to motivation to implement | Substantial contribution by decision-making processes to motivation to implement |

**6. Character of goal setting or ordering:**

Manner in which usually done

| 1 2 3 4 | 5 6 7 8 9 10 | 11 12 13 14 15 | 16 17 18 19 20 |
|---|---|---|---|
| Orders issued | Orders issued; opportunity to comment may or may not exist | Goals are set or orders issued after discussion with subordinate(s) of problems and planned action | Except in emergencies, goals are usually established by means of group participation |

Are there forces to accept, resist, or reject goals?

| 1 2 3 4 | 5 6 7 8 9 10 | 11 12 13 14 15 | 16 17 18 19 20 |
|---|---|---|---|
| Goals are overtly accepted, but are covertly resisted strongly | Goals are overtly accepted, but often covertly resisted to at least a moderate degree | Goals are overtly accepted, but at times with some covert resistance | Goals are fully accepted both overtly and covertly |

| Organizational Variable | System I | System II | System III | System IV |
|---|---|---|---|---|
| **7. Character of control processes:** | | | | |
| Extent to which the review and control functions are concentrated | Highly concentrated in top management | Relatively highly concentrated, with some delegated control to middle and lower levels | Moderate downward delegation of review and control processes; lower as well as higher levels feel responsible | Quite widespread responsibility for review and control, with lower units at times imposing more rigorous reviews and tighter controls than top management |

| 1 | 2 | 3 | 4 | 5 | 6 | 7 | 8 | 9 | 10 | 11 | 12 | 13 | 14 | 15 | 16 | 17 | 18 | 19 | 20 |
|---|---|---|---|---|---|---|---|---|---|---|---|---|---|---|---|---|---|---|---|

| Organizational Variable | System I | System II | System III | System IV |
|---|---|---|---|---|
| Extent to which there is an informal organization present and supporting or opposing goals of organization | Informal organization present and opposing goals of formal organization | Informal organization usually present and partially resisting goals | Informal organization may be present and may either support or partially resist goals of formal organization | Informal and formal organization are one and the same; hence all social forces support efforts to achieve organization's goals |

| 1 | 2 | 3 | 4 | 5 | 6 | 7 | 8 | 9 | 10 | 11 | 12 | 13 | 14 | 15 | 16 | 17 | 18 | 19 | 20 |
|---|---|---|---|---|---|---|---|---|---|---|---|---|---|---|---|---|---|---|---|

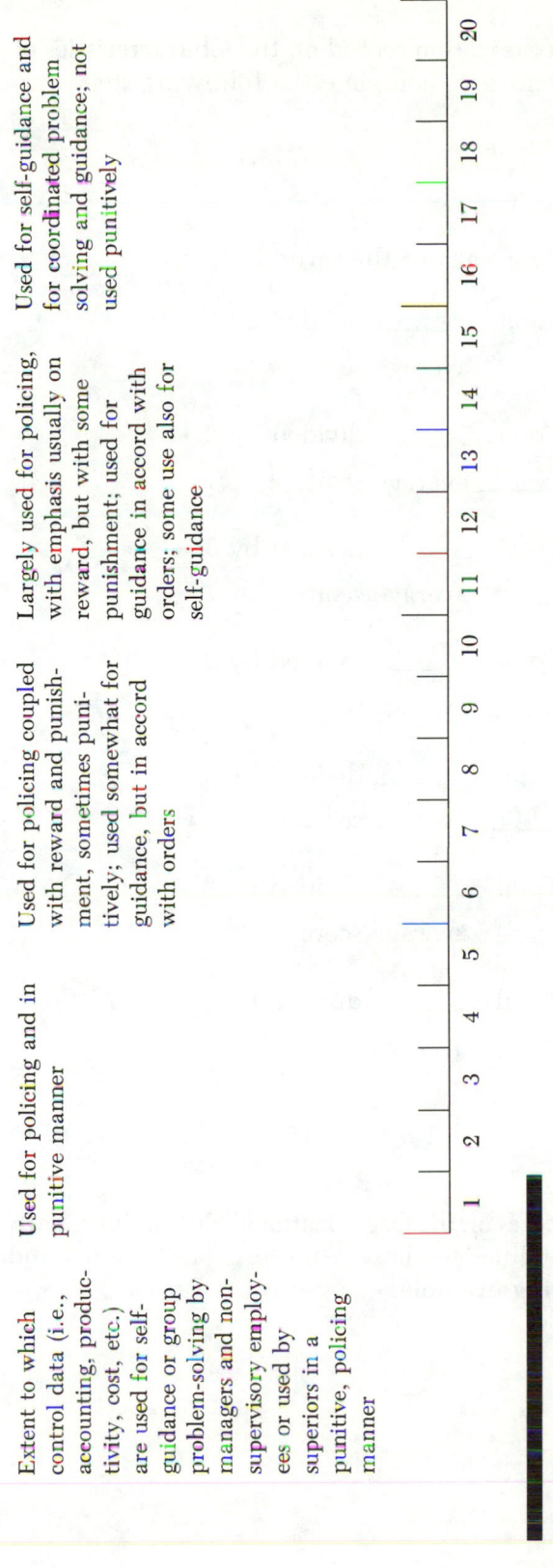

Extent to which control data (i.e., accounting, productivity, cost, etc.) are used for self-guidance or group problem-solving by managers and non-supervisory employees or used by superiors in a punitive, policing manner

Used for policing and in punitive manner

Used for policing coupled with reward and punishment, sometimes punitively; used somewhat for guidance, but in accord with orders

Largely used for policing, with emphasis usually on reward, but with some punishment; used for guidance in accord with orders; some use also for self-guidance

Used for self-guidance and for coordinated problem solving and guidance; not used punitively

1  2  3  4  5  6  7  8  9  10  11  12  13  14  15  16  17  18  19  20

*Source:* The Human Organization: Its Management and Value *by Rensis Likert, copyright © 1967, McGraw-Hill, Inc. Reprinted with permission.*

# SCORING

To find how well your organization scored on the Characteristics of Different Management Systems test, complete the following steps.

### Step One

Obtain an average score for each of the seven key areas:

Leadership processes:     Total _____ divided by 3 =
_____ average score

Motivational forces:      Total _____ divided by 2 =
_____ average score

Communication
processes:                Total _____ divided by 5 =
_____ average score

Interaction processes:    Total _____ divided by 2 =
_____ average score

Decision-making
processes:                Total _____ divided by 5 =
_____ average score

Goal setting:             Total _____ divided by 2 =
_____ average score

Control processes:        Total _____ divided by 3 =
_____ average score

### Step Two

Enter the seven average scores on the Organizational Evaluation Chart. Connect them with straight lines to show a pattern of strengths and weaknesses as in the following example.

# EXAMPLE

| Organizational Variable | System I | System II | System III | System IV |
|---|---|---|---|---|
| Leadership | 1 2 3 4 5 | 6 7 8 9 10 | 11 12 13 14 15 | 16 17 18 19 20 |
| Motivation | 1 2 3 4 5 | 6 7 8 9 10 | 11 12 13 14 15 | 16 17 18 19 20 |
| Communication | 1 2 3 4 5 | 6 7 8 9 10 | 11 12 13 14 15 | 16 17 18 19 20 |
| Interaction | 1 2 3 4 5 | 6 7 8 9 10 | 11 12 13 14 15 | 16 17 18 19 20 |
| Decision making | 1 2 3 4 5 | 6 7 8 9 10 | 11 12 13 14 15 | 16 17 18 19 20 |
| Goal setting | 1 2 3 4 5 | 6 7 8 9 10 | 11 12 13 14 15 | 16 17 18 19 20 |
| Controls | 1 2 3 4 5 | 6 7 8 9 10 | 11 12 13 14 15 | 16 17 18 19 20 |

## ORGANIZATIONAL EVALUATION CHART

| Organizational Variable | System I | System II | System III | System IV |
|---|---|---|---|---|
| Leadership | 1 2 3 4 5 | 6 7 8 9 10 | 11 12 13 14 15 | 16 17 18 19 20 |
| Motivation | 1 2 3 4 5 | 6 7 8 9 10 | 11 12 13 14 15 | 16 17 18 19 20 |
| Communication | 1 2 3 4 5 | 6 7 8 9 10 | 11 12 13 14 15 | 16 17 18 19 20 |
| Interaction | 1 2 3 4 5 | 6 7 8 9 10 | 11 12 13 14 15 | 16 17 18 19 20 |
| Decision making | 1 2 3 4 5 | 6 7 8 9 10 | 11 12 13 14 15 | 16 17 18 19 20 |
| Goal setting | 1 2 3 4 5 | 6 7 8 9 10 | 11 12 13 14 15 | 16 17 18 19 20 |
| Controls | 1 2 3 4 5 | 6 7 8 9 10 | 11 12 13 14 15 | 16 17 18 19 20 |

# INTERPRETATION

Total the average scores for the seven organizational variables, and match the final score with the corresponding management system.

| | Management Systems | Evaluations |
|---|---|---|
| 105–140 | System IV | Enlightened; successful; best organizational climate |
| 70–104 | System III | Supportive; positive; good organizational climate |
| 35–69 | System II | Impoverished; needs work; unsatisfactory organizational climate |
| 7–34 | System I | Exploitive; failing; poor organizational climate |

# ENLIGHTENED ORGANIZATIONS

Historically, organizational structures have resembled the diagram in Figure 3.2.

This form of organization has been used by church, military, and government organizations down through the years because of basic assumptions people have held: top people are smarter than bottom people; bottom people owe respect and obedience to top people; bottom people must be forced to behave; bottom people should not know about the ideas and plans of top people; and top people are more worthy and valuable than bottom people.[6]

The form and assumptions of classical organizations worked well in earlier times because top people did know more than bottom people. For the most part, only the people at the top could read and write and knew history and mathematics. Also, bottom people accepted the supremacy of nobility, religious figures, and other people in authority. Poverty and powerlessness left bottom people little choice except to conform to the wishes of powerful top people. Finally, people at the bottom were considered expendable.[7]

**FIGURE 3.2**

Classical Organization Structure and
Processes

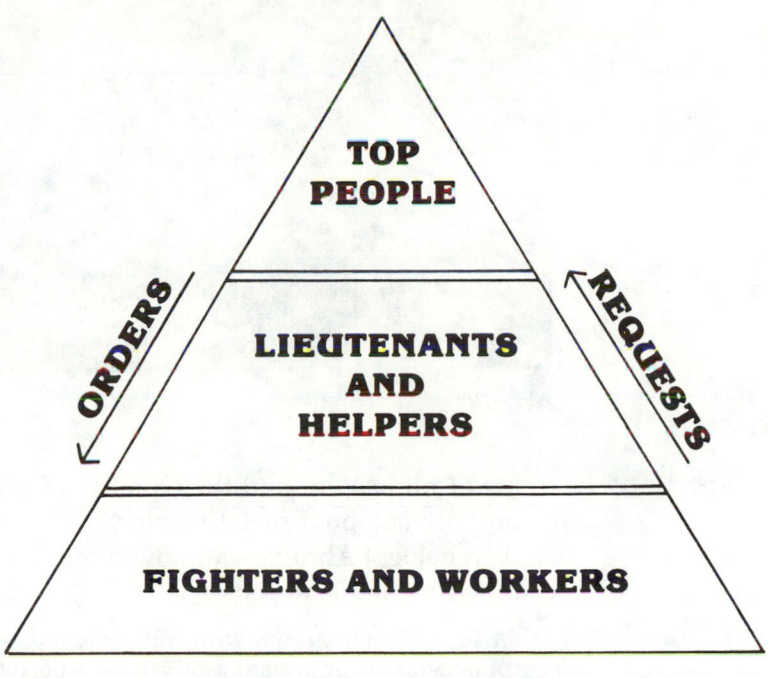

As conditions changed in Western culture, particularly in the United States, traditional assumptions about human behavior became less valid. Free public education is available in America today, equalizing knowledge and opportunity for more and more people, and information is easily accessible for everyone as newspapers, magazines, and radios keep us informed of daily events. Television has significantly equalized the experiences of people from all classes in that what they see and hear is much the same. Also, social stature based on education and occupation has become increasingly important. An individual's work, as opposed to his or her family history, is the primary determinant of social status in America today.

In addition, welfare programs, minimum-wage laws, unemployment insurance, savings accounts, and installment buying have helped to reduce the economic gap between the poor and the rich. At the same time, these economic factors have allowed for individuality in living habits and lifestyles, making it more difficult to treat people as collective types.[8]

Finally, the efforts of groups such as labor unions and social reform movements have decreased the absolute power advantage of those at the top. Group efforts have produced government-supported reforms such as civil rights legislation and equal employment opportunity among the races, sexes, and ages. Today, the duty of government to protect the civil

AFL-CIO

rights of all people, and the equality of all people before the law, are commonly accepted social ideals.[9]

Psychologist Abraham Maslow summarizes the meaning of these social changes in American society:

> . . . People are growing and growing, either in their actual health of personality or in their aspirations, especially in the United States, and especially women and underprivileged groups. The more grown people are . . . the less well people will function in the authoritarian situation, and the more they will hate it. Partly this comes about from the fact that when people have a choice between a high and a low pleasure, they practically always choose the high pleasure if they have previously experienced both. What this means is that people who have experienced freedom can never really be content again with slavery, even though they made no protest about the slavery before they had the experience of freedom. This is true with all higher pleasures; those people who have known the feeling of dignity and self-respect for the first time can never again be content with slavishness, even though they made no protest about it before being treated with dignity.[10]

In spite of changes in society and changes in the attitudes of workers, the assumptions of exploitive, System I organizations remain remarkably unchanged from those held by organizations centuries ago. These organizations assume:[11]

- Management's job should be to set quotas, to control activities, and to achieve results by dispensing rewards and punishments.

- Showing respect and obedience to management, and keeping one's place in the pecking order, should be the duty of all employees.

- Employees should not have access to the plans and budgets of the organization because employees are untrustworthy or not smart enough to understand them.

- Employees need strict rules and formal discipline to keep them in line.

- Employees are supposed to serve management. The welfare and pleasure of upper level personnel should be the primary concern of lower level personnel.

- Ideas should originate with top management and travel downward. Creativity and change should not be expected, encouraged, or rewarded at lower levels of the organization.

- Employees are expendable.

Contrast the assumptions of exploitive, System I organizations with today's successful organizations. Although the chart of responsibilities and reporting relationships looks similar, vastly different assumptions and practices are followed, and these result in a superior quality of work and a superior quality of work life. See Figure 3.3.

---

**FIGURE 3.3**

**Enlightened, System IV Organization Structure and Processes**

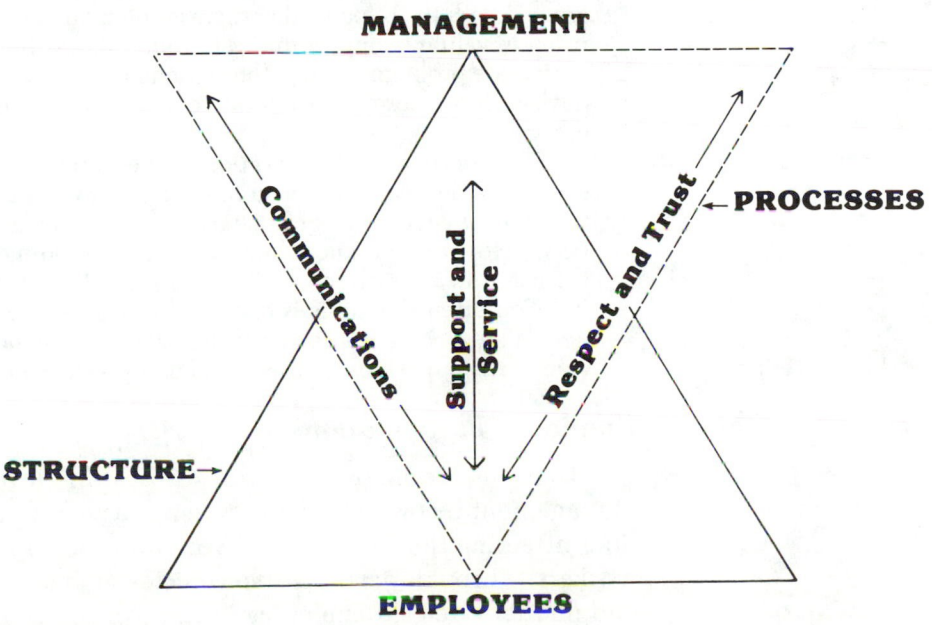

The following are the assumptions and practices of enlightened, System IV organizations. As you read these, consider your own organization. Ask what is good and what needs to be improved. Also, consider your own role. As upper manager, middle manager, front-line supervisor, or employee, what can you do to help the climate of your organization and therefore the quality of work and the quality of work life?

## Focus of Concern

The primary goal of every level of management is to facilitate the work of subordinates. Supporting and serving lower level subordinates is a major concern. Management consultant Harry Levinson describes the importance of showing support to employees:

> The ability to provide psychological and moral support is one of the basic dimensions of good leadership. It is also a "sine qua non" of organizational life. Despite its importance, the most glaring deficiency in contemporary organizational functioning is the almost universal inadequacy of support. Executives habitually neglect the importance of being available to their people. They think it is silly to have to "hold people's hands." Wanting their subordinates to take initiative and to act independently, they try to model a self-reliant stance. All this is very rational, but it is not valid psychologically. People need to have access to their superiors, to be able to read their faces, to see recognition of their own existence reflected in their superior's eyes. Managing by objectives does not alter this fundamental human condition. People need contact and support, and executives at all levels should recognize this as one of their primary tasks.
>
> Support for lower level executives is frequently discussed, but not necessarily delivered. The suggestion that managers and supervisors meet with subordinates for a few minutes before starting the day's work is often greeted with the response that there is not enough time. But such meetings provide valuable opportunities to touch bases, lay out the day's work, anticipate problems, and gather momentum. They also serve to start the day with a sense of cooperative helpfulness, mutual support, and optimism.
>
> Even in day-to-day operations, when there is no moral or strategic crisis, people benefit from support in the form of feedback. As a rule, they do not get enough of it. One can ask people in almost any organization, "How do you know how well you are doing?" Ninety percent of them are likely to respond, "If I do something wrong, I'll hear about it." Too often this topic is discussed as if praise were the answer; it is not. What people are saying is that they do not have sufficient support from their superiors. Praise without support is an empty gesture.[12]

## Employee Participation

Decisions are made at the lowest possible level in the organization. Management recognizes that most employees want to participate in decisions affecting their immediate work and their relationships with fellow workers. Through participative vehicles such as committees, task forces, and quality circles, democracy in the workplace is practiced. Crawford Greenewalt, management author, describes the importance of broad employee involvement:

Organization success is not due to one person, not to the few geniuses that cross the stage from time to time, but arises out of the creation of an atmosphere that induces every man or woman connected with the enterprise, no matter what their position, to perform his or her task with a degree of competence and enthusiasm measurably greater than what could be called their normal expectation. . . . Business success, then, can be measured by summing up the small increments of extra effort on the parts of all the people who are joined together in a given enterprise.[13]

## Respect

Employees seek dignity in the work experience. In the home, at school, and in the broader community, our society encourages self-respect and independent thinking. Although employees may accept subordinate positions in the work setting, they resent being treated as inferior people who cannot think for themselves. This reduces both morale and productivity. Enlightened, System IV organizations treat each worker in each job classification with equal respect.

## Communication

System IV managers are aware that the more workers know about the job (costs, schedules, competitive position, etc.), the better quality of work they will usually perform. Therefore, regular communication sessions about goals, working conditions, and work-related issues are conducted throughout the work force — top, middle, and frontline. Communications flow freely, and the information is accurate.

## Job Assignments

If employee satisfaction and quality performance are to be achieved, the job must match the level of ability, the temperament, and the interests of the worker. Enlightened managers remember the adage that one person's poison is another's cup of tea and, as much as possible, they make job assignments based on the unique qualities of each employee.

## Orientation

Although guided by the belief that the greatest good for the greatest number is best, and realizing that the interests of the individual sometimes must be subordinated to the greater good of the majority, the dominant orientation of System IV organizations is that organizations exist to serve people, not that people exist to serve organizations.

## Innovation

System IV managers encourage new ideas at every level of responsibility and reward employees who make suggestions. In this way, the organization combats inflexibility. Change is generated within the organization in a constructive manner, and responsiveness to change outside the organization is improved.

## Motivation

System IV managers recognize that after income has reached a level sufficient to meet the economic needs of employees, other kinds of rewards become more important: (a) job security; (b) acceptance from co-workers; (c) respect and recognition; and (d) self-expression, respectively. Policies, procedures, and programs are provided to meet these needs.

## Human Understanding

Employees are recognized as multidimensional individuals who have goals and values of their own and who are subject to the demands and constraints of other institutions — family, social, recreational, educational, and professional groups — all vying for their time, effort, and loyalty. Employees are viewed as more complex, less predictable, and far less manageable than the economic beings of yesterday. Therefore, policies and programs are available to accommodate a life away from the job.

## Individuality

System IV managers consider the unique characteristics of employees and tap the productive possibilities of each: the needs of some to lead and of others to follow; the needs of some for privacy and of others for interaction; the needs of some for stability and of others for variety; the needs of some for freedom and of others for structure; the dependable delivery of some and the creative ability of others; the open-mindedness of some and the rigid allegiances of others. Enlightened organizations realize that workers are like the instruments in an orchestra. Each is different, so each is treated individually to maximize personal satisfaction and job performance.

## Education

Many of today's workers are products of a culture of immediacy, exponents of a society that expects instant gratification, whether earned or not. System IV managers recognize this and cope with the problem through patience and education.

## Human Resources

Talented people are recognized as the key to the success of an organization. As such, System IV organizations assign the highest priority to the recruitment and development of qualified personnel at every level of responsibility.

## Goal Setting

The goal-setting process involves broad employee participation in setting high but attainable objectives in line with the mission of the organization. Job duties and day-to-day activities are based on individual and work group objectives; these objectives are based on organization-wide goals;

organization-wide goals are established to support the mission or purpose of the organization; and the mission is based on shared values.

## Controls

Employees share responsibility for controlling the organization. The emphasis is on self-control and problem solving rather than on policing and punishment. There is a saying that people like to be led, but they hate to be controlled. Close supervision, restrictive policies, and an autocratic leadership style lead to resentment, resistance, and rebellion.

## Trust

Many employees have said of their organization: "Our problems are well known, and we even know what to do about them, but we are afraid to criticize. Who wants to get their head chopped off?" System IV managers encourage constructive criticism. They use many methods— attitude surveys, performance audits, suggestion systems, small-group meetings, grievance procedures, quality circles, and day-to-day communications—to constantly review the appropriateness of policies and practices. In management's openness to criticism, the guiding light is not who said what, but what is the truth.

When enlightened, System IV assumptions and practices are followed, both the individual and the organization benefit. Consider one example:

> A manufacturing organization decided to treat its employees more like adults. The firm was not following any behavioral theory, but simply wanted to remove conditions that made employees feel regimented and that seemed counterproductive. Time clocks, buzzers, and bells were removed, and employees were put on salary instead of hourly wages. Rigid rules were eliminated, and routine disciplinary action was replaced with counseling. Employees were encouraged to participate in decisions affecting them personally. As a result of this change in climate, absenteeism was reduced about fifty percent, and turnover declined materially. Perhaps even more important, worker resistance to change declined substantially.[14]

Enlightened, System IV organizations produce the highest quality of work and offer their employees the highest quality of work life. In their influential book, *In Search of Excellence: Lessons From America's Best-Run Companies*, Thomas J. Peters and Robert H. Waterman, Jr., report on the nature of these organizations:

> . . .The findings from excellent companies amount to an upbeat message. There is good news from America. Good management practice today is not resident only in Japan. But, more important, the good news comes from treating people decently and asking them to shine, and from producing things that work.
>
> Scale efficiencies give way to small units with turned-on people. Precisely planned R&D efforts aimed at big bang products are replaced by armies of dedicated champions. A numbing focus on cost gives way to an enhancing focus on quality. Hierarchy and three-piece suits give way to first names, shirtsleeves, hoopla, and project-based flexibility.

Working according to fat rule books is replaced by everyone's contributing.

Even management's job becomes more fun. Instead of brain games in the sterile ivory tower, it's shaping values and reinforcing through coaching and evangelism in the field — with the worker and in support of the cherished product.[15]

How do they do it? How do the companies featured in *In Search of Excellence*, like Bechtel, Boeing, Caterpillar, Dana, Delta Air Lines, Digital Equipment, Emerson Electric, Fluor, Hewlett-Packard, IBM, Johnson & Johnson, McDonald's, Procter & Gamble, 3M, and others, succeed so impressively? What are the secrets they use? Peters and Waterman summarize the eight attributes that characterize all of these companies. The same attributes apply in public service organizations as well. They are as follows:[16]

*A bias for action.* Even though these companies may be analytical in their approach to decision-making, they are not paralyzed by that fact (as so many others seem to be). In many of these companies the standard operating procedure is "Do it, fix it, try it." Says a Digital Equipment Corporation senior executive, for example, "When we've got a big problem here, we grab ten senior guys and stick them in a room for a week. They come up with an answer and implement it." Moreover, the companies are experimenters supreme. Instead of allowing 250 engineers and marketers to work on a new product in isolation for fifteen months, they form bands of 5 to 25 and test ideas out on a customer, often with inexpensive prototypes, within a matter of weeks. What is striking is the host of practical devices the excellent companies employ, to maintain corporate fleetness of foot and counter the stultification that almost inevitably comes with size.

## ILLUS. 3.2

Enlightened organizations succeed because of a strong commitment to people.

*Courtesy of The Procter & Gamble Company*

*Close to the customer.* These companies learn from the people they serve. They provide unparalleled quality, service, and reliability — things that work and last. They succeed in differentiating — à la Frito-Lay (potato chips), Maytag (washers), or Tupperware — the most commodity-like products. IBM's marketing vice president, Francis G. (Buck) Rodgers, says, "It's a shame that, in so many companies, whenever you get good service, it's an exception." Not so at the excellent companies. Everyone gets into the act. Many of the innovative companies get their best product ideas from customers. That comes from listening intently and regularly.

*Autonomy and entrepreneurship.* The innovative companies foster many leaders and many innovators throughout the organization. They are a hive of what we've come to call champions; 3M has been described as "so intent on innovation that its essential atmosphere seems not like that of a large corporation, but rather a loose network of laboratories and cubbyholes populated by feverish inventors and dauntless entrepreneurs who let their imaginations fly in all directions." They don't try to hold everyone on so short a rein that they can't be creative. They encourage practical risk-taking, and support good tries. They follow Fletcher Byrom's ninth commandment: "Make sure you generate a reasonable number of mistakes."

*Productivity through people.* The excellent companies treat the rank and file as the root source of quality and productivity gain. They do not foster we/they labor attitudes or regard capital investment as the fundamental source of efficiency improvement. As Thomas J. Watson, Jr. said of his company, "IBM's philosophy is largely contained in three simple beliefs. I want to begin with what I think is the most important: our respect for the individual. This is a simple concept, but in IBM it occupies a major portion of management time." Texas Instruments' chairman Mark Shepherd talks about it in terms of every worker being "seen as a source of ideas, not just acting as a pair of hands"; each of his more than 9,000 People Involvement Program, or PIP, teams (TI's quality circles) does contribute to the company's sparkling productivity record.

*Hands-on, value driven.* Thomas Watson, Jr. said, "The basic philosophy of an organization has far more to do with its achievements than do technological or economic resources, organizational structure, innovation, and timing." Watson and HP's William Hewlett are legendary for walking the plant floors. McDonalds' Ray Kroc regularly visited stores and assesses them on the factors the company holds dear, Q.S.C.&V. (Quality, Service, Cleanliness, and Value).

*Stick to the knitting.* Robert W. Johnson, former Johnson & Johnson chairman, put it this way: "Never acquire a business you don't know how to run." Or as Edward G. Harness, past chief executive at Procter & Gamble, said, "This company has never left its base. We seek to be anything but a conglomerate." While there are a few exceptions, the odds for excellent performance seem strongly to favor those companies that stay reasonably close to businesses they know.

*Simple form, lean staff.* As big as most of the companies we have looked at are, none when we looked at them were formally run with a matrix organization structure, and some that had tried that form had abandoned it. The underlying structural forms and systems in the excellent companies are elegantly simple. Top-level staffs are lean; it is not uncommon to find a corporate staff of fewer than 100 people running multi-billion-dollar enterprises.

*Simultaneous loose-tight properties.* The excellent companies are both centralized and decentralized. For the most part, they have pushed autonomy down to the shop floor or product development team. On the other hand, they are fanatic centralists around the few core values they hold dear. 3M is marked by barely organized chaos surrounding its product champions. Yet one analyst argues, "The brainwashed members of an extremist political sect are no more conformist in their central beliefs." At Digital the chaos is so rampant that one executive noted, "Damn few people know who they work for." Yet Digital's fetish for reliability is more rigidly adhered to than any outsider could imagine.

Peters and Waterman go on to write that most of the eight attributes of excellent organizations are not startling and that some could be called "motherhoods." They quote Rene McPherson, president of Dana Corp., saying: "Almost everybody agrees, 'people are our most important asset.' Yet almost no one really lives it. Excellent companies live their commitment to people."[17] This, in summary, is the nature of any enlightened organization. It is an old truth, and it applies today: the human side counts.

## SUMMARY

Every industry and profession has its own unique technology. This includes special equipment, materials, knowledge, and skills. The technical side of work is important for individual and organizational effectiveness. But equally important are three central themes that run through all jobs regardless of type or level. These three themes are the meaning of work, employee morale, and organizational climate.

The goal of this book has been to describe these important themes and to show how they apply in your own work and organization. Our goal has been to personalize the subject in the hope that you will use the ideas discussed to achieve the highest possible quality of work and quality of work life. To these ends, we wish you well.

## RECOMMENDED RESOURCES

The following readings, cases, applications, and films are suggested for greater insight into the material in Part Three:

| | |
|---|---|
| **Readings** | — The Un-Manager |
| | Quality of Work Life — Learning from Tarrytown |
| | Organizational Revitalization |
| | Four-Star Management |
| | A Business and Its Beliefs: The Ideas That Helped Build IBM |
| **Cases** | — Phil Hancock Tries Changing the World . . . a Little Bit at a Time |

| Applications | — Organizational Norms Questionnaire |
| | Management Effectiveness Audit |
| | In Search of Excellence |
| Films | — The Management of Human Assets |
| | Organizational Climate |
| | In Search of Excellence: Lessons from America's |
| | Best-Run Companies |

## REFERENCE NOTES

1  Rensis Likert, *New Patterns of Management* (New York: McGraw-Hill, Inc., 1961), 222–36.

2  Likert, *New Patterns of Management*, 99, 197–211.

3  Likert, *New Patterns of Management*, 197–211; and David G. Bowers, *Systems of Organization: Management of the Human Resource* (Ann Arbor: University of Michigan Press, 1976), 106–7.

4  Rensis Likert, *News Ways of Managing Conflict* (New York: McGraw-Hill, Inc., 1976), 52, 98.

5.  Likert, *New Ways of Managing Conflict*, 17.

6  "The Corporate Dropout," *Iron Age* (1 January 1970).

7  "The Corporate Dropout."

8  John F. Cube and William F. Kenkel, *Social Stratification in the United States* (New York: Appleton-Century-Crofts, 1954), 340–41, and Robert J. Harris, *The Quest for Equality: The Constitution, Congress and the Supreme Court* (Westport, Conn.: Greenwood Press, 1977), 1.

9  Harris, *The Quest for Equality*.

10  Abraham H. Maslow, "The Necessity for Enlightened Management Policy," *Eupsychian Management: A Journal* (Homewood, Ill.: Richard D. Irwin, Inc., and The Dorsey Press, 1965), 261.

11  Likert, *New Patterns of Management*.

12  Levinson, *Executive*, 187–89.

13  Levinson, *Executive*, 216.

14  "The Unregimented Workforce," *Management in Practice*, American Management Association (September 1974), 1–2, as found in Keith Davis, *Human Behavior at Work: Organizational Behavior*, 6th ed. (New York: McGraw-Hill, Inc., 1981), 108.

15  Thomas J. Peters and Robert H. Waterman, Jr., *In Search of Excellence: Lessons from America's Best-Run Companies* (New York: Harper & Row, Publishers, Inc., 1982), xxv.

16  Peters and Waterman, *In Search of Excellence*, 14–16.

17  Peters and Waterman, *In Search of Excellence*, 16.

# STUDY QUIZ

As a test of your understanding and the extent to which you have achieved the objectives in Part Three, complete the following questions. See Appendix D for the answer key.

1. System I managements are characterized by:

    a. genuine concern for employee welfare
    b. financial security
    c. recurrent financial crises
    d. high employee morality

2. System I managements are characterized by:

    a. lack of employee loyalty
    b. organizational success
    c. financial solvency
    d. involvement in decision making

3. System III managements are characterized by:

    a. employee participation and involvement
    b. poor communication
    c. inefficiency and waste
    d. high absenteeism

4. One of the principles adhered to in a System IV organization is that:

    a. every employee must be treated equally, without regard for level of performance
    b. destructive power should be identified and eliminated where it exists
    c. human resources must be viewed as the organization's greatest asset
    d. organizational goals must be mandated and clarified by top management

5. In the best organizations, constructive criticism is encouraged from:

    a. leadership
    b. consultants
    c. analysts
    d. every worker

6. Who or what is the primary determinant of organizational climate?

    a. Employees
    b. Management
    c. The public
    d. Government

7. Likert suggests that U.S. organizations, as a whole, are:

   a. between System I and System II
   b. between System II and System III
   c. between System III and System IV

8. Likert estimates that a shift from System II or III to System IV would improve morale and productivity by:

   a. 5 to 10 percent
   b. 10 to 20 percent
   c. 20 to 40 percent

9. System III managements are characterized by:

   a. good communication
   b. poor communication
   c. financial ruin
   d. employee turnover

10. System IV managements are characterized by:

    a. high efficiency
    b. low efficiency
    c. poor communication
    d. financial failure

11. In addition to the meaning of work and the level of morale, the quality of work life depends on the:

    a. climate of the day
    b. number of policies
    c. union strength available
    d. climate of the organization

12. The primary goal of every level of management should be to facilitate the work of:

    a. financial officers
    b. employee representatives
    c. company directors
    d. subordinate workers

13. Which of the following is not a principle of System IV management?

    a. Human resources should be viewed as the organization's greatest asset
    b. Every individual should be treated with understanding, dignity, warmth, and support
    c. The constructive rather than the destructive power of groups should be tapped

    d. High performance goals should be set at every level of the organization

    e. Advancement should be based on experience and seniority

14. People in upper levels of responsibility tend to evaluate conditions more favorably than do people in lower levels.

    a. True

    b. False

15. All of the following are key organizational variables identified by Likert except:

    a. leadership processes

    b. motivational forces

    c. communication processes

    d. employee longevity

16. The characteristics of America's best run companies identified by Peters and Waterman include all of the following except:

    a. a bias for action

    b. closeness to the customer

    c. high pay, low tolerance

    d. productivity through people

    e. hands-on, value-driven approach

## DISCUSSION QUESTIONS AND ACTIVITIES

1. What is the climate of your organization? Discuss its strengths and weaknesses.

   _____

   _____

   _____

2. What role does management play in determining the organizational climate in your company? Relate examples of managers and their influence.

   _____

   _____

   _____

3. Consider the folklore of your organization. What are the stories people tell about people and events? Are these positive or negative? What does this say about the company's success?

   _____

   _____

   _____

4. Gather into groups to discuss organizational climate. What are the factors important to group members — reward systems, standards of performance, warmth and support, leadership, stress levels, etc.? Who has experienced an exploitive or impoverished organizational climate? Who has experienced a supportive or enlightened climate? Discuss.

5. Give true-life examples of good organizational climate. What do managers do? What do employees do? What influence does organizational climate have on the success of those organizations?

# READINGS

**Editor's Note:** *Some of the facts in the readings chosen for this book may appear to be out of date; however, the articles have been selected because of the overall importance of the subject matter.*

# Work

Whether work should be placed among the causes of happiness or among the causes of unhappiness may perhaps be regarded as a doubtful question. There is certainly much work which is exceedingly irksome, and an excess of work is always very painful. I think, however, that, provided work is not excessive in amount, even the dullest work is to most people less painful than idleness. There are in work all grades, from mere relief of tedium up to the profoundest delights, according to the nature of the work and the abilities of the worker. Most of the work that most people have to do is not in itself interesting, but even such work has certain great advantages. To begin with, it fills a good many hours of the day without the need of deciding what one shall do. Most people, when they are left free to fill their own time according to their own choice, are at a loss to think of anything sufficiently pleasant to be worth doing. And whatever they decide on, they are troubled by the feeling that something else would have been pleasanter. To be able to fill leisure intelligently is the last product of civilization, and at present very few people have reached this level. Moreover the exercise of choice is in itself tiresome. Except to people with unusual initiative it is positively agreeable to be told what to do at each hour of the day, provided the orders are not too unpleasant. Most of the idle rich suffer unspeakable boredom as the price of their freedom from drudgery. At times they may find relief by hunting big game in Africa, or by flying round the world, but the number of such sensations is limited, especially after youth is past. Accordingly the more intelligent rich men work nearly as hard as if they were poor, while rich women for the most part keep themselves busy with innumerable trifles of whose earth-shaking importance they are firmly persuaded.

Work therefore is desirable, first and foremost, as a preventive of boredom, for the boredom that a man feels when he is doing necessary though uninteresting work is as nothing in comparison with the boredom that he feels when he has nothing to do with his days. With this advantage of work another is associated, namely that it makes holidays much more delicious when they come. Provided a man does not have to work so hard as to impair his vigor, he is likely to find far more zest in his free time than an idle man could possibly find.

The second advantage of most paid work and of some unpaid work is that it gives chances of success and opportunities for ambition. In most work success is measured by income, and while our capitalistic society continues, this is inevitable. It is only where the best work is concerned that this measure ceases to be the natural one to apply. The desire that men feel to increase their income is quite as much a desire for success as for the extra comforts that a higher income can procure. However dull work may be, it becomes bearable if it is a means of building up a reputation, whether in the world at large or only in one's own circle. Continuity of purpose is one of the most essential ingredients of happiness in the long run, and for most men this comes chiefly through their work. In this respect those women whose lives are occupied with housework are much less fortunate than men, or than women who work outside the home. The domesticated wife does not receive wages, has no means of bettering herself, is taken for granted by her husband (who sees practically nothing of what she does), and is valued by him not for her housework but for quite other qualities. Of course this does not apply to those women who are sufficiently well-to-do to make beautiful houses and beautiful gardens and become the envy of their neighbors; but such women are comparatively few, and for the great majority housework cannot bring as much satisfaction as work of other kinds brings to men and to professional women.

The satisfaction of killing time and of affording some outlet, however modest, for ambition, belongs to most work, and is sufficient to make even a man whose work is dull happier on the average than a man who has no work at all. But when work is interesting, it is capable of giving satisfaction of a far higher order than mere relief from tedium. The kinds of work in which there is some interest may be arranged in a hierarchy. I shall begin with those which are only mildly interesting and end with those that are worthy to absorb the whole energies of a great man.

Two chief elements make work interesting: first, the exercise of skill, and second, construction.

Every man who has acquired some unusual skill enjoys exercising it until it has become a matter of course, or until he can no longer improve himself. This motive to activity begins in early childhood: a boy who can stand on his head becomes reluctant to stand on his feet. A great deal of work gives the same pleasure that is to be derived from games of skill. The work of a lawyer or a politician must contain in a more delectable form a great deal of the same pleasure that is to be derived from playing bridge. Here of course there is not only the exercise of skill but the outwitting of a skilled opponent. Even where this competitive element is absent, however, the performance of difficult feats is agreeable. A man who can do stunts in an aëroplane finds the pleasure so great that for the sake of it he is willing to risk his life. I imagine that an able surgeon, in spite of the painful circumstances in which his work is done, derives satisfaction from the exquisite precision of his operations. The same kind of pleasure, though in a less intense form, is to be derived from a great deal of work of a humbler kind. All skilled work can be pleasurable, provided the skill required is either variable or capable of indefinite improvement. If these conditions are absent, it will cease to be interesting when a man has acquired his maximum skill. A man who runs three-mile races will cease to find pleasure in this occupation when he passes the age at which he can beat his own previous record. Fortunately there is a very considerable amount of work in which new circumstances call for new skill and a man can go on improving, at any rate until he has reached middle age. In some kinds of skilled work, such as politics, for example, it seems that men are at their best between sixty and seventy, the reason being that in such occupations a wide experience of other men is essential. For this reason successful politicians are apt to be happier at the age of seventy than any other men of equal age. Their only competitors in this respect are the men who are the heads of big businesses.

There is, however, another element possessed by the best work, which is even more important as a source of happiness than is the exercise of skill. This is the element of constructiveness. In some work, though by no means in most, something is built up which remains as a monument when the work is completed. We may distinguish construction from destruction by the following criterion. In construction the initial state of affairs is comparatively haphazard, while the final state of affairs embodies a purpose: in destruction the reverse is the case; the initial state of affairs embodies a purpose, while the final state of affairs is haphazard, that is to say, all that is intended by the destroyer is to produce a state of affairs which does not embody a certain purpose. This criterion applies in the most literal and obvious case, namely the construction and destruction of buildings. In constructing a building a previously made plan is carried out, whereas in destroying it no one decides exactly how the materials are to lie when the demolition is complete. Destruction is of course necessary very often as a preliminary to subsequent construction; in that case it is part of a whole which is constructive. But not infrequently a man will engage in activities of which the purpose is destructive without regard to any construction that may come after. Frequently he will conceal this from himself by the belief that he is only sweeping away in order to build afresh, but it is generally possible to unmask this pretense, when it is a pretense, by asking him what the subsequent construction is to be. On this subject it will be found that he will speak vaguely and without enthusiasm, whereas on the preliminary destruction he has spoken precisely and with zest. This applies to not a few revolutionaries and militarists and other apostles of violence. They are actuated, usually without their own knowledge, by hatred: the destruction of what they hate is their real purpose, and they are comparatively indifferent to the question of what is to come after it. Now I cannot deny that in the work of destruction as in the work of construction there may be joy. It is a fiercer joy, perhaps at moments more intense, but it is less profoundly satisfying, since the result is one in which little satisfaction is to be found. You kill your enemy, and when he is dead your occupation is gone, and the satisfaction that you derive from victory quickly fades. The work of construction, on the other hand, when completed is delightful to contemplate, and moreover is never so fully completed that there is nothing further to do about it. The most satisfactory purposes are those that lead on indefinitely from one success to another without ever coming to a dead end; and in this respect it will be found that construction is a greater source of happiness than destruction. Perhaps it would be more correct to say that those who find satisfaction in construction find in it greater satisfaction than the lovers of destruction can find in destruction, for if once you have become filled with hate you will not easily derive from construction the pleasure which another man would derive from it.

At the same time few things are so likely to cure the habit of hatred as the opportunity to do constructive work of an important kind.

The satisfaction to be derived from success in a great constructive enterprise is one of the most massive that life has to offer, although unfortunately in its highest forms it is open only to men of exceptional ability. Nothing can rob a man of the happiness of successful achievement in an important piece of work, unless it be the proof that after all his work was bad. There are many forms of such satisfaction. The man who by a scheme of irrigation has caused the wilderness to blossom like the rose enjoys it in one of its most tangible forms. The creation of an organization may be a work of supreme importance. So is the work of those few statesmen who have devoted their lives to producing order out of chaos, of whom Lenin is the supreme type in our day. The most obvious examples are artists and men of science. Shakespeare says of his verse: "So long as men can breathe, or eyes can see, so long lives this." And it cannot be doubted that the thought consoled him for misfortune. In his sonnets he maintains that the thought of his friend reconciled him to life, but I cannot help suspecting that the sonnets he wrote to his friend were even more effective for this purpose than the friend himself. Great artists and great men of science do work which is in itself delightful; while they are doing it, it secures them the respect of those whose respect is worth having, which gives them the most fundamental kind of power, namely, power over men's thoughts and feelings. They have also the most solid reasons for thinking well of themselves. This combination of fortunate circumstances ought, one would think, to be enough to make any man happy. Nevertheless it is not so. Michaelangelo, for example, was a profoundly unhappy man, and maintained (not, I am sure, with truth) that he would not have troubled to produce works of art if he had not had to pay the debts of his impecunious relations. The power to produce great art is very often, though by no means always, associated with a temperamental unhappiness, so great that but for the joy which the artist derives from his work, he would be driven to suicide. We cannot, therefore, maintain that even the greatest work must make a man happy; we can only maintain that it must make him less unhappy. Men of science, however, are far less often temperamentally unhappy than artists are, and in the main the men who do great work in science are happy men, whose happiness is derived primarily from their work.

One of the causes of unhappiness among intellectuals in the present day is that so many of them, especially those whose skill is literary, find no opportunity for the independent exercise of their talents, but have to hire themselves out to rich corporations directed by Philistines, who insist upon their producing what they themselves regard as pernicious nonsense. If you were to inquire among journalists in either England or America whether they believed in the policy of the newspaper for which they worked, you would find, I believe, that only a small minority do so; the rest, for the sake of a livelihood, prostitute their skill to purposes which they believe to be harmful. Such work cannot bring any real satisfaction, and in the course of reconciling himself to the doing of it, a man has to make himself so cynical that he can no longer derive whole-hearted satisfaction from anything whatever. I cannot condemn men who undertake work of this sort, since starvation is too serious an alternative, but I think that where it is possible to do work that is satisfactory to a man's constructive impulses without entirely starving, he will be well advised from the point of view of his own happiness if he chooses it in preference to work much more highly paid but not seeming to him worth doing on its own account. Without self-respect genuine happiness is scarcely possible. And the man who is ashamed of his work can hardly achieve self-respect.

The satisfaction of constructive work, though it may, as things are, be the privilege of a minority, can never the less be the privilege of a quite large minority. Any man who is his own master in his work can feel it; so can any man whose work appears to him useful and requires considerable skill. The production of satisfactory children is a difficult constructive work capable of affording profound satisfaction. Any woman who has achieved this can feel that as a result of her labor the world contains something of value which it would not otherwise contain.

Human beings differ profoundly in regard to the tendency to regard their lives as a whole. To some men it is natural to do so, and essential to happiness to be able to do so with some satisfaction. To others life is a series of detached incidents without directed movement and without unity. I think the former sort are more likely to achieve happiness than the latter, since they will gradually build up those circumstances from which they can derive contentment and self-respect, whereas the others will be blown about by the winds of circumstance now this way, now that, without ever arriving at any haven. The habit of viewing life as a whole is an essential part both of wisdom and of true morality, and is one of the things which ought to be encouraged in education. Consistent purpose is not enough to make life happy, but it is an almost indispensable condition of a happy life. And consistent purpose embodies itself mainly in work.

## QUESTIONS

1. What does work mean to you?

   _____

   _____

   _____

2. How would you define success in your work life?

   _____

   _____

   _____

3. Do you think the meaning of work is changing in Western civilization? In what ways?

   _____

   _____

   _____

# The Shoeshine Boy

When I got home, Ella said there had been a telephone call from somebody named Shorty. He had left a message that over at the Roseland State Ballroom, the shoeshine boy was quitting that night, and Shorty had told him to hold the job for me.

"Malcolm, you haven't had any experience shining shoes," Ella said. Her expression and tone of voice told me she wasn't happy about my taking that job. I didn't particularly care, because I was already speechless thinking about being somewhere close to the greatest bands in the world. I didn't even wait to eat any dinner.

The ballroom was all lighted when I got there. A man at the front door was letting in members of Benny Goodman's band. I told him I wanted to see the shoeshine boy, Freddie.

"You're going to be the new one?" he asked. I said I thought I was, and he laughed, "Well, maybe you'll hit the numbers and get a Cadillac, too." He told me that I'd find Freddie upstairs in the men's room on the second floor.

But downstairs before I went up, I stepped over and snatched a glimpse inside the ballroom. I just couldn't believe the size of that waxed floor! At the far end, under the soft, rose-colored lights, was the bandstand with the Benny Goodman musicians moving around, laughing and talking, arranging their horns and stands.

A wiry, brown-skinned, conked fellow upstairs in the men's room greeted me. "You Shorty's homeboy?" I said I was, and he said he was Freddie. "Good old boy," he said. "He called me, he just heard I hit the big number, and he figured right I'd be quitting." I told Freddie what the man at the front door had said about a Cadillac. He laughed and said, "Burns them white cats up when you get yourself something. Yeah, I told them I was going to get me one—just to bug them."

Freddie then said for me to pay close attention, that he was going to be busy and for me to watch but not get in the way, and he'd try to get me ready to take over at the next dance, a couple of nights later.

As Freddie busied himself setting up the shoeshine stand, he told me, "Get here early . . . your shoeshine rags and brushes by this footstand

*Source:   Malcolm X with the assistance of Alex Haley,* The Autobiography of Malcolm X *(New York: Grove Press, Inc., 1965). Reprinted by permission of Random House, Inc.*

. . . your polish bottles, paste wax, suede brushes over here . . . everything in place, you get rushed, you never need to waste motion. . . ."

While you shined shoes, I learned, you also kept watch on customers inside, leaving the urinals. You darted over and offered a small white hand towel. "A lot of cats who ain't planning to wash their hands, sometimes you can run up with a towel and shame them. Your towels are really your best hustle in here. Cost you a penny apiece to launder—you always get at least a nickel tip."

The shoeshine customers, and any from the inside rest room who took a towel, you whiskbroomed a couple of licks. "A nickel or a dime tip, just give 'em that," Freddie said. "But for two bits, Uncle Tom a little—white cats especially like that. I've had them to come back two, three times a dance."

From down below, the sound of the music had begun floating up. I guess I stood transfixed. "You never seen a big dance?" asked Freddie. "Run on awhile, and watch."

There were a few couples already dancing under the rose-colored lights. But even more exciting to me was the crowd thronging in. The most glamorous-looking white women I'd ever seen—young ones, old ones, white cats buying tickets at the window, sticking big wads of green bills back into their pockets, checking the women's coats, and taking their arms and squiring them inside.

Freddie had some early customers when I got back upstairs. Between the shoeshine stand and thrusting towels to me just as they approached the wash basin, Freddie seemed to be doing four things at once. "Here, you can take over the whiskbroom," he said, "just two or three licks—but let 'em feel it."

When things slowed a little, he said, "You ain't seen nothing tonight. You wait until you see a spooks' dance! Man, our own people carry *on*!" Whenever he had a moment, he kept schooling me. "Shoelaces, this drawer here. You just starting out, I'm going to make these to you as a present. Buy them for a nickel a pair, tell cats they need laces if they do, and charge two bits."

Every Benny Goodman record I'd ever heard in my life, it seemed, was filtering faintly into where we were. During another customer lull, Freddie let me slip back outside again to listen. Peggy Lee was at the mike singing. Beautiful! She had just joined the band and she was from North Dakota and had been singing with a group in Chicago when Mrs. Benny Goodman discovered her, we had heard some customers say. She finished the song and the crowd burst into applause. She was a big hit.

"It knocked me out, too, when I first broke in here," Freddie said, grinning, when I went back in there. "But, look, you ever shined any shoes?" He laughed when I said I hadn't, excepting my own. "Well, let's get to work. I never had neither." Freddie got on the stand and went to work on his own shoes. Brush, liquid polish, brush, paste wax, shine rag, lacquer sole dressing . . . step by step, Freddie showed me what to do.

"But you got to get a whole lot faster. You can't waste time!" Freddie showed me how fast on my own shoes. Then, because business was tapering off, he had time to give me a demonstration of how to make the shine rag pop like a firecracker. "Dig the action?" he asked. He did it in slow motion. I got down and tried it on his shoes. I had the principle of it. "Just got to do it faster," Freddie said. "It's a jive noise, that's all. Cats tip better, they figure you're knocking yourself out!"

## QUESTIONS

1. Different jobs have different characteristics and traditions. What are the unique characteristics and traditions of jobs you have held?

_____

_____

_____

2. What type of work would you enjoy? Why?

_____

_____

_____

# Who Will Do the Dirty Work Tomorrow?

In the computer age, millions of men and women still earn wages by carrying food trays, pushing brooms, shoveling dirt, and performing countless other menial tasks in ways that haven't changed much in centuries. Traditionally, these jobs have been taken by people with no choice: high-school dropouts, immigrants with language difficulties, members of racial minorities, women, and young people (as well as unemployed family heads in desperate straits and disproportionate numbers of ex-convicts, alcoholics, the mentally retarded, and people with personality disorders). But various currents of change — including egalitarianism, rising expectations, and ever-more-generous government programs of support for nonworkers — are tending to make it harder to fill such jobs as time goes by. Some observers, indeed, foresee an eventual drying up of the pool of labor available to do menial work.

Yet many of these "jobs of last resort," as they have been called, involve essential tasks that it would be difficult to dispense with or to mechanize. Under the pressure of rising wages, the U.S. has traveled far down the road of reducing menial labor, which currently engages somewhere between 10 and 15 percent of the working population. But we are approaching the limits of how far we can go, or wish to go.

## NO REPLACEMENT FOR ELBOW GREASE

On farms, for example, machines have replaced most manual toil. But a visit to California's Imperial Valley, one of the most efficient agricultural regions in the U.S., reveals that a surprising amount of "stoop" labor still survives. At construction sites, machines now do most of the heavy digging, but men with shovels still must work behind them. Much of the restaurant industry has shifted to self-service and throwaways, but growing numbers of Americans want to dine out in conventional fashion, with the food served on china plates.

*Source: Edmund Faltermayer, "Who Will Do the Dirty Work Tomorrow?"* Fortune *(January 1974). Reprinted with permission.*

In an effort to simplify cleaning, developers have modified the design of new office buildings, stores, and hotels, and industry now supplies improved chemicals and equipment. But Daniel Fraad Jr., chairman of Allied Maintenance Corp., which cleans offices, factories, and passenger terminals across the U.S., sees few remaining breakthroughs in productivity. Years ago, he says, his company abandoned a mechanical wall-washing device after it was found to be less efficient than a man with a sponge. Says Fraad, himself a former window washer: "In the final analysis, cleaning is elbow grease."

All this helps explain why the century-long process in which Americans have been moving out of low-status jobs is decelerating and may even be reversing. Productivity in the remaining menial occupations is growing more slowly than in most other fields, and shorter working hours often necessitate larger working staffs even where the amount of work remains the same. According to the Department of Labor, the percentage of Americans who were either "nonfarm laborers" or "service workers" was higher in 1972 than in 1960.

Declines in some menial jobs, most notably maids and housekeepers, have been more than offset by increases in other occupations. The 1970 census showed 1,250,000 "janitors" at work in the U.S., up from 750,000 a decade earlier. In the same period the ranks of unskilled hospital workers, i.e., "nursing aides, orderlies and attendants," rose by nearly 80 percent to 720,000, and the number of "garbage collectors" doubled. And the trend seems likely to continue. Between now and 1985, the Bureau of Labor Statistics has predicted, openings in many low-status jobs will increase faster than total employment.

## DESPERATION IN DALLAS

But who, in this era when the Army feels compelled to abolish K.P., will want to wait on tables, empty bedpans or, for that matter, bury the dead? In some cities it's already hard to keep menial jobs filled. In the booming Dallas region, with its unemployment rate of only 2.1 percent, jobs for waitresses, private guards, trash collectors, and busboys were recently going begging.

One restaurant owner who is short of "bus help" revealed that his current roster consists of an illiterate black man in his fifties, a white girl who is somewhat retarded, a divorced white man in his sixties with personality problems, and an unattached white man in his forties "who goes out and gets drunk each day after he finishes his shift."

In slack labor markets such as Boston, where the unemployment rate has been running above the recent national figure of 4.7 percent, employers are experiencing troubles of a different sort. There seem to be enough people to fill most menial jobs, but they just don't stay around.

At the popular Sheraton-Boston Hotel, the turnover among chambermaids is about 150 percent a year. On pleasant weekends, when absenteeism runs high, the hotel hurriedly telephones local college students on a standby list. Down in the kitchens, turnover among dishwashers on the night shift exceeds a phenomenal 400 percent a year. Sometimes, the hotel has to ask the local U.S.O. to send over Navy men on shore leave who want to earn some extra money by helping out in the kitchens.

## THE INCENTIVES *NOT* TO WORK

In Boston, as in many other cities outside the South, liberal welfare benefits make it possible for a great many people to stay out of the labor market if they don't like the work and wages available. Stricter administration of welfare, currently being attempted in a number of states, may remove some cheaters and induce some other recipients to work. Under a 1971 provision of federal law, welfare mothers with no preschool children are required to register for work. But it would be unrealistic to expect a tightening effective enough to make any large number of welfare recipients take menial jobs.

A number of factors besides increasingly generous welfare have been eroding the supply of people available for menial work. Perhaps the leading expert on this subject is economist Harold Wool of the National Planning Association. Wool points out that during the Sixties society's efforts to keep young people in school reduced the number of dropouts entering the labor force. At the same time, he says, the U.S. drew down much of its remaining "reserve" of rural labor migrating to cities.

Most important of all, minority groups, especially blacks, began pushing in earnest toward equality in employment. According to Wool's reckoning, black young men with at least one year of college (but not teen-agers or young women) have actually achieved occupational parity with their white counterparts. This remarkable social achievement has been too little noticed.

Today a great many young black people refuse to take jobs they consider demeaning. Wool observes that while a decade ago 20 percent of the black young women who had graduated from high school worked as domestics, only 3 percent were settling for that kind of work in 1970. "The service-type job," he says, "has become anathema to many blacks, even on a temporary basis." This helps explain why some service jobs are hard to fill even in cities where unemployment among young black people runs at dismayingly high rates.

It seems clear, then, that in years ahead the traditional supply of menial workers will not meet the demand. Some work will go undone. Many prosperous families whose counterparts even a decade ago would have employed household help now get along without any. Corners are clipped in services. Some restaurants, for example, have reduced the number of items on their menus, which among other things trims the customer's decision-making time and enables the waitress to move along faster.

## THE $12,866-A-YEAR TRASHMEN

But a lot of menial work will have to be done, one way or another. Society will have to respond to the tightening of the labor supply by improving pay and working conditions. Right now there are many places where the federal minimum wage of $1.60 an hour cannot buy work. In northern cities, even members of the so-called "secondary labor force" — women and young people whose pay supplements a family's principal source of income — are usually not willing to work for $1.60. For those groups, $2 to $2.50 is the real market "minimum" needed to balance supply and demand.

It may be a portent of things to come that New York City now pays its unionized sanitation men $12,886 a year (plus an ultraliberal pension). Hardly anybody ever quits, and thousands of men are on a waiting list for future job openings. At Chrysler Corp., unskilled "material handlers," whose job includes pushing carts around the plant floor by hand, get $4.90 an hour, which draws plenty of young married men, both white and black.

At Boston's Massachusetts General Hospital, the minimum starting pay for "dietary service aides" and "building service aides" is $2.78, more than local hotels pay busboys and chambermaids. But even so, few native Bostonians, black or white, are entering such jobs these days. Most of the hospital's recent hires for entry-level jobs are immigrants from Jamaica and other Carribean islands, or recent black arrivals from the rural south.

## HIGH STANDARDS FOR SWABBING DOWN

Higher pay, if it's high enough, clearly helps improve the status of menial work. Another way to improve its status is to raise the quality and complexity of the work itself. Some of the credit for a fairly low turnover rate at Massachusetts General Hospital goes to a training program begun in 1968 for those "building service aides," who previously had gone by the relatively servile titles of "maid" and "houseman."

The one-month program, which involves eighty hours in a classroom and a loose-leaf manual resembling one used by higher-skilled workers at the hospital, is not mere industrial-relations gimmickry. "Janitorial work in a hospital is different than in an office building," says Ruth MacRobert, the hospital's personnel director. "Here they need to learn aseptic techniques, and the fact that they can't use slippery compounds that might cause a patient to trip and fall. If there's a spill, they can't leave broken glass lying around. It's a lot different than swabbing down a deserted office. Who cares if the John Hancock Building is wet and slippery after hours?"

A pleasanter work climate can also help make low-status work less lowly. Lack of amenity on the job is particularly noticeable in the clangorous kitchens where some of the country's 2,860,000 food service workers earn their living. Jan Lovell, president of the Dallas Restaurant Association, believes his industry is improving the work atmosphere but will have to do more in order to survive. In the most menial jobs, he says, "we used to have a tradition of taking the dregs of society off the street and working them twelve hours a day." This, he says, was bad for management as well as the worker.

"A few years ago it wasn't unusual for a restaurant to buy a $12,000 dishwashing machine and then hire two drunks or wetbacks at $75 a week who might forget to turn the water on. Today you pay one guy $150 a week who does the work of two. But maybe we also need to put in a radio and a rug on the floor. The restaurant business has been hot, dirty, and sweaty. Who needs it?"

## TO REPLACE A "VANISHING BREED"

Still another strategy is to make menial jobs a stepping-stone to something better. Texas Instruments, for example, offers a prospect of advancement to anyone who signs on to push a broom. Six years ago, in an effort to get better-quality work (and save money too), T.I. terminated contracts with outside cleaning firms and created a staff of its own to clean its factories and offices in the Dallas area. As in so many menial occupations, the staff has a nucleus of mature people who never aimed much higher in life, a majority of them black men in their fifties and sixties who in one supervisor's words are "a vanishing breed."

To lure younger replacements, the company offers a starting wage of $2.43 an hour, exactly the same as in production, and allows anyone to seek a transfer after six months. And like other T.I. employees, the sweepers are entitled to an exceptional fringe benefit: 90 percent of the cost of part-time education.

In a way, though, "promotability" makes it even harder to maintain a staff. Over the course of a year about 40 percent of T.I.'s "cleaning service attendants" move on to other jobs within the company, in addition to the 36 percent who quit or retire. One recently arrived janitor who is already looking around is Willie Gibson, a soft-spoken, twenty-year-old high-school graduate. Willie has been talking to "the head man in the machine shop" about the possibilities of a transfer. "There ain't nothing wrong with cleaning," he says, "It's got to be done. But me, I feel I can do better."

Texas Instruments is forced to search ceaselessly for replacements, who these days include Mexican-Americans and a few whites as well as blacks. Recruiting methods have included the announcement of janitorial vacancies from the pulpit of a black church.

## A MAGNET FOR ILLEGALS

Until the early 1920's, immigration provided an abundant supply of menial workers. And recent years have seen something of a resurgence. Legal immigration has grown to 400,000 a year and now accounts for a fifth of the country's population growth. While many of the newcomers are professionals from the Philippines and India, the ranks also include a great many unskilled men and women from Mexico, the West Indies, and South America.

In addition, it is estimated that between one million and two million illegal aliens are at large in the U.S., mostly employed in low-status jobs. And the number of illegal aliens, whatever it may be, is undoubtedly growing. "Suddenly, in the last few months, there have been more of the illegals," says an official of the Texas Employment Commission in Dallas. The hiring of illegal immigrants is against the law in Texas, and the federal Immigration and Naturalization Service periodically rounds some of them up and deports them. But the very low unemployment rate in Dallas, the official says, acts as a magnet pulling in the illegals, who work mainly in small enterprises that are not scrupulous about observing the law.

In northern cities, illegal immigration began to increase during the late 1960's. New York City alone may have as many as 250,000 illegals, including Chinese and Greeks as well as Haitians, Dominicans, and other Latin Americans. Such people can be an employer's dream. Often they have no welfare or unemployment compensation to fall back on, since applying for such assistance could reveal their existence to the authorities. In an era of liberal income-maintenance programs for the native population, says New York State Industrial Commissioner Louis Levine, such people "have a total incentive to work."

## TOWARD SELF-SUFFICIENCY IN DIRTY WORK

To rely on increasing numbers of immigrants to perform menial jobs, however, is to put off true long-range solutions to the problem. Sooner or later, every mature nation intent upon keeping its cultural identity will have to figure out a way to get most of the work done with its own native-born.

The U.S. cannot, and should not, close the door to all immigration, but a crackdown on illegal immigrants seems overdue. In addition to penalties against employers who hire illegal immigrants, an effective crackdown might require some device such as identity cards for all citizens. While repugnant to many Americans, such controls have long been a fact of life in France.

The U.S. is in a better position than most countries to move toward a state of "self-sufficiency in dirty work." Americans are generally free of Europe's ingrained class consciousness, and under certain conditions are rather flexible about the jobs they will take. And in recent years, in fact, white Americans have been moving into low-status jobs as black Americans move out. Most of these native-born recruits to menial work are women or young people.

In view of all the attention given to the women's liberation movement in recent years, it may seem paradoxical that many women have been moving into the lower end of the occupational scale. But there is not really any paradox. The desire of *some* women to pursue careers in managerial and professional fields should certainly not preclude employment of a different kind of woman in a different kind of situation — the woman who is not a breadwinner and does not want a career, but who does want the freedom to divide her life between housekeeping and periods of work that entail no encumbering commitments between employer and employee.

A lot of these women are in jobs that are fairly pleasant, and whose "menialness" has more to do with society's prevailing view than the nature of the work itself. Some restaurant work falls into this category. That is the opinion, for example, of Peggy Easter, a middle-aged white woman who waits on tables at Jan's Restaurant, a moderate-priced but clean and well-run establishment in a Dallas suburb. "Some people look down on this kind of work," she says. "But there's an art to this, and I like the hectic, fast pace because I have lots of nervous energy."

Like many waiters and waitresses, Mrs. Easter works only part time, coming in for three and a half hours each day during lunchtime. Her only child is married and her husband works full time as a diesel mechanic. With growing numbers of married women wanting to get out of the house, it is reasonable to expect that more Peggy Easters will turn up in the years ahead.

## A BULGE FROM THE BABY BOOM

Young white people have moved into low-status jobs in even greater numbers than women. In 1960, according to census data, only 8 percent of the country's janitors were young whites under twenty-five. By 1970 that figure had jumped to 22 percent. Some of the movement of white young men *down* the occupational status scale (which partly accounts for that "parity" between blacks and whites who went to college) is a result of the postwar baby boom. Many of the young janitors, kitchen workers, and construction laborers are part-time workers from the ballooning population of high-school and college students. Others are full-time employees who, meeting heavy competition for jobs from their numerous contemporaries, have taken menial jobs until they can find something better. Another factor here is that many young whites live in the suburbs, where fast-food and other service jobs have grown more rapidly than in the cities.

Because the baby boom began waning in the late 1950's, the bulge in the number of employable young people will begin to recede during the middle and late 1970's. During the current decade as a whole, the sixteen to twenty-four age group will increase by 16 percent — somewhat less than the entire labor force, and far less than the phenomenal 48 percent growth during the Sixties.

To some extent, however, this demographic slowdown could be offset by a reduction in school hours, particularly in the high-school years. A growing number of educators and sociologists favor more part-time exposure of teen-agers to the working world, where they can benefit by rubbing shoulders with adults. One principal at a high school in the Northeast confided not long ago that all the basic material in his three-year curriculum, including the courses necessary for entering college, could be given in half the time. Not many principals, perhaps, would go that far, but certainly high-school education is now a very inefficient process. Any reduction in classroom time, of course, would make more teen-agers available for work, and much of that would be work generally considered menial.

## AGAINST THE GRAIN

In any event, it seems reasonable to expect that young people will be taking on more of those dirty jobs. According to a well-entrenched American tradition, almost unthinkable in much of Europe, it is healthy for sons and daughters of the middle class to wait on tables, scrub pots, and even clean toilets as part of their "rites of initiation" into the world of work. Late in the nineteenth century, the American author Edward Bellamy, in the Utopian novel *Looking Backward*, foresaw a day when all the onerous tasks of society would be performed by young people during a three-year period of obligatory service.

A formal period of "national youth service," a proposal that has been revived in recent years, runs against the American grain. But less extreme policies to encourage the employment of more young people would be a step in the right direction. Lots of young people might welcome earlier introduction to the world of work, especially high-school students, who these days seem increasingly inclined to work anyway.

## "DIRTY WORK CAN BE FUN"

Charles Muer, who operates a chain of restaurants headquartered in Detroit, employs young part-time workers extensively and considers it entirely feasible that they could take over most of the kitchen work. "You might have to pay them more," he says, "but productivity would be high. Kids are strong and enthusiastic, and dirty work can be fun, especially if you enjoy your co-workers and the management is nice."

Others are skeptical. "You've got to screen young people," says a hospital administrator, "and you can't leave them off by themselves where they'll goof off." Some tasks cannot and should not be performed by the young, particularly those involving nighttime shifts or long commuting distances. And some parents, of course, would object to their children's taking jobs they consider demeaning. John R. Coleman, the president of Haverford College whose experiences last year as an incognito ditchdigger and trash collector are described in his book *Time Out*, advises many of his students to get a taste of menial work. The parents most likely to be upset by such an idea, Coleman says, are "people unsure of their own status."

There's another and perhaps more formidable impediment. Until now the large number of young people bumping from one job to another as they slowly settle into careers has provided much of the labor pool for temporary dead-end work. (See "A Better Way to Deal with Unemployment," *Fortune*, June, 1973.) But some of the desirable education reforms now being tested are designed to enable high-school graduates to jump right into jobs with career ladders. If "career education" or something like it becomes widespread, it may become necessary to get that menial work out of students *before* they graduate. That would entail new social arrangements of some kind.

In an ideal world, all menial work would be a passing thing, whether for adults seeking a temporary change from their normal routine or for young people who can count on better jobs later on. It won't turn out quite that way, of course. Some people, because of limited ability or sheer inclination, will mop floors or wait on tables throughout their working lives. If recent trends continue, however, their pay will rise and with it their self-esteem — and, of course, the costs of their labor, at a time when lots of other things are also getting costlier.

## THE AIRLINE ROUTE

An indication of the direction things will move in can be seen in the way some airlines get their planes cleaned up between runs. The American Airlines system, for example, embodies nearly all of the features that society will probably have to incorporate into its low-status jobs. At New York's LaGuardia Airport a force of 185 "cabin service clerks" (an old designation rather than a recent euphemism) cleans floors, scrubs lavatories, and empties the ashtrays into which airline passengers grind their cigarettes. The men go about their work briskly, with no indication that they consider it demeaning. Two-thirds of them are white, the rest black and Puerto Rican. Their pay starts at $4.57 an hour, with a maximum of $5.15.

The job is not a dead end. Some recent hires are college graduates who, in the words of H. Lee Nichols, the staff's black manager, "get a foot in the door with an airline by taking a job like this." Most of these workers move on, replaced by a steady supply of new men attracted by the pay and the prospects for advancement. After all, Nichols says, "five years of cleaning ashtrays, if you have any drive, can get to you."

**QUESTIONS**

1. Have you ever had a menial job? What was your attitude about doing this type of work? Discuss.

   _____

   _____

   _____

2. Would you be in favor of some kind of "work-fare" program to replace aspects of the current welfare system? Explain.

   _____

   _____

   _____

# What Job Attitudes Tell About Motivation

Emerson once wrote, "This time, like all times, is a good one if we but know what to do with it." With slight rephrasing, this philosophy could aptly express the typical organization's quandary with respect to the role of job attitudes: job attitudes are always present, if only we knew what they meant!

Every manager is continually being confronted with evidence that his subordinates hold a variety of attitudes toward him, toward the organization, and, especially, toward their jobs. What most managers are not sure of is how they should react to these attitudes. Should they ignore them entirely? Should they systematically try to measure them? If they decide to measure the attitudes, a whole set of other questions arises. What kinds of attitudes are important to measure? What interpretations should be put on the results of attitude studies? For example, is high job satisfaction good? Does information on job satisfaction tell anything about motivation? Finally, the organization is faced with a whole series of questions about what kinds of action, if any, it should take as a consequence of the existing attitudes. In a sense, then, management is frequently faced with the dilemma of what its own attitude should be toward employees' attitudes.

Our position on these questions can be summarized as follows: Job attitudes *are* important and merit the attention of businessmen. They are *not* important, however, in the ways that most top executives ordinarily think about them. In the succeeding pages we shall try to answer the specific questions raised above, utilizing previous evidence, some recently articulated theoretical notions, and data from our own investigations dealing with managerial job attitudes. Finally, we shall put forth some suggested guidelines for organizational action on how to utilize attitude data more effectively.

# A SHORT HISTORY

Industry's flirtation with job attitudes has had an interesting history and one that sheds considerable light on the current ambiguous feelings about their importance. During the early part of this century, most business leaders doggedly avoided giving any attention at all to this aspect of employee behavior. Instead, the focus was on the principles of scientific management with their concern for maximizing operator efficiency. And since these principles were built around the "man as a machine" analogy, and since machines obviously do not have attitudes, it was logical for companies to ignore job attitudes in their search for new approaches to increased human efficiency. This neglect on the part of the owner or manager was reinforced by the activities of early personnel specialists, especially industrial psychologists. Their attention was focused on quite another area — namely, on improving the selection of employees so that only competent ones would be hired. If any attention was given to the attitudes and behavior of employees once they were on the job, it consisted almost entirely of developing certain kinds of blue-collar skill training.

## Romantic Period

The lowly status of job attitudes changed rapidly and decisively in the 1930's and 1940's. During these years the topic was pursued with great ardor by businessmen, the chief reason being the dramatic impact on both business and academic circles of the findings of Elton Mayo and Fritz J. Roethlisberger in the now classic Hawthorne studies. Suddenly, it became apparent to everyone that human performance in the job situation was not solely a function of the aptitudes or skills that the employee brought to the workplace. The massive number of interviews carried out by investigators at the Hawthorne plant (some 20,000) vividly illustrated that the average worker did indeed think about his job, had various kinds of reactions to it, and, most importantly, believed his feelings affected how hard he worked. A number of managers and personnel specialists jumped to the conclusion that "if we can improve job satisfaction and morale, we can improve job performance."

Immediately, businessmen set about to take advantage of this newly found insight. Companies took action on two fronts. First, they initiated attempts to measure the state of employee feelings in order to know where to concentrate their efforts in improving employee satisfaction. Secondly, they set about to train their managers, especially first-level supervisors, to pay attention to the attitudes and feelings of their subordinates so that performance could thereby be improved. Meanwhile, personnel staff specialists began to set up studies which would demonstrate that, if companies did in fact improve morale, there would be consequent increases in performance.

## Era of Disenchantment

But as often happens in the case of precipitous and intense affairs, disenchantment soon began to set in. There were those critics of the human relations movement who saw the concern with job satisfaction and morale as degenerating into a wishy-washy "make people happy" approach. For example, William Whyte in *The Organization Man* asked, "What about . . . the tyranny of the happy work team? What about the adverse effects of high morale?"[1] Similarly, Malcolm McNair, in his well-known HBR [*Harvard Business Review*] article, claimed that "devoting too much effort in business to trying to keep everybody happy results in conformity, in failure to build individuals."[2]

In effect, these critics were arguing that, even if high job satisfaction could be shown to have some relationship to employee performance, there were associated negative consequences which were being overlooked. Quite aside from the anti-human relations attacks, many companies were beginning to question whether it was worthwhile to bother with trying to improve job satisfaction. The costs involved in measuring job satisfaction, and especially in trying to increase it, often seemed to be disproportionate to the presumed gains in performance. In short, the payoff did not seem to be nearly as large as many had thought it would be.

Social scientists, especially those with an interest in seeing that attitude research was supported and encouraged by business organizations, were also slow in coming to the same realization. They finally began to suspect the validity of their hypothesis that increases in job satisfaction would result in direct improvements in performance. Two scholarly reviews of the scientific literature published in the mid-1950's appeared to demonstrate conclusively that satisfaction-performance relationships were much weaker than most people had assumed.[3] These reviews proved to have sobering effects on psychologists and others engaged in personnel research; the reviews were followed by a marked decrease in the reporting of satisfaction-performance studies in scientific journals. Having found the simple "satisfaction increases performance" hypothesis seemingly unsupported by the evidence, scholars joined managers in abandoning much of their interest in assessing employees' job satisfaction.

## Mistakes in Retrospect

Several important lessons can be learned from this brief review of the rise and fall of interest in job attitude research:

- The early assumptions about the effects of high levels of job satisfaction were greatly oversimplified, if not clearly incorrect. Any view that, because a worker is satisfied, he *must* be a highly productive performer is obviously naive. The first lesson to be learned is not that job satisfaction is an inconsequential variable, but rather that its relationship to performance is more complex than previously recognized.

- Both companies and psychologists concentrated their attentions too narrowly on "satisfaction" as the only type of attitude that should be measured and dealt with. Other attitudes or views that might be held by employees were generally ignored in the attempts to see whether their liking for their jobs could be improved.

### Second Look at Evidence

Before proceeding to other points, let us take another look at the accumulated evidence. While it is true that very few well-controlled investigations found highly positive relationships between satisfaction and performance, the *trend* of the relationships nevertheless seems to be in that direction. For example, one authority has reviewed some 20 studies and found that in most of the cases where data on satisfaction and performance were gathered, higher satisfaction was associated with better job performance.[4] Such consistency is highly significant in a statistical sense, and indicates that some sort of meaningful relationship probably exists between these two variables.

Also, most studies of the relationship between satisfaction and such measures of job behavior as turnover and absenteeism (but not performance) have obtained definite results in the expected direction. That is, high satisfaction is associated with low turnover and with low absenteeism.

The foregoing suggests that the demise of interest in measuring job satisfaction may be quite premature. In other words, even without any new research studies or theoretical analyses, the available data alone would appear to justify a concern with this type of attitude. Given this conclusion, the question remains: What should management do with job satisfaction information? We shall try to answer that now.

## CHANGING THE FOCUS

The first step in understanding this subject is to stop putting the satisfaction cart before the performance horse, so to speak. It appears wiser to think of job satisfaction as something that is likely to result *from* performance behavior rather than as the cause of good or bad performance.

The reasoning goes like this: Satisfaction comes about when certain of our needs or desires are fulfilled. (Let us use the shorthand term "rewards" to refer to those things we receive from others or gain by our own actions that help fulfill our needs.) Thus, in an organization where we work, job satisfaction is generated when we receive rewards from our job situation. Such rewards are of many types and are provided in many ways. Some of them are intrinsic, such as when we feel a sense of accomplishment at having carried through a difficult task successfully; in such a case we can, in effect, administer the reward ourselves. Other rewards are clearly extrinsic, provided by people other than ourselves—such as when the boss gives us a promotion, or when the organization awards us a year-end bonus.

Psychologically speaking, then, the degree to which we feel satisfied should be roughly proportionate to the amount of rewards we believe we are receiving from our job environment. A crucial point in this chain of reasoning is often overlooked: the amount of rewards we receive *may* be unrelated to how well we have performed. To put it another way, high-quality performance is not the only means, nor necessarily the most important means, by which we are able to obtain rewards from our work.

## Contrasting Situations

Here it will help to make the point if we consider two situations, one involving a blue-collar worker, the other a manager. The illustrations that follow are hypothetical but realistic:

**Nonmanagerial worker.** His base rate of pay is determined completely by a fixed schedule that provides exactly the same amount of pay for all employees holding that type of job. Short of totally unacceptable performance, his pay will not be lowered. It also is not likely to be raised easily by above-average performance. However, it *is* likely to increase as a result of seniority. The degree of his job security also is probably determined by his seniority and contract provisions, not by the day-to-day quality of his performance.

The employee's opportunities to gain considerable amounts of intrinsic rewards from performing his job duties in a superior fashion are frequently limited by the mechanical, machine-controlled nature of his work. Furthermore, his chances to assume new, more interesting duties (with higher pay) by working harder on his current job are probably sharply curtailed both in terms of the way in which the organization has arranged the work flow and by union contracts that might exist. In short, the bulk of his rewards are determined not by how good or poor his job performance is, but by factors that are largely or totally beyond his personal control.

Although our example is hypothetical, it typifies a large percentage of rank-and-file work situations in which it is nearly impossible for workers to receive varying amounts of rewards, and therefore of satisfaction, in relation to their performance. If this be the case, then the failure of most previous studies to find strong, positive relationships between satisfaction and performance is not at all surprising; it is, in fact, perfectly predictable and logical, since almost all of them were carried out at the rank-and-file level of organizations.

**Manager.** Rewards for this man are more nearly proportionate to the quality and quantity of his performance. Compared to the blue-collar worker's situation, at least, rewards from factors beyond the manager's control are of less importance than rewards due to his own work.

Why is this relationship likely to be found at the managerial level in a company? Because it is here, if anywhere, that the organization has the potential flexibility to give rewards commensurate with performance.

For one thing, in a given group of managers there is the opportunity to pay different salaries based on performance even though all the men are carrying out the same assigned tasks, or equivalent tasks. Other extrinsic rewards, such as status and authority, can also be dispensed in differing amounts to those working in the same kinds of jobs. Likewise, managers, as compared with nonmanagers, tend to have more flexibility in gaining intrinsic rewards from their jobs based on their efforts and performance. Their jobs usually involve considerably greater variety and hence more opportunity to achieve a sense of completion and worthwhile accomplishment.

## Findings of New Study

The picture drawn from the foregoing observations can be substantiated by research data. We have recently completed a study of managers in five companies of differing types and character. A noteworthy feature of the study is that it is one of the first satisfaction-performance studies to use a sample of executives instead of nonmanagerial employees.[5] The results show:

- Managers who are ranked high by their superiors report significantly greater satisfaction than do the low-ranked managers. However, the degree of relationship between high performance and high satisfaction, though somewhat larger than in most previous studies made on nonmanagement workers, is not as large as it reasonably could be.

- The greatest differences between the high- and low-performance groups, in terms of perceived rewards, occur in those areas where personal needs are deepest and most intangible. The best performing managers do not report receiving much greater rewards in pay or security, but they do report significantly more rewards in areas concerned with opportunities to express autonomy and to obtain self-realization in the job.

The import of this is that the five organizations in our sample seem to be allowing their best management performers to gain more self-fulfillment and self-realization from work than low performers do, but they do not appear to be providing perceptibly different *extrinsic* rewards to the two groups. This was confirmed when we found that, at a given management level in any of the companies studied, pay does not show an appreciable relationship to rated job performance.

## Meaning for Management

In light of the foregoing analyses and findings, the tough question for top management to face up to is this: Does the organization actively and visibly give rewards directly in proportion to the quality of job performance for all of its employees, rank-and-file as well as managers? *If* it does, and *if* employees realize this, then high satisfaction should be more closely associated with superior performance. To the extent that satisfaction and performance are positively related in a given situation, management knows that the best performers believe they are receiving the most rewards.

On the other hand, a company's failure to find job satisfaction related to job performance for a sample of its employees may mean that it is not in fact differentially rewarding its best performers. Such a failure might also suggest that employees are not working on jobs where good performance is intrinsically satisfying and interesting. Looked at in this way, the role of job satisfaction is quite different from that formerly assigned to it by the human relations advocates. Its role is not to serve as a stimulus to employees' job performance but rather as a gauge of how good a job the organization itself is doing in rewarding employees in proportion to the quality and quantity of their performance. Data on job satisfaction also suggest something about how challenging and stimulating employees feel their jobs are.

*The company which takes this kind of view of job satisfaction adopts an approach which is different from the usual one.* Its aim is not necessarily to increase everyone's satisfaction, and thereby to make "everyone happy," but rather to make sure that the best performing employees are the most satisfied employees. Its goal, in other words, is not to maximize satisfaction, but to maximize the *relationship* between satisfaction and performance.

## ROLE OF OTHER ATTITUDES

In the past, as previously pointed out, most companies and researchers have acted as if satisfaction is the only kind of job attitude worth measuring. But it is our contention that other types of attitudes or beliefs are just as important, if not more so, in understanding and modifying employee motivation. These are attitudes that do what job satisfaction was naively assumed to do: namely, affect the amount of effort a person puts into his job.

To begin with, let us make the reasonable assumption that people want to obtain various kinds of rewards from their jobs — a certain level of pay, self-fulfillment, security, status, personal growth, and the like. Furthermore, let us assume that each person attaches different degrees of importance to these various potential rewards. We can say that people place different "values" on different rewards.

Concurrently, we can also assume that in a given job situation an employee will have notions about how likely he is to receive these rewards in return for exerting extra amounts of effort in his job. Such beliefs can be labeled "effort-reward expectations." In some cases, the individual will have low expectations that more effort on his part will provide him with increased rewards. For example, the blue-collar worker described earlier probably feels it is quite unlikely that above-average performance on his part will lead to greater security or a chance to perform a more satisfying set of tasks. On the other hand, the typical manager described might have higher expectations because he feels the organization will, to a certain degree, pay off for the effort he puts into his job.

The conceptual formulations we have discussed can be portrayed as shown in *Exhibit I*. Here performance is seen as resulting from effort. (Aptitudes and skills are regarded as constants in this formulation, as we are focusing solely on the attitude or motivational bases of performance.) Effort is seen as resulting from the interaction of reward values and effort-reward expectations in the following way: the more a reward is valued and the higher the expectation that effort will lead to this reward, the greater will be the effort exerted (and hence the better will be the performance).[6]

## Putting Results to Use

The formulation diagrammed in *Exhibit I* does more than put several variables into a theoretical relationship. It tells an organization what types of attitudes should be measured and worked with if performance is to be improved through increased effort. These attitudes can be stated as questions:

1. How much does the employee value various possible rewards?

2. What are the probabilities, in his opinion, that a high degree of effort on his part will lead to the rewards he wants?

If an organization has accurate data on these two attitudes, it should be able to predict who will put forth the most effort in his job and, even more important, what might be done by the organization to increase this effort. Consider the following:

- In our study of managers, several of the questions we asked related to pay. One concerned the importance of pay to the manager; another concerned how closely he felt his pay was based on job performance factors (such as effort). The answers to these questions were then compared to superiors' ratings of the amount of effort each man put forth on his job. The results showed that the highest rated managers were those who saw their pay most closely tied to their

---

**EXHIBIT I**

**Role of attitudes other than satisfaction in performance**

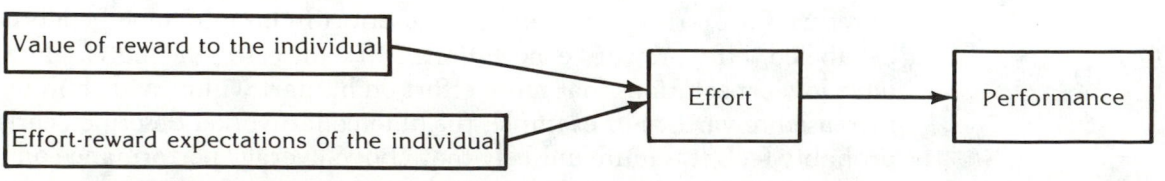

effort—that is, who had the highest effort-reward expectations. Additionally, and significantly, this relationship between expectations and rated effort was strongest for those managers *who attached the most importance to pay*.

Systematic monitoring of the effort-reward expectations held by employees will provide pertinent data on the motivation levels present in the organization. Changes in these expectations could indicate whether employee motivation has increased or decreased over a set period of time. Also, differences among parts of the organization would help pinpoint those areas where motivation is weakest.

The data on effort-reward expectations could be gathered from individuals by interview, questionnaire, and/or other appropriate methods known to personnel specialists. The data should be grouped by departments and work units for examination. In evaluating changes in employees' expectations over time, averages for the departments or units would be used.

The collection of such information may, in turn, lead to the following kinds of questions: What can companies do if they find from their attitude studies that their employees do not have high effort-reward expectations? What can they do about motivational soft spots in the organization? Where should they look in order to improve the effort-reward expectancies of employees? We shall discuss these questions in the following section.

## REWARD PRACTICES

A key to the whole attitude picture for an organization revolves around its reward practices—which may or may not be similar to its reward policies. Because of this, job attitudes can be utilized as a set of indicators of an organization's ability to motivate its employees. Let us elaborate. For a company or firm to produce high levels of motivation, top management should make sure that:

1. The rewards given are those most desired in return for performing the job well.

2. Superior performers are given more extrinsic rewards (e.g., salary and bonuses) and are provided with more opportunities to gain intrinsic rewards (e.g., challenging and varied work) than inferior performers are given.

3. Most individuals in the organization *see* and *believe* that good performance leads to both extrinsic and intrinsic rewards.

Each of these steps involves careful attention to certain details, and, as we hope to show, relevant attitude data should indicate whether such attention is being given to them.

## Offering What Is Desired

The first step in building effective reward practices is for the company to make sure that the rewards it is providing are ones which are widely desired. This is a seemingly simple point that is often neglected. In day-to-day operations we frequently forget that, regardless of the value the giver or observer places on a reward, its motivational influence comes about only as a result of the value the *receiver* places on it. In effect, rewards that the company considers highly positive inducements may not be so regarded by many of the persons receiving them. Yet how many times do companies check this out?

Attitude measurement provides management with a potential tool to confirm its assumptions about *what* is motivating, or will motivate, various groups and individuals in the work force. Eventually, a company may want to consider systematically selecting the kinds of employees who will value the particular rewards that it can give most readily and feasibly.

## Favoring Superior Performers

Knowledge of the kinds of rewards that are most highly valued, and by whom, is only an initial step in developing psychologically meaningful reward practices. The next step involves the crucial, and sometimes difficult, process of attaching rewards to performance such that superior performers receive more than average or mediocre ones do.

**Measuring differences.** This involves developing methods to discriminate between good and poor performance. Of course, this is far from an easy job. Typically, in management, performance measurement involves judgments that are subjective in nature. Sometimes, it is true, objective data are available — for instance, in sales management — but often in these cases the interpretation of the "facts" is complicated because factors beyond the subordinate's control influence the final results. (An example would be where one sales manager's area has greater sales potential than another man's area.) Hence, the boss or other evaluator is often right back where he started — namely, facing the necessity of making subjective, nonprovable assessments.

Given this situation, we would like to suggest that organizations make greater use of self-ratings in measuring individual performance. This should serve to increase the accuracy of performance measurements and, perhaps even more important, their acceptance. Under such a system, the superior and subordinate would jointly establish the subordinate's performance goals for an ensuing period. The two should also agree on how progress toward these goals is to be measured and on what kinds of rewards are to be given if the goals are achieved. Finally, at the end of the period, the two men would *jointly* participate in assessing the results and determining how much progress the subordinate has made during the period. This approach does not mean that the boss gives up his role as the final arbiter; it simply provides him with other important information which he can incorporate into his decisions and which may help to increase his subordinates' confidence in them.

**Providing rewards.** Besides being able to distinguish among performance differences, management must be able to provide commensurate rewards. A man may know that he is regarded as one of the best employees, but this knowledge will do little to enhance his performance if his superior cannot provide him with sufficient rewards or opportunities to gain rewards. Quite often, the organization has so restricted the freedom of individual superiors to dispense rewards of any type that they are completely hamstrung in tying rewards closely to performance. The net effect is to reduce by a considerable amount the possibilities of motivating employees.

However, granted that the boss has the power to provide appropriate rewards, will he go ahead and actually give them out? The process frequently breaks down at this point. For instance, the boss may hesitate to act because of the threat of competition from below or because of the possible complaints he will receive from those who do not get what they desire. The main role that higher management can play in dealing with these types of situations is to endeavor to provide concrete rewards to superiors who do not shrink from evaluating and rewarding outstanding subordinate performance. It has been well established by research that the right types of reward policies higher up the line can have positive impacts on those practiced lower down in the organization.

## Maintaining Credibility

A good performance reward system must have credibility. Oftentimes it seems that management will pay a great deal of attention to setting up elaborate compensation schemes and then will proceed to nullify its efforts by actions designed to disguise the whole procedure.

For one thing, as we have already mentioned, many organizations miss the opportunity to increase managers' trust and confidence in the evaluation procedure by neglecting to secure judgments from all relevant sources. Usually only the immediate superior or a group of superiors evaluates a manager's performance. While this is traditional, it may not be adequate for the organization's needs in the future. As the requirements for sophisticated technical expertise increase throughout wide areas of management, many subordinates may come to expect that the boss's perspective is not necessarily the only one that should be used in performance evaluation.

Subordinate ratings, which we advocated earlier for purposes of making valid measurements, could be particularly useful in developing credibility. By taking them into account, management could determine in advance the motivational impact of giving rewards to particular individuals. It would then be better able to dispense rewards in such a way that the system would be respected and trusted by most members of the organization.

**Is secrecy necessary?** Another practice which serves to weaken credibility in the reward process is secrecy. Companies often go to great lengths to maintain a shroud of secrecy surrounding their reward practices, especially as they relate to managers' pay. It is next to impossible for the typical manager to know to what degree the organization is actually giving larger monetary rewards in proportion to above-average performance. Even worse, the top-notch performer who *is* getting paid substantially more than his peers may not be aware of just how much more he is receiving.

While there may be some valid reasons for retaining secrecy in the managerial salary system, one of them certainly cannot be that it promotes credibility in the reward process. If anything, secrecy about who gets what in terms of salary and bonuses works to reduce credibility in the whole program, and to this extent weakens the motivational possibilities of linking higher pay to better performance.

Our viewpoint here is not that pay secrecy be summarily chucked out the corporate window and replaced by a policy of publicizing what everyone is being paid. Rather, we are advocating that companies take a serious look at the disadvantages described and consider whether they are outweighed by the presumed advantages of secrecy. At the very least, it would seem that companies might undertake some small-scale and relatively controlled experiments to test executives' assumptions about secrecy. In such experimentation, attitude measurement — both of satisfactions and of effort-reward expectations — could be usefully employed to calculate the impact of the changes.

If a company's reward practices are considered valid by those affected, this should serve to reduce a boss's reluctance to evaluate subordinates candidly, since resentments from those receiving low evaluations will be minimized. The boss is most vulnerable to complaints from below when the whole reward process — not just his own evaluations — is regarded skeptically and suspiciously.

## CONCLUSION

Having reviewed the basic components in the chain of steps linking rewards to performance in the eyes of the members of an organization, we can summarize the effects of inadequate reward practices — that is, practices severing or reducing the link between rewards and performance. The effects are portrayed in *Exhibit II*. When the *satisfaction* of a number of individuals is measured and compared with their *performance* ratings, a weak or low association of satisfaction with performance will be found. At the same time, many individuals will have weak beliefs that increased *effort* on their part will result in increased *rewards* (and, hence, satisfaction). Such perceptions, if they are held, are likely to reduce the motivations of people to try to improve their performance.

Evidence that satisfaction is not related to performance should be regarded as a signal for management to investigate effort-reward expectations.

**EXHIBIT II**

**Consequences of inadequate reward practices**

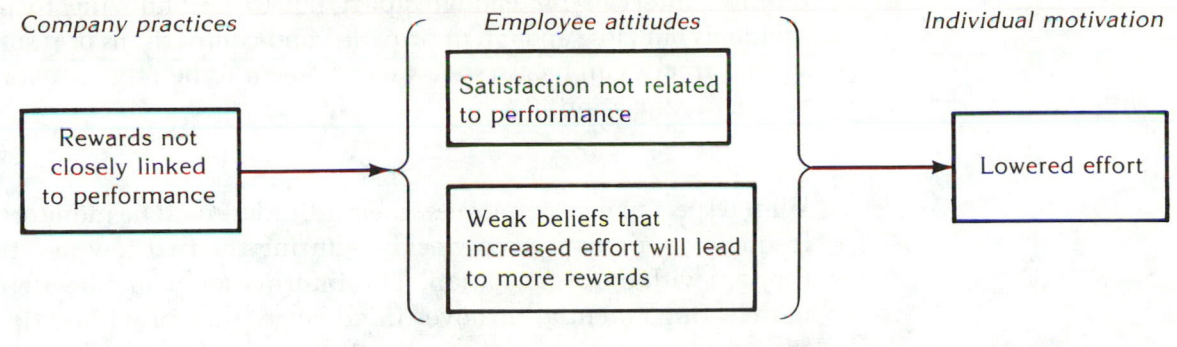

Evidence that these expectations are weak indicates a need for some of the actions and procedures described earlier in this article.

## Program of Action

To sum up, we recommend the following steps to top management:

1. Try to assess the satisfaction level of managers, supervisors, and, if desired, other employees.

2. Compare individual satisfaction levels with individual performance assessments, in order to determine the extent to which satisfaction is related to performance.

3. From a motivational point of view, there is no particular utility in trying to increase the satisfaction of all employees in the organization. There *is*, on the other hand, considerable utility in trying to increase the strength of the *relationship* between satisfaction and performance.

4. In addition to measuring the relationship between satisfaction and performance, attempt to measure systematically other types of attitudes — expecially, attitudes about what people want from their jobs and whether they hold strong effort-reward expectancies.

5. If such effort-reward expectancies are found to be weak or low, a company should undertake an examination of its reward practices (as opposed to its reward policies), looking particularly hard at how individuals *perceive* these practices.

6. If changes in reward practices are made, assessment of their impact should be carried out by planned *continuous* monitoring of

satisfaction-performance relationships and of effort-reward expectancies.

Even if present practices already appear good as indicated by current attitude data, continuous assessment at appropriate intervals — intervals far enough apart not to be annoying to individuals but close enough to provide valid comparisons of results so that trends can be assessed — would seem to be of great value to the organization.

7. With respect to new employees, their attitudes could be monitored frequently — perhaps even weekly — during the first few months they are with the organization. This information would be useful in detecting potential turnover in advance, thus providing time for corrective action.

All men seek one goal: success or happiness. The only way to achieve true success is to express yourself completely in service to society. First, have a definite, clear, practical ideal — a goal, an objective. Second, have the necessary means to achieve your ends — wisdom, money, materials, and methods. Third, adjust your means to that end.

Aristotle, 384–322 B.C.

## REFERENCE NOTES

1 New York, Simon & Schuster, 1956, p. 401.

2 "What Price Human Relations?" HBR March–April 1957, p. 20.

3 See Arthur H. Brayfield and Walter H. Crockett, "Employee Attitudes and Employee Performance," *Psychological Bulletin*, September 1955; and *Frederick Herzberg*, et al, *Job Attitudes: Review of Research and Opinion* (Pittsburgh, Psychological Service of Pittsburgh, 1957).

4 See Victor H. Vroom, *Work and Motivation* (New York, John Wiley & Sons, Inc., 1964), Chapter 6.

5 For a detailed report of the findings, see our book, *Managerial Attitudes and Performance* (Homewood, Illinois, Richard D. Irwin, Inc., 1968).

6 For a similar approach to work motivation, see Victor H. Vroom, op. cit.

## QUESTIONS

1. What is your opinion about job attitudes and job performance? Is there a relationship between the two? Describe.

   _____

   _____

   _____

2. Do you think there is value in measuring employee morale? What problems and opportunities do you see?

   _____

   _____

   _____

# Personnel Directors Are the
# New Corporate Heroes

The personnel department has been represented on many a corporate organization chart as an orphaned box—one that came from nowhere and didn't seem to fit anywhere. To many businessmen, including many chief executives, the people who worked in "personnel" appeared to be a bunch of drones whose apparent missions in life were to create paperwork, recruit secretaries who couldn't type, and send around memos whose impertinence was exceeded only by their irrelevance. As a result of this perception, personnel directors, whatever their individual competence, suffered the *sui generis* image of being good-old-Joe types—harmless chaps who spent their careers worshiping files, arranging company picnics, and generally accomplishing nothing whatsoever of any fundamental importance.

In some cases, this depressing image was accurate. Companies *have* been known to use their personnel departments as a sort of dumping ground for executive misfits, or for burned-out vice presidents who needed just a little while longer on the payroll to be eligible for their pensions. But there have always been some personnel directors who found the job a springboard to higher corporate office, and in some companies the executive in charge of personnel management has traditionally been regarded not as an outcast but as an heir apparent.

The current chairman and chief executive of Delta Airlines, W. T. Beebe, was once Delta's senior vice president for personnel. Both Richard D. Wood, the chairman of Eli Lilly & Co., and one of his predecessors as chief executive served as corporate personnel directors on their way to the top—and a former president had followed the same route. Right now, the top Lilly executive responsible for personnel, Harold M. Wisely, holds the rank of executive vice president and has a seat on the company's board of directors.

*Source: Herbert E. Meyer, "Personnel Directors Are the New Corporate Heroes,"* Fortune *(February 1976). Reprinted with permission.*

# A STEP TOWARD THE TOP

In the last few years, many companies have joined Delta and Lilly in putting their personnel departments in the hands of powerful senior executives. That old chestnut about a transfer to personnel being a one-way ticket to oblivion is no longer true. Absolutely no one at First National City Bank viewed it as a setback for Lawrence M. Small when he was transferred from the commercial-banking division to head the personnel division in August, 1974. Indeed, it was universally regarded as one very impressive step up the ladder; the job carries the title of senior vice president, and Small was only thirty-two years old at the time. And at I.B.M., to cite just one other example, the former director of personnel resources, David E. McKinney, is now president of the Information Records Division, an important marketing and manufacturing unit.

Those good-old-Joes of yesteryear would be stunned by the amount of power and prestige today's personnel directors can claim within their companies. At Dow Chemical Co., for example, the man in charge of personnel, Herbert Lyon, reports directly to President Ben Branch, the chief executive. Lyon is a member of Dow's board of directors, and is responsible for, among other things, global product planning and corporate administration. At Warnaco Inc., most of the executives promoted to jobs in top management during the last three years were singled out for advancement by John Limpitlaw, the company's vice president for personnel.

The executives who are being put in charge of personnel departments today are hard-driving business managers who speak what they call "bottom-line language"; they are as interested in profits as any other executives. George A. Rieder, senior vice president for personnel at Indiana National Bank in Indianapolis, provides an almost textbook example of how today's personnel executives perceive their role. "I'm not a personnel manager," Rieder says, in a tone of voice conveying scorn for that traditional title. "I'm a business manager with responsibilities for personnel."

Rieder quickly adds that this difference is much more than merely semantic. "It's a difference of style, scope and approach. I view myself as a businessman first, whose job has as much of an impact on the bottom line around here as anybody else's. To be effective I have got to understand every aspect of my company's business, and I have got to participate actively in major management decisions before they're made." As a senior vice president, Rieder reports to John R. Benbow, the bank's president, and participates actively in day-to-day management of the business.

# "GOOD ONES ARE WORTH A LOT"

Salary scales provide a measure of the growing importance of personnel. When the average salaries of executives in different specialties are compared — manufacturing, finance, and so on — personnel directors come out as the lowest paid. But they've begun catching up, because they are getting bigger raises than other executives. According to the American Management Association, the average compensation for personnel directors of industrial companies with sales of $500 million to $1 billion was $61,400 in 1975. Executives in charge of manufacturing for those companies got an average of $83,400, chief financial officers got $103,400 and chief executives $225,700. But since 1970, the average compensation of personnel directors has increased by 20 percent, compared with just 13.5 percent for chief financial officers, 15 percent for manufacturing executives, and 18 percent for chief executives.

It's likely that personnel directors will continue to receive larger raises than other kinds of executives, according to Pearl Meyer, a compensation expert who is executive vice president of Handy Associates. "These poor guys in personnel won't be at the bottom of the scale for too much longer," Mrs. Meyer predicts. "Companies are recognizing that good ones are worth a lot." Last year, when Chase Manhattan Bank went looking for an executive to head its human-resources division (modern corporations don't have personnel departments anymore), the bank put out word that for the right man, it would pay up to $120,000. Chase was obviously not in the market for a mere picnic planner. (The right man turned out to be Alan Lafley, from General Electric.)

Clearly, things are not at all what they used to be in the once dull world of personnel or, if you please, human-resource management. And just as clearly, much of the pressure for change came from the economic environment in which corporations have been operating. As Warnaco's John Limpitlaw points out, "The business climate out there today is a whole lot different from what it was ten years ago." In the economy of the 1970's, just about everybody has found the going tough and profits hard to come by. The cost of labor—union contracts, executive salaries, pension plans, and so on—keeps moving up.

Furthermore, many companies that had expanded geometrically during the 1960's discovered that their acquisition programs had left them with a tangle of incompatible compensation plans, and with scores of highly paid executives who now seemed to be in the wrong jobs or, worse, were superfluous. And with the stock market remaining in the doldrums, stock-option plans that had looked like money machines during the 1960's suddenly seemed most unsatisfactory; new compensation plans had to be devised to keep key executives contented. The job of personnel director took on new dimensions—especially as chief executives began scrambling to minimize the adverse effects of the recession.

Companies eager to increase their workers' productivity—and which were not?—discovered that an alert personnel director was in a unique position to contribute to the company's welfare. For example, George Sherman, the vice president of industrial relations at Cleveland's Midland-Ross Corp., got to wondering just why productivity rates in Japanese factories were so high. He flew to Japan, visited some factories, and concluded that part of the answer lay in the use of committees, made up of both workers and supervisors, that met regularly to hear suggestions for meeting production goals. On his return to the U.S., Sherman got clearance to form Japanese-style committees of workers and supervisors at the company's electrical-equipment plant in Athens, Tennessee. One modification of the Japanese plan involved the offer of a cash bonus to both workers and managers if productivity really did increase beyond the goal set by Midland-Ross. One year and 400 suggestions later, productivity at the Athens plant was up by 15 percent. The company was able to cancel plans to invest $250,000 in added manufacturing capacity, because output increased without it. Now Sherman expects to set up similar committees at other plants.

## TIME OFF WHEN IT COUNTS

An idea developed by I.B.M.'s vice president for personnel, Walton Burdick, further illustrates how a personnel executive can help his company, and its workers, through a difficult economic period. Burdick developed a policy allowing I.B.M.'s employees to defer vacation time for as long as they wanted. Postponement was actively urged during years of booming business activity, thus keeping a lid on the number of employees. The payoff for both I.B.M. and its employees came during the past year when the recession took a bite out of I.B.M.'s production. Workers who had saved up weeks or even months of vacation time were encouraged (rather firmly, one gathers) to use it.

I.B.M. Chairman Frank Cary credits the policy of deferred time off for helping the company get through a rough period without any layoffs. "You can't put a dollar sign on this sort of thing," Cary says. "The real benefit is in terms of morale. Our people know our policies are designed to keep them on the payroll. It makes them a lot more willing to go along with organizational changes we propose from time to time."

Pressure on American corporations from their not-so-silent partner, Uncle Sam, has done a great deal to add luster to the job of personnel director. In the last twenty years, there have been more than a hundred individual pieces of federal legislation directly affecting the relationship between corporations and their employees — e.g., the Work Hours Act of 1962, the Occupational Safety and Health Act of 1970, and the Employees Retirement Income Security Act of 1974. There has been a whole basket of laws and regulations to outlaw discrimination, including the Civil Rights Act of 1960, the Equal Pay Act of 1963, and the Age Discrimination in Employment Act of 1967.

## SUITS THAT CONCENTRATE THE MIND

Personnel directors complain that the federal rules and regulations are poorly conceived, sloppily written, and almost impossible to comply with because they change so rapidly. But many of those same personnel directors concede that the federal government's antidiscrimination activities have done wonders for their own prestige and power. To paraphrase Samuel Johnson, there is something about being sued for a lot of money that concentrates a chief executive's mind wonderfully. While some antidiscrimination suits involve just one aggrieved person and not much money, there have also been some class-action suits whose costs to corporations have been considerable. American Telephone & Telegraph Co. has settled two antidiscrimination suits — one for $38 million and another for $25 million — and nine steel companies settled one for a total of $31 million. The threat of class-action suits by aggrieved employees or disgruntled job applicants has made chief executives very much interested in having their personnel directors come up with ways to avoid even the appearance of discrimination. "Boy, do they listen to us now," says one personnel expert rather cheerfully.

In addition to setting affirmative-action goals, such as for the number of women and blacks to be hired during the coming year, and the number to be promoted into various levels of management, personnel directors develop procedures to make sure the goals are reached. That may involve new hiring systems or special training programs for those already hired and marked for fast promotion. Personnel directors must spend a lot of time these days with supervisors at all levels, helping them to meet their targets.

At Chemetron Corp., Melvin Shulman, corporate director of human resources, works directly with Chief Executive John P. Gallagher to set the affirmative-action goals and develop the procedures for reaching them. Then he works with Chemetron's line executives to make sure they understand what those goals are, and also that they understand how serious could be the consequences of failing to reach them. Says Shulman: "I tell them of the possible damage to the company, but in a sense I'm making sure they realize that their own careers here are involved. When they understand how directly the chief executive is involved, and that in effect I'm representing him, they're more than willing to get cracking."

Personnel directors probably would have come in from the cold even without the help of a topsy-turvy economy or a flood of legislation. It would have happened because attitudes within the American corporation itself have been changing steadily for at least a generation — the attitude of chief executives toward their subordinates as well as the attitude of employees at all levels toward the companies for which they work.

It is so commonplace now for chief executives to deliver speeches extolling "people" as their companies' most important resource that one tends to dismiss the phrase as cant. For some chief executives, of course, it may be. But a growing number of them really do realize that the quality and morale of their employees can make the difference between success and failure for their companies. One chief executive who is especially articulate on the importance of a company's human resources is Delta Airlines' Tom Beebe. "The name of the game in business today is personnel," he says emphatically. "You can't hope to show a good financial or operating report unless your personnel relations are in order and I don't care what kind of a company you're running. A chief executive is nothing without his people. You've got to have the right ones in the right jobs for them, and you've got to be sure employees at every level are being paid fairly and being given opportunities for promotion. You can't fool them, and any chief executive who tries is going to hurt himself and his company."

Since Beebe is a former personnel man, there is some temptation to pooh-pooh his views as those of a man loyal to his old specialty. But one cannot argue with success. Delta hasn't had a strike in twenty years, and as airlines go, it is uncommonly profitable.

## COURSES FOR THE COMERS

Every chief executive has to be especially concerned about bringing along capable successors. One company that is justifiably famous for the breadth and quality of its management-training programs is I.B.M. Frank Cary works closely with Walton Burdick, the vice president for personnel, to develop those programs and to assign the executive "graduates" to appropriate jobs within I.B.M. "It's the chief executive's responsibility to make sure the company has personnel policies and practices that can select the best people, then train them for management positions," says Cary.

Dresser Industries' senior vice president for industrial relations, Thomas Raleigh, spends a lot of time with President John V. James developing and administering the company's executive-training programs. At the recently established Dresser Leadership Center, a campus-like training center near the company's Dallas headquarters, executives enroll for courses lasting one to four weeks. They take courses in business management, and also study aspects of Dresser's energy-related business that may be unconnected to their immediate assignments. And Raleigh gets a chance to size up Dresser officials who work far from Dallas.

Few personnel managers work only with executives, of course, and the changed attitudes of employees toward their companies present a constant flow of new challenges. Today's blue- and white-collar workers want more from their jobs than just a paycheck; they want satisfaction, and they want to be treated fairly. Specifically, they want a salary that's fair in relation to their co-workers' salaries, and they want a fair chance for promotion that's based on an objective evaluation of their performances rather than the subjective whims of their immediate supervisors, or on their sex or skin color.

When Harold Johnson joined Philadelphia's INA Corp. as vice president for personnel a few months ago — he was formerly with American Medicorp Inc. — the insurance company did not have a fully developed system for setting the salaries of new employees. Nor were there clear ground rules for awarding raises, or for evaluating employee performance. "Things worked pretty much according to the whims of individual supervisors," says Johnson. "There were no company wide standards at all. The employees were unhappy because they felt their salaries were sometimes unfair, and because they felt top management wasn't aware of the quality work they were doing. And top management needed a tool to help identify the high performers so they could be promoted, or selected for advanced training."

INA Chairman Ralph Saul has ordered Johnson to develop a system to identify the company's most promising executives, and to establish corporate salary scales so that employees in similar jobs will be paid within an established range. Johnson is also devising an evaluation system to assure that raises will be awarded in a consistent way, based on individual performance. Once the system is in effect, Johnson will be responsible for getting supervisors to use it. Saul has told Johnson that the latter's own job performance will be measured in part by how quickly he can get the new pay and evaluation system working.

## POWER FOR THE TEAM

In many companies, the personnel director's responsibilities have become so complex that they can only be shouldered by topflight business managers who have the backing of the chief executive. The people who do the job like to say that in the years to come, a tour of duty in the personnel department (more likely the division of human resources) will be mandatory for any executive who aims to be chairman. Though that may prove to be an exaggeration, it is true that more companies are transferring up-and-coming executives into personnel for a while, en route to greater things. Dow Chemical's Herbert Lyon says it's a good thing for personnel departments to have a mix of professional experts, who have worked exclusively in personnel, and generalists who are brought in for a tour of duty from other parts of the company. I.B.M.'s Walton Burdick agrees, and adds that in his view the professional personnel types — of whom he is one — benefit even more than the generalists from having a mix. "It gives the specialists a better sense of what's really going on out there," he explains.

Citibank's Larry Small reflects a perspective common to executives who have moved into personnel but who do not expect to remain in it forever. "I'm not a personnel guy," he says carefully, displaying the annoyance of a man who has explained this to others before and who knows he'll have to explain it again to somebody else. "I'm a businessman — a manager. I just happen to be handling personnel at the moment, because it's a very important part of managing a business today."

As more and more personnel departments become populated with managers like Small, what were once enclaves will increasingly be seen as key corporate divisions. And the executives who run them, whether they are called personnel directors or executive vice presidents for human resources, will finally be recognized for what they now are and what in retrospect they always should have been — power-wielding members of their companies' management teams.

**QUESTIONS**

1. What do you see as the pluses and minuses of a career in personnel?

   _____

   _____

   _____

2. If you were a personnel director, what policies and programs would you promote?

   _____

   _____

   _____

# The Un-Manager

Early on the morning of July 26, 1976, 23-year-old Jack Dougherty drove the five miles from his apartment to the Newark, Del., headquarters of W.L. Gore & Associates Inc. He noticed the horses grazing on either side of the road, and for a while he held the image in his mind. But he was preoccupied. It was his first day on the job, and the recent MBA from the College of William and Mary was bursting with resolve. "I was beginning my career," he says. "I told myself that all the fooling around had stopped. I was all business."

Dressed in a dark blue suit and smiling broadly, Dougherty presented himself to Bill Gore, the founder of the company. He shook hands firmly but warmly, looked Gore in the eye, and said he was ready for anything. "That's fine, Jack, fine," Gore told him. "Why don't you look around and find something you'd like to do." "That," Dougherty says, "was probably the one thing I wasn't ready for. I was shocked, but he was so relaxed about everything that I decided to go along with it. He said maybe I should start at the Cherry Hill plant, where a lot of the new products were, and I figured they'd probably have something set up for me over there. But they didn't. I was confused for the next three weeks."

Jack spent his time earnestly interrogating various product managers who were more than happy to explain their activities in great detail. Finally, Dougherty careened into the office of Joe Tanner, who was busy marketing the latest wunderkind from the Gore laboratories. It was a white, gossamer-thin membrane with pores too small for a molecule of water to penetrate yet large enough to transmit certain vapors.

It was called Gore-tex, Tanner said, and when it was bonded to a fabric, lo and behold, the fabric became waterproof but "breathable," a combination of qualities that had long eluded researchers. He was only making tents with it now, Tanner continued, but it wouldn't be long until the great out-of-doors would see legions of campers wearing Gore-tex parkas, backpacks, and other gear. Dougherty heard them marching. "I liked what I heard," he says. The next morning, the new employee, dressed in jeans, was helping feed fabric into the maw of a huge laminator. Dougherty had found his "something to do." Today, Dougherty is responsible for all advertising and marketing in the fabrics group, the third largest segment of the company's business.

Bill Gore claims that Jack Dougherty's success, like the success of the company itself, is the happy consequence of a system of un-management Gore calls the "lattice organization." It is so named because every individual within it deals directly with every other, one on one, in relationships best described as a cross-hatching of horizontal and vertical lines. Unlike traditional "pyramid" management structures with carefully defined chains of command, Gore's lattice contains no titles, no orders, and no bosses. Associates, as all Gore employees are called, are allowed to identify an area where they feel they will be able to make their best contribution. Then, they are encouraged to maximize their individual accomplishments. "We don't manage people here," Bill Gore says. "People manage themselves. We organize ourselves around voluntary commitments. There is a fundamental difference in philosophy between a commitment and a command."

Hearing about the lattice without seeing it in operation can leave a suspicion that Bill Gore may have created a kind of self-indulgent commune where the profits of commerce are largely irrelevant. But the suspicion doesn't last long; the numbers won't allow it. During the past five years, Gore's sales and earnings have been growing at a compounded annual rate of nearly 40%. In the fiscal year ended March 31, 1982, the company's worldwide sales approached $125 million from five basic product groups: wire and cable, medical, Gore-tex fabrics, Gore-tex fibers, and industrial filter bags. The company has some 2,000 associates in 20 plants worldwide and 7 more plants under construction.

"Money is essential," Bill Gore says. "Without it, you don't have an enterprise." When someone suggested recently that Gore's determined drive for profits seemed incompatible with his more rarified ideas about human relationships, Gore said: "That's because there's something wrong with your education, sir. Actually, making money is a creative activity. It means people are applauding you for making a good contribution. In fact, it gives us the freedom to be what we are."

Wilbert L. Gore was born in Meridian, Idaho, near Boise. He is 70 but looks 50. His face is tan and creased from a lifetime of outdoorsmanship, primarily backpacking. He is trim and compact, standing about five feet, seven inches tall, He is calm and totally devoid of pretense. When he was studying for his degree in chemical engineering at the University of Utah, he won the Rocky Mountain Conference diving title from the one-meter board. Bill recalls growing up "with a lot of love around me."

At age six, Bill began his mountain wanderings in the Wasatch Range in Utah. And it was in those mountains, at a church summer camp, that he later met his future wife, Genevieve. Vieve, as she is called, says that in those days, every time she came around, Bill would execute a series of back somersaults. Friends say they are inseparable. One company advertisement features a photograph of them in full backpacking gear against a cratered, mountainous landscape. The caption reads: "The force behind the dream."

The dream itself first started taking shape from 1945 to 1957, when Bill worked on a task force in the research labs of E.I. Du Pont de Nemours. As Bill remembers it, the task-force approach to problem-solving had just been introduced at Du Pont. It had become increasingly popular in scientific research after prototype groups had proven their effectiveness during World War II. Bill's group, which at times included 20 researchers from various scientific disciplines, was intent on fabricating useful products from a polymer Du Pont had patented in 1937 called polytetrafluoroethylene, or PTFE. Years later, consumers would know PTFE as "Teflon," of nonstick-frying fame.

At the time, though, PTFE was little more than a puzzle. It had all the markings of a super-substance: It was strong, impervious to chemical solvents, abrasion-resistant, stable over a wide range of temperatures, and a nearly perfect electrical insulator. But in polymer form, PTFE could be neither injection-molded nor extruded by melt-processing techniques, the two traditional methods of fashioning, say, a plastic bowl. It could be "ram" extruded, a process of taking a lump of PTFE, a battering ram of some sort, and then smashing the PTFE through an orifice. Tape and tubing could be made that way, but little else. "The task force," Bill says, "was exciting, challenging, and loads of fun. Besides, we worked like Trojans. I began to wonder why entire companies couldn't be run the same way."

But even as Bill's group burned the midnight oil, another task force succeeded in creating a thermoplastic copolymer of PTFE that could be conventionally fabricated. "Du Pont felt that was good enough," Bill says, "and our group was dissolved. Everybody went back to their departments." Gore did, too, but nights, holidays, and weekends, he went to his basement. "I had a pretty good shop set up," he says, "so I started fooling around with polymer PTFE down there."

Bill continued to pursue his career at Du Pont and tinker in the basement for a year or so. One night in the fall of 1957, Bob Gore, a junior studying chemical engineering at the University of Delaware, dropped in on his father in the basement lab. He was surprised when his father launched into a long lecture on PTFE. Not only did Bill recite the litany of qualities he considered superior to those of the thermoplastic copolymer, but he also related their importance to another technological revolution that was unfolding at an astonishing pace—computers.

Ever since he first entered a few numbers into a computer named Eniac, a forerunner of Univac, Bill had followed the evolution of computers and transistors with growing excitement. He felt that some of PTFE's characteristics made it an ideal insulator for electrical wires in computers. It would make them easier to build, he said, and would ultimately increase their efficiency. And that, he concluded, could mean a very profitable market.

Bill explained that he had tried various ways to make a PTFE coating but had failed. He held up an aborted section of ribbon cable and pointed out where his attempts had broken down. "Then I noticed some sealant tape made by the 3M company," Bob says. "Dad had said it was ram-extruded PTFE so I asked him: 'Why don't you try this tape?' Dad said that would mean laminating the wires between two sections of tape and everybody knew you couldn't bond PTFE to itself. I went to bed."

As near as Bob can recall, it was around 4 a.m. when his father shook him awake. "I really didn't grasp what he was talking about," Bob says, "except I knew my father was very excited. I was sitting on the edge of my bed blinking at him, and he was waving this small piece of cable around saying: 'It works. It works.' "

"That's right," Bill says, "I stayed up all night to try out his suggestion. My son proved everybody wrong. But I really think it was 6 a.m. Bob used to sleep late." The next night, father and son returned to the lab and made ribbon cable "just as beautiful as can be."

During the next four months, Bill Gore tried to persuade Du Pont to take on the PTFE ribbon cable as a new product. "By that time in my career," he says, "I knew people who could make a decision. But it came through loud and clear that Du Pont regarded itself as a supplier of plastic raw materials and not as a fabricator." Soon after he learned of the company's decision, Bill and Vieve talked about starting their own wire and cable business. Bill said that if they mortgaged their house and took $4,000 from savings, they could make a go of it for two years. If they weren't successful by then, he said, he could probably get his job back at Du Pont or possibly teach at a university.

On January 1, 1958, their 23rd wedding anniversary, Bill and Vieve started another partnership. "All of our friends told us not to do it," Vieve Gore says, "and that's a very difficult thing. But this man of mine had it in his head. He just had to do it. We had that basement festooned with lights. We put drill holes in the floor and drill holes in the walls. It's hard to describe what it's like to bring your husband home and turn him loose."

When Bill Gore left Du Pont, he was 45 years old with five children to support. He left behind a career that spanned 17 years, a good salary, and security. But he also took a lot with him. During the next 24 years, virtually every new product Gore & Associates introduced was based on the PTFE polymer, bought from Du Pont, that Bill first encountered on the task force. And, just as important, Gore set out to recreate in his own company the sense of excited commitment, personal fulfillment, and self-direction that he had experienced on the Du Pont task force. "From the very beginning," Bill says, "we were using the principles of the lattice. After all, there was just Vieve and me, and we had been using them for years."

The two years the Gores had given themselves quickly slipped away. They needed business badly. The few odd orders that trickled into the basement just weren't paying the bills. "We came very close to calling it quits," Vieve says. But help was on the way.

One afternoon, Vieve stopped sifting PTFE powder to answer a phone call from a man who said he was with the city of Denver's water department. He said he had a sample of ribbon cable and was very interested but needed answers to a few technical questions. "Obviously Bill was the technical expert," Vieve says, "but he was out on an errand. I didn't know what to say. First, he asked for the product manager and I said he was out at the moment, then he asked for the sales manager, and finally for the president. They were all out, I told him. Before I could ask if I could help, he was hollering: 'What kind of a company is this anyway?'"

It took a little diplomacy, but eventually the Gores got an order for about $100,000 worth of ribbon cable to be used as part of a system that monitored pressure in water mains. "That order put us over the hump," Bill says. 'We took off from there."

By the time Bob Gore joined the company in 1963 with a Ph.D. in chemical engineering, it was clear the wire and cable business had taken hold. The company was properly ensconced in a new plant on Paper Mill Road in Newark, horses grazed lazily in pastures nearby, and the sun was shining on W.L. Gore & Associates. But all was not well. There were profits in the till, but there were also cracks in the lattice.

One warm Monday morning in the summer of 1965, Bill Gore was taking his usual stroll through the plant "to look around and say hello" when he suddenly realized that he no longer knew everyone's name. "I'm not talking about just one person," he says, "but several. I said to myself, 'Hey, the game has changed.' " Actually, the game was still the same, but there were many more players. The company had grown from simple connubial bliss to close to 200 employees. That growth was, in itself, a basement dream come true, something every entrepreneur hopes for. But, as often happens, it was still somewhat disconcerting.

"As the number of associates grew," Bill says, "we had to find a way to help people get started and then to follow their progress. This was particularly important when it came to compensation." At the same time, Bill wanted to avoid smothering the company in thick layers of formal "management," a common response to organizational problems that he felt stifled individual creativity. Instead, he promoted a kind of "buddy system," a casual Big Brother or Big Sister relationship in which a more experienced associate took a specific and personal interest in the contributions, problems, and goals of a new associate.

Gradually, the "buddy" system matured into the "sponsor" system, a largely semantic difference that, nonetheless, accurately suggests a more sophisticated sense of advocacy and involvement. Everyone at Gore has a sponsor and frequently more than one. The associate who starts out in, say, fabric inspection and quality control and then becomes interested in fabric lamination will have a sponsor in each department and perhaps still others as the associate's responsibilities grow.

Ultimately this associate will also become a sponsor, because at Gore leaders are not appointed but are allowed to "happen." "Leaders are so defined," Bill Gore says, "because they have followers. And why people follow one person and not another, I don't really know. Sometimes it's based on superior knowledge or skill, but there are many other nonobjective and perhaps even mystical factors."

The sponsorship system was a harmonious addition to Bill Gore's evolving method of un-management. It was flexible, expandable, and well suited to accommodate the future needs of a growing company — but it wasn't enough. During that tour when Bill discovered that he didn't know everyone's name, he also realized that neither did anyone else. Even more alarming, he fould a subtle shift in perspective; the once tightly knit group had lost its sense of identity. Although he wasn't sure of the cause, his memories of the DuPont task force strongly suggested that it had to do with the number of people in the group. Apparently, he reasoned, as that number approached 200, a group somehow became a crowd in which individuals grew increasingly anonymous and significantly less cooperative.

In part to test his theory and in part to reach midwestern markets, Bill Gore opened a second plant in 1967 in Flagstaff, Ariz. As people shifted to Flagstaff the number of associates at the Newark plant dropped to 150. "That did the trick," Bill says. "People started smiling more. You could tell they felt better even by the way they said 'hello.' " In the years that followed, the accuracy of his intuition was proven time and again. Each time the magic number was breached, group cohesiveness and cooperation declined. Each time, Bill would open another plant. In fact, he has opened 18 more plants since 1967, at an average cost of almost $4.5 million. The openings are all the more remarkable because the company never used a dime of debt until 1980.

The thought obviously pleases Bill Gore; he smiles faintly and says: "Opening plants costs money, but it makes money." Then he goes on to say that his goal in the next five years is to become one of the country's biggest companies. Almost impishly he waits for the message to sink in. Obviously growth of that magnitude means a cloudburst of new plant openings. "Yes, I know," he says contentedly. "We've already got seven under construction. Now do you see why profits are essential?"

The middle '60s marked a period of transition for W.L. Gore & Associates. By 1969, as the company approached $6 million in sales, Bill Gore had confronted the problem of growth and had found some innovative solutions consistent with his vision of a lattice organization. The sponsorship system, for example, preserved both order and individual freedom. And the realization that size had a measurable impact on group dynamics was another theoretical and then practical breakthrough. As a result, the lattice itself was evolving. These developments couldn't have been better timed. Bob Gore was about to have another brainstorm.

In the fall of 1969, Bob was troubled by a growing suspicion that the company's wire and cable business was slowing down because of market saturation and increasing competition. The anxiety made him restless and soon he found himself working nights in the lab toying with PTFE. If he could stretch PTFE, he reasoned, he could introduce air into its molecular structure, giving a greater volume per pound of raw material without affecting its performance. This, in turn, could sharply reduce the company's fabricating costs and ultimately increase profit margins on coated wire and cable products. That way, any sales slowdown could be offset by increasing profitability. The scientific community had already determined that PTFE couldn't be stretched very far. But since he had proven conventional wisdom wrong once before, Bob decided to go ahead.

For three days, he took slender rods of PTFE about a foot long and preheated them in the lab's ovens. Then, ever so gently, he pulled on both ends of the rod. Each time, the rod snapped in two. He tried again and again. He tried different temperatures. He tried to adjust the force of his easy pull. Nothing worked.

Finally, the days of futile, frustrating effort caught up with him. One evening in October, Bob Gore, dressed in a white lab coat and heavy asbestos gloves, took a rod from the oven, grabbed each end, and angrily yanked his clenched fists apart. The foot-long rod stretched the full length of his extended arms. "I couldn't believe it," he says. "I went right home. I didn't say anything to anybody because I thought it might be a fluke. I knew what I had done, but I just couldn't believe it. I always entered my results in a journal, but that night I didn't write anything. I must've been really worked up."

Early the next morning, Bob hurried to the lab so he could repeat his experiment before anyone else arrived. After several successful attempts, he called in his father and colleagues. With a quick flourish of his arms, he revealed the fruits of his labor. "We were all very quiet," Bill Gore says. "We were all trained scientists so we recognized the importance of what Bob had done. I was very proud."

Word spread rapidly throughout the company that Bob Gore had discovered a "miracle product." Even today, associates who were there recall the time with a certain breathless sense of wonder. "Everybody seemed to have an idea how to use it," says Burt Chase, business leader of the wire and cable division. "Bob kept a small gray file-card box in his office so people could drop off their ideas. I remember one that said we should string tennis racquets with expanded PTFE. We were all caught up in the excitement." The list of suggested ideas was so exhaustive that when the patent was filed on May 21, 1970, it correctly anticipated every product application that would be introduced during the next 12 years, with the sole exception of vascular grafting. In only six months, the miracle product, now called Gore-tex, had totally reshaped the company's future. A wire and cable company had been transformed into a multifaceted high-technology company reaching for a tantalizing variety of markets. At least that is how it appeared in the white heat of the moment. Translating imagination into viable commercial products was another matter.

Gore's first product using expanded PTFE was made by a process that didn't bathe the company in the glory of high-tech precision but was, nonetheless, a fitting example of the resourcefulness that would characterize the development of Gore-tex. This product was, and is, a joint sealant that is put on pipe flanges to ensure a tight fit.

Bob Gore affectionately describes the sealant's method of manufacture as the "sneaker process." Two men would come to work wearing sneakers; they would each grab an end of a preheated length of PTFE; they would nod to each other when ready, and then they would run like crazy to opposite ends of the warehouse. Voilà, they had made Gore-tex sealant tape. "Now that was something to see," Bob Gore says. "I guess it was about 100 feet, wall to wall, and those guys really flew. It wasn't fancy, but it worked."

While the boys were sprinting out in the warehouse, Bob and his colleagues were creating machines that could mass-produce the Gore-tex membrane in wide sheets and then bond it to fabrics. But it was slow work, and to keep the miracle product alive and growing, the associates foraged for new applications wherever and whenever they could.

In 1971, for example, Bill Gore chanced on the company's second largest division on a snow-covered slope in Colorado where he was skiing with friends, including Dr. Ben Eiseman of the Denver General Hospital. "We were just about to start a run," Bill Gore says, "when I absentmindedly pulled a small tubular section of Gore-tex out of my pocket and looked at it. 'What is that stuff?' Ben asked. So I told him about its properties. 'Feels great,' he said. 'What do you use it for?' 'Got no idea,' I said. 'Well give it to me,' he said, 'and I'll try it in a vascular graft on a pig.' Two weeks alter, he called me up. Ben was pretty excited. 'Bill,' he said, 'I put it in a pig and it works. What do I do now?' I told him to get together with Pete Cooper in our Flagstaff plant, and I let them figure it out." Although a major problem would have to be solved four years later, 375,000 patients throughout the world now walk around with Gore-tex vascular grafts. "Cardiovascular disease is one of the major health problems of mankind," says medical products leader Jack Hoover. "The use of Gore-tex to treat it has only just begun."

By 1973, Bob's engineering team had devised machines that could stretch Gore-tex wide enough to cover the standard commercial dimensions of several different fabrics. All their tests indicated that, at long last, the secret of a waterproof, breathable garment had been discovered. Bill Gore couldn't have been happier, but he wasn't going to wear it; he wanted to sleep in it. For years, Bill had yearned for a light, waterproof tent that would save him lower back pain on long mountain treks. Gore-tex looked like the answer to a veteran camper's prayer.

Since Vieve had routinely handcrafted their backpacks and tents, Bill commissioned her to stitch up a tent from sections of Gore-tex he had bonded to mosquito netting. Then they set off for the mountains of the Wind River Range in the wilds of Wyoming. "One night," Bill says, "it started to rain just after we had gone to bed. And it rained harder. Vieve and I felt around the tent and it was bone dry. We were very pleased with ourselves. But then the rain turned partly to hail. The hail punched tiny holes through the Gore-tex, and later there must've been two inches of water in the tent. We didn't sleep well that night."

As it turned out, Bill and Vieve's soggy night at Wind River was more than a temporary inconvenience; it was the first sign that Gore-tex had entered a time of troubles. During the next five years, Gore-tex would suffer a variety of technical growing pains. Some were minor, but others were critical, even potentially fatal to the reputation of a miracle product, and all would test the resiliency of the lattice.

In June 1975, Dr. Charles Campbell, senior resident at the University of Pittsburgh, reported to Jack Hoover that a Gore-tex arterial graft he had placed in a patient had developed an aneurism, a bubblelike protrusion of the arterial wall that meant it wasn't strong enough to withstand the pressure of the blood within it. If the aneurism continued to expand, it would eventually burst, and the patient could die.

The problem had to be solved quickly and permanently if the company's plans for vascular grafts were ever to be realized. "I'm told from time to time," Bill Gore says, "that a lattice organization can't meet a crisis well because it takes too long to reach a consensus when there are no bosses. But this isn't true. Actually, a lattice, by its very nature, works particularly well in a crisis. A lot of useless effort is avoided because there is no rigid management hierarchy to conquer before you can attack a problem."

Only days after his call, Dr. Campbell flew to Newark to present his findings to Bill and Bob Gore and several other associates drawn from production and research. The meeting adjourned after two hours of discussion, and the associates went their separate ways to consider solutions. But one of the associates, Dan Hubis, already had an idea he thought might work. If he could wrap another layer of Gore-tex around a section of graft, he reasoned, he might be able to increase the rupture tolerance of the entire section. Hubis, a former Elkton, Md., policeman who had joined Gore in 1966 to work on new production methods, immediately started testing his idea in the lab.

He tried various wrapping techniques, and after each try he forced compressed air through the specimen section to see if it would hold. On his twelfth try, after three hours of work, he found the right method. Hubis had resolved a potentially serious setback in only one afternoon. "It was quick because it had to be," Hubis says. "I don't remember any clapping or cheering, but I know we were very happy." Bill Gore was pleased, too; not only was it a noteworthy technical accomplishment, but it also proved the worth of the lattice. "There were several people with different skills all working on a common problem," Bill says. "They came together quickly, and no one was slowed down because they had to get the approval of some higher-up before they could proceed. The creativity of such a group is much greater than the sum of its members."

As 1976 began, W.L. Gore & Associates still looked like the wire and cable company founded 18 years earlier. It was more elaborate, of course, with more people, more markets, and a broader product line, but at least 90% of sales and profits were still being drawn from the basic wire and cable business. After several years of research and development, Gore-tex was only a modest success, contributing some $2 million in sales from uses in microfiltration, industrial filter bags, joint sealant, and medical products. But even though Gore & Associates may have looked like the same old company, it didn't look that way for long, because in 1976, Gore-tex took off and took the whole company with it. "From that time," says Shanti Mehta, Gore's financial leader, "the company's sales and earnings have grown at least 35% a year. Gore-tex products were soon contributing almost 50% of our business."

The initial surge was led by the medical products division as Hubis's strengthened graft won widespread acceptance in the medical community — eventually it would control 70% of the market. Then the Goretex fabric division kicked in with its first commercial product, a tent.

A mountaineer named Bill Nicolai had nearly frozen to death in the Picket Range of Washington State's North Cascades in the fall of 1971. Like the Gores, Nicolai had problems with his tent, only his was shredded to streamers in a storm. And also like the Gores, he wasn't going to let it happen again. That winter he created a two-man expedition tent especially designed to withstand nature's high-altitude perversities. He called it the Omnipotent, in praise of its virtues, and then he founded a company, Early Winters Ltd., to make it and sell it.

But the Omnipotent was a costly and complex affair meant for very serious climbers, and Nicolai soon learned that there just weren't that many people around who habitually spent their time on the roof of the world. For several years, Early Winters, like its customers, lived close to the edge of disaster. Even by January 1976, the company — one product, five employees, and rented space in a former neighborhood grocery store in Seattle — was still struggling to survive. Then Joe Tanner walked through the door. Since February 1974, when he joined Gore, Tanner had been traveling around the country literally trying to give Gore-tex away to anyone who would agree to make something with it. A few companies were willing to give it a try, but afterwards they balked when they were asked to buy it. Then Tanner found Nicolai.

"I'd never met the man before," says Nicolai. "But there he was telling me about this stuff that was waterproof and breathed. He wanted me to make a tent with it. Of course, I'd heard all this before, but I had nothing to lose; my tent wasn't selling very well." Nicolai took some Goretex laminate, quickly fashioned a prototype tent, and headed for the hills. "The fantastic thing about it was that it worked," he says. "I took it camping at Icicle Creek in the Cascades. That night it was drizzling and 29 degrees Fahrenheit — perfect for condensation. When I woke up in the morning, I felt the side of the tent and it was bone dry. A shiver went down my spine." Nicolai's new tent, christened Light Dimension, was an instant success.

Although the Omnipotent is still favored by professional climbers, the Light Dimension reached a much bigger market because it set up quickly and was light, compact, and, at $195, some $60 less than its big brother. Sales at Early Winters jumped from $6,000 a month to $35,000, enabling Nicolai to introduce several new products. Today, the company's tents, parkas, and other equipment produce annual sales of roughly $10 million.

There was only one man who could have matched Nicolai smile for smile, and that was Joe Tanner. Two years of hope, disappointment, tests, and more hope had finally paid off. That summer he explained to a young business school graduate recently hired at Gore that even though he was making only tents with Gore-tex laminate, it wouldn't be long until the great out-of-doors was draped with Gore-tex. During the next two years, as word of waterproof, breathable fabrics spread from Nicolai's store, Tanner signed up some half-dozen larger and better-known manufacturers.

Gore supplied the membrane and the lamination process, but it left design, cutting, and sewing to the manufacturers. Companies like Sierra West, Banana Equipment, and Recreational Equipment Inc. started making parkas, rainwear, sleeping bags, and a variety of outdoor accessories with Gore-tex. Once again, the sun was shining on W.L. Gore & Associates. But the summer of 1978, which began so full of promise for the Gore-tex fabrics division, gradually darkened into deepest gloom. "It was a nightmare," says Peter Gilson, the division's business leader. "Parkas were being returned because they leaked."

Gilson had just joined Gore. He was 38 years old, but he already had 15 years of conspicuous accomplishment in the fabrics business at Du Pont. But even with all his experience, Gilson was bewildered when leaky parkas started showing up in groups of threes and fours. "We had no idea why they leaked," he says. "At first we thought the customers hadn't sealed the seams properly or maybe they punctured it somehow. We sensed we had a problem, but because the parkas straggled in, we weren't sure how big it was." But there was one thing that Gilson did know: The entire company's reputation and credibility were on the line.

In September, Gore researchers discovered that certain oils in human sweat could clog the pores in the Gore-tex membrane, which, in turn, altered the surface tension of the membrane, allowing water molecules to pass through. In short, sweaty parkas leaked. But they also discovered that such "contaminated" parkas could be restored if they were washed in a detergent and double-rinse cycle or, in extreme cases, in a denatured alcohol bath. This became known as the "Ivory Snow Solution" and it was passed on to every Gore-tex manufacturer and dealer. For a while, there was hope that this solution would remedy the relatively few complaints being reported. Then, in November, Gilson received a disturbing letter from a part-time employee of Sierra West who also worked as a mountain guide. He told Gilson about a recent experience when he led a small group of campers into the Sierras and they were hit by a freak storm. "His name was Butch," Gilson says, "and I remember he wrote: 'My parka leaked, and my life was in danger.' That scared the hell out of us. Clearly our solution was no solution at all to someone on a mountaintop."

Gilson, at Gore only a few months, was faced with a decision that could cause serious damage to the entire company. Bill Gore calls decisions of this type "waterline decisions," using the image of a sinking ship. At any other time, Gore associates are allowed to solve their problems independently; free to seek advice or not, as they see fit. But if the problem could twist toward the company's waterline, associates must consult with other associates before proceeding. As evidence mounted, it became clear that the contamination problem was larger in scope and carried more serious consequences than had first been imagined.

Gilson sat down at a conference table with Bob Gore and four other associates. The circumstances were undeniably grave, but otherwise the meeting merely reflected the normal metabolism of a healthy lattice organization. Once again, associates with different skills had been brought together to solve a common problem. Bob Gore was there for his scientific expertise and the others brought talents in marketing, manufacturing, and quality control. The more they talked, the more they realized that there was only one thing they could do. "We took all of the noninsulated Gore-tex garments off the market," Gilson says. "We brought back, at our own expense, a fortune in pipeline material. Anything that was in the stores, at the manufacturers, or anywhere else in the pipeline, we stopped."

Meanwhile, Bob Gore set out to find a permanent answer to the contamination problem. One month after the garments were taken off the market, Bob Gore came out of the lab having restructured the molecular configuration of the membrane to exclude the oils that were causing the contamination. By late December, parkas made with improved, second-generation Gore-tex laminates were already on dealers' racks. In addition, Gilson told dealers that any time a customer returned a leaky parka, they should replace it with a second-generation model and bill the company. "In the four years since 1978, we've taken back roughly $3.5 million of first-generation products. But hindsight tells us that we made the right decision. We didn't lose our credibility. We haven't lost even one customer."

As time passed, Gilson's perspective changed to give equal weight to what was gained as well as to what hadn't been lost. In four years, Gore's customer list grew from the original 6 to 125, including names like North Face, C.B. Sports, and Sierra Designs. Gore-tex fabrics blossomed into a profusion of products. There are Gore-tex jogging shoes, hiking boots, and high-fashion boots for women; Gore-tex hats and gloves; and trench coats, ski jackets, and golf jackets. There are even Gore-tex space suits on the space shuttle, Columbia. The fabrics division has grown "substantially faster" than the company as a whole, and Gilson expects it to double its size in the current fiscal year alone. And, he says, there is more growth on the way. This year the Army and the Marine Corps will begin outfitting troops in Gore-tex wet-weather parkas, pants, and headgear. "That," says Gilson, "is a sizable piece of business."

Still, the scare of '78 hasn't been entirely forgotten. Bill Gore, for example, likes to test a sample of every new garment personally to assure himself that it doesn't leak. Sometimes, he is spotted wandering around the grounds of the Newark plant during a rainstorm wearing a colorful, hooded parka, but at other times, when nature fails, he is perfectly content to wear a similar parka out to the garden behind his house and stand there with a hose over his head.

Ever since Bob Gore yanked a new future out of preheated goop, W.L. Gore & Associates has risen at a pace and in directions that no observer could have anticipated. But just as the company seems focused on a future of dramatic growth with fabrics as the largest and fastest-growing business in the company, yet another Gore prepares to yank something spectacular out of the goop.

"It will be the desalination of sea water; you know, making it drinkable," says Bill Gore. "We haven't talked much about it, because it's still in development. But my son, Dave, is going to give a paper on it next month."

Dave Gore is a 37-year-old physicist who has been working on the process for almost three years in Flagstaff. He says the idea first impressed him when he was a child watching his father scamper around the roof of the house setting up solar-distillation experiments. "It's always been a big dream of mine," he says. "It would have impact. You can make the desert bloom." But it was the invention of the Gore-tex membrane that made the dream come true.

Basically, Dave's process, which he calls "membrane distillation," involves passing water vapor from salt water through a Gore-tex membrane. Impurities are left behind and then the vapor condenses against a cold surface to recover potable water. He claims membrane distillation is considerably more efficient and less expensive than any other technique currently available. Even though he has only small units being tested, Dave says he is about ready to market them commercially. "We'll start with the $100 million-a-year market for pure laboratory water," he says, "and then we'll move to making drinking water from seawater. Worldwide, the market is probably worth billions. It's a little bit mind-boggling when you think of all the possibilities."

Could it be that virtually anything is possible in some kind of corporate paradise structured on the lattice? Is the lattice the answer to every problem? "No," says Bill Gore. "For example, established companies would find it very difficult to use the lattice. Too many hierarchies would be destroyed. When you remove titles and positions and allow people to follow who they want, it may very well be someone other than the person who has been in charge. The lattice works for us, but it's always evolving. You have to expect problems."

Sometimes, it appears, the lattice can even make life difficult for those it serves. Burt Chase, head of wire and cable, says the unhappiest moment of his 20-year career was caused by a sponsor who wouldn't sponsor. "I still don't know what his problem was," Chase says. "At the time, I was selling on the West Coast, and I had three men working with me. Time after time I'd tell my sponsor that if he didn't come through for me on one thing or another, I'd have to let the men down. He'd nod and say: 'Uh, huh, I'll take care of it.' But he never did. Finally, I had to go directly to Bill Gore. I guess Bill told him that there were some very unhappy men out there and that woke him up. Anyway, it's still a potential problem that we work very hard at avoiding."

And sometimes customers don't quite know what to make of it. "I was taken aback that something that loose could really work," says Eric Reynolds, founder of Marmot Mountain Works Ltd. of Grand Junction, Colo., and a major Gore customer. "I was also taken by the romance of it all, the idea of free spirits working together. But the more I've seen of it the more I think that the lattice works best in research and development projects. I think the lattice has its problems with the day-to-day nitty-gritty of getting things done on time and getting products out the door. I don't think Bill quite realizes how the lattice system affects customers. I mean, after you've established a relationship with someone about product quality, you can call up one day and suddenly find that someone new to you is handling your problems. It's frustrating to find a lack of continuity. But I have to admit that I've personally seen at Gore remarkable examples of people coming out of nowhere and excelling."

Associates asked to describe the lattice in operation act as if they have just been teased with an insoluble riddle. They do their best to capture a phenomenon that at times requires them to invent a new vocabulary. But in the end it becomes clear that the lattice to them is like breathing, something done every second and rarely thought about. "You don't come to work here and say 'Okay, now we've got to do the lattice system,' " says Carmela Avallone, head of fabric inspection. "The lattice is a feeling, a state of mind." And ultimately, they say, that feeling finds its way back to Bill and Vieve Gore.

Late one afternoon, Bill and Vieve were swapping stories about their adventures in the mountains of the world. Vieve suddenly changed the subject and began talking about a meeting the company had held for the associates on the previous Saturday. Some 600 associates filled an auditorium at the University of Delaware, she said, to listen to a detailed presentation about the company's results for the year and plans for the future. This was done regularly, she said, but this year was a little different. "My son, Bob, got up to speak," she said. "And then behind him were slides projected that he had put together showing Bill as a young man. There was even a picture of him going off a diving board. Bob looked at the pictures for a while and then he turned to the associates and said: 'My father was a young man once,' and that's how he introduced Bill."

As Vieve was telling the story she never stopped looking at her husband, and at the end of it she had tears in her eyes. And he never looked away from her, because they were talking really only for each other. He was looking at her and smiling faintly with utter tenderness. Vieve didn't say any more, but Carmela Avallone finished the story later. "When Bill got up," she said, "everyone started clapping, and then they stood up, and it went on and on, and there weren't many dry eyes that day."

"It's much better to use friendship and love," Bill Gore once said, "than slavery and whips. The results will always be much better."

## QUESTIONS

1. If you were the manager of a company, what organizational structure would you use?

   _____

   _____

   _____

2. What management principles would you use in dealing with employees?

   _____

   _____

   _____

# Quality of Work Life — Learning from Tarrytown

Imagine that an executive of one of our largest corporations is told that one of his plant managers wants to spend over $1.6 million on a program that has no guarantee of any return in greater efficiency, higher productivity, or lower costs. Then imagine how he would react if he were told that the union is in on the program up to its ears and that the purpose of the program is referred to as "improving the quality of work life."

If the reader imagines that the average top corporate manager would say the plant manager had lost his senses and ought to be fired, the reader is probably in the majority. The striking fact, however, is that one particular executive, the head of what is probably the largest division of any manufacturing company in the world (18 plants and almost 100,000 employees) knew just what was going on and approved the idea enthusiastically.

This is the story of the General Motors car assembly plant at Tarrytown, New York. In 1970, the plant was known as having one of the poorest labor relations and production records in GM. In seven years, the plant turned around to become one of the company's better run sites.

Born out of frustration and desperation, but with a mutual commitment by management and the union to change old ways of dealing with the workers on the shop floor, a quality of work life (QWL) program developed at Tarrytown. "Quality of work life" is a generic phrase that covers a person's feelings about every dimension of work, including economic rewards and benefits, security, working conditions, organizational and interpersonal relationships, and its intrinsic meaning in a person's life.

For the moment, I will define QWL more specifically as a *process* by which an organization attempts to unlock the creative potential of its people by involving them in decisions affecting their work lives. A distinguishing characteristic of the process is that its goals are not simply extrinsic, focusing on the improvement of productivity and efficiency per se; they are also intrinsic, regarding what the worker sees as self-fulfilling and self-enhancing ends in themselves.

In recent years, the QWL movement has generated wide-scale interest. Just since 1975, more than 450 articles and books have been written on the subject, and there are at least four national and international study and research centers focusing on quality of work life as such. Scores of industrial enterprises throughout the United States are conducting experiments, usually on a small scale; and in an eight-month world study tour a few years back of more than 50 industrial plants in Japan, Australia, and Europe, I found great interest in "industrial democracy."

So what is special about the Tarrytown story? First, it has the earmarks of success. Second, it illustrates some underlying principles of successful organizational change that can be applied in a variety of work environments. Third, although a number of promising experiments are going on in many General Motors plants and in other companies, this QWL program has involved more human beings—more than 3,800—than any other I know of. Finally, and this is speculative, I believe that Tarrytown represents in microcosm the beginnings of what may become commonplace in the future—a new collaborative approach on the part of management, unions, and workers to improve the quality of life at work in its broadest sense.

## TARRYTOWN—THE BAD OLD DAYS

In the late 1960s and early 1970s, the Tarrytown plant suffered from much absenteeism and labor turnover. Operating costs were high. Frustration, fear, and mistrust characterized the relationship between management and labor. At certain times, as many as 2,000 labor grievances were on the docket. As one manager puts it, "Management was always in a defensive posture. We were instructed to go by the book, and we played by the book. The way we solved problems was to use our authority and impose discipline." The plant general superintendent acknowledges in retrospect, "For reasons we thought valid, we were very secretive in letting the union and the workers know about changes to be introduced or new programs coming down the pike."

Union officers and committeemen battled constantly with management. As one union officer describes it, "We were always trying to solve yesterday's problems. There was no trust and everybody was putting out fires. The company's attitude was to employ a stupid robot with hands and no face." The union committee chairman describes the situation the way he saw it: "When I walked in each morning I was out to get the personnel director, the committeeman was shooting for the foreman, and the zone committeeman was shooting for the general foreman. Every time a foreman notified a worker that there would be a job change, it resulted in an instant '78 (work standards grievance). It was not unusual to have a hundred '78s hanging fire, more than 300 discipline cases, and many others."

Another committeeman adds, "My job was purely political. It was to respond instantly to any complaint or grievance regardless of the merits, and just fight the company. I was expected to jump up and down and scream. Every time a grievance came up, it lit a spark, and the spark brought instant combustion."

Workers were mad at everyone. They disliked the job itself and the inexorable movement of the high-speed line — 56 cars per hour, a minute and a half per operation per defined space. One worker remembers it well, "Finish one job, and you always had another stare you in the face." Conditions were dirty, crowded, and often noisy. Employees saw their foremen as insensitive dictators, whose operating principle was "If you can't do the job like I tell you, get out."

Warnings, disciplinary layoffs, and firings were commonplace. Not only did the workers view the company as an impersonal bureaucratic machine, "They number the parts and they number you," but also they saw the union itself as a source of frustration. "The committeeman often wrote up a grievance but, because he was so busy putting out fires, he didn't tell the worker how or whether the grievance was settled. In his frustration, the worker would take it out on the foreman, the committeeman, and the job itself."

In the words of both union and management representatives, during this period "Tarrytown was a mess."

## Beginnings of Change

What turned Tarrytown around? How did it start? Who started it and why?

Because of the high labor turnover, the plant was hiring a large number of young people. The late 1960s was the time of the youth counterculture revolution. It was a time when respect for authority was being questioned. According to the plant manager, "It was during this time that the young people in the plant were demanding some kind of change. They didn't want to work in this kind of environment. The union didn't have much control over them, and they certainly were not interested in taking orders from a dictatorial management."

In April 1971, Tarrytown faced a serious threat. The plant manager saw the need for change, and also an opportunity. He approached some of the key union officers who, though traditionally suspicious of management overtures, listened to him. The union officers remember liking what they heard. "This manager indicated that he wanted to create a philosophy of management different from what had gone on before. He felt there was a better way of doing things."

The plant manager suggested that if the union was willing to do its part, he would put pressure on his own management people to change their ways. The tough chairman of the grievance committee observed later that "this guy showed right off he had a quality of work life attitude— we didn't call it that at that time—inside him. He was determined that this attitude should carry right down to the foremen, and allow the men on the line to be men."

The company decided to stop assembling trucks at Tarrytown and to shuffle the entire layout around. Two departments, Hard Trim and Soft Trim, were to be moved to a renovated area of the former truck line.

At first, the changes were introduced in the usual way. Manufacturing and industrial engineers and technical specialists designed the new layout, developed the charts and blueprints, and planned every move. They then presented their proposals to the supervisors. Two of the production supervisors in Hard Trim, sensing that top plant management was looking for new approaches, asked a question that was to have a profound effect on events to follow: "Why not ask the workers themselves to get involved in the move? They are experts in their own right. They know as much about trim operations as anyone else."

The consensus of the Hard Trim management group was that they would involve the workers. The Soft Trim Department followed suit. The union was brought in on the planning and told that management wanted to ask the workers' advice. Old timers in the union report "wondering about management's motives. We could remember the times management came up with programs only to find there was an ulterior motive and that in the long run the men could get [the short end of the deal]." Many supervisors in other departments also doubted the wisdom of fully disclosing the plans.

Nevertheless, the supervisors of the two trim departments insisted not only that plans *not* be hidden from the workers but also that the latter would have a say in the setup of jobs. Charts and diagrams of the facilities, conveyors, benches, and materials storage areas were drawn up for the workers to look at. Lists were made of the work stations and the personnel to man them. The supervisors were impressed by the outpouring of ideas: "We found they did know a lot about their own operations. They made hundreds of suggestions and we adopted many of them."

Here was a new concept. The training director observes, "Although it affected only one area of the plant, this was the first time management was communicating with the union and the workers on a challenge for solving *future* problems and not the usual situation of doing something, waiting for a reaction, then putting out the fires later." The union echoes the same point: "This demonstrated how important it is to solve problems before they explode. If not solved, then you get the men riled up against everything and everybody."

Moving the two departments was carried out successfully with remarkably few grievances. The plant easily made its production schedule deadlines. The next year saw the involvement of employees in the complete rearrangement of another major area of the plant, the Chassis Department. The following year a new car model was introduced at Tarrytown.

## Labor-Management Agreement

In 1972, Irving Bluestone, the vice president for the General Motors Department of the United Automobile Workers Union (UAW), made what many consider to be the kick-off speech for the future of the quality of work life movement. Repeated later in different forms, he declared:

"Traditionally management has called upon labor to cooperate in increasing productivity and improving the quality of the product. My view of the other side of the coin is more appropriate; namely, that management should cooperate with the worker to find ways to enhance the dignity of labor and to tap the creative resources in each human being in developing a more satisfying work life, with emphasis on worker participation in the decision-making process."[1]

In 1973, the UAW and GM negotiated a national agreement. In the contract was a brief "letter of agreement" signed by Bluestone and George Morris, head of industrial relations for GM. Both parties committed themselves to establishing formal mechanisms, at least at top levels, for exploring new ways of dealing with the quality of work life. *This was the first time QWL was explicitly addressed in any major U.S. labor-management contract.*

The Tarrytown union and management were aware of this new agreement. They had previously established close connections with William Horner of Bluestone's staff and with James Rae, the top corporate representative of the Organization Development Department. It was only natural that Tarrytown extend its ongoing efforts within the framework of the new agreement. Furthermore, Charles Katko, vice president and general manager of the GM Assembly Division, gave his enthusiastic endorsement to these efforts.

Local issues and grievances, however, faced both parties. In the past, it had not been uncommon for strike action to be taken during contract negotiations. The manager and the union representatives asked themselves, "Isn't there a better way to do this, to open up some two-way communication, gain some trust?" The union president was quick to recognize "that it was no good to have a 'love-in' at the top between the union and management, especially the Personnel Department. We had to stick with our job as union officers. But things were so bad we figured 'what the hell, we have nothing to lose.' "

The union president's observation about that period is extremely significant in explaining the process of change that followed:

"We as a union knew that our primary job was to protect the worker and improve his economic life. But times had changed and we began to realize we had a broader obligation, which was to help the workers become more involved in decisions affecting their own jobs, to get their ideas, and to help them to improve the whole quality of life at work beyond the paycheck."

The negotiations were carried out in the background of another effort on management's part. Delmar Landon, director of organizational research and development at General Motors, had been independently promoting an organizational development effort for a number of years. These efforts were being carried out in many plants. Professionally trained communication facilitators had been meeting with supervisors and even some work groups to solve problems of interpersonal communication.

What General Motors was attempting to do was like the OD programs that were being started up in many industries and businesses in the United States. But, as with many such programs, there was virtually no union involvement. As the training director put it, "Under the influence of our plant manager, the OD program was having some influence among our managers and supervisors, but still this OD stuff was looked upon by many as a gimmick. It was called the 'happy people' program by those who did not understand it." And, of course, because it was not involved, the union was suspicious.

Nevertheless, a new atmosphere of trust between the union and the plant manager was beginning to emerge. Local negotiations were settled without a strike. There was at least a spark of hope that the Tarrytown mess could be cleaned up. Thus the informal efforts at Tarrytown to improve union-management relations and to seek greater involvement of workers in problem solving became "legitimatized" through the national agreement and top level support. Other plants would follow.

## THE TESTING PERIOD

In April 1974, a professional consultant was brought in to involve supervisors and workers in joint training programs for problem solving. Management paid his fees. He talked at length with most of the union officers and committeemen, who report that "we were skeptical at first but we came to trust him. We realized that if we were going to break through the communications barrier on a large scale, we needed a third party."

The local union officials were somewhat suspicious about "another management trick." But after talking with Solidarity House (UAW's headquarters), they agreed to go along. Both parties at the local level discussed what should be done. Both knew it would be a critical test of the previous year's preliminary attempts to communicate with one another on a different plane. Also, as one union person says, "We came to realize the experiment would not happen overnight."

Management and the union each selected a coordinator to work with the consultant and with the supervisors, the union, and the workers. The consultant, with the union and the management coordinators, proposed a series of problem-solving training sessions to be held on Saturdays, for eight hours each day. Two supervisors and the committeemen in the Soft Trim Department talked it over with the workers, of whom 34 from two shifts volunteered for the training sessions that were to begin in late September 1974. Management agreed to pay for six hours of the training, and the men volunteered their own time for the remaining two hours.

Top management was very impressed by the ideas being generated from the sessions and by the cooperation from the union. The regular repairmen were especially helpful. Not long after the program began, the workers began developing solutions to problems of water leaks, glass breakage, and molding damage.

## Layoff Crisis

In November 1974, at the height of the OPEC oil crisis, disaster struck. General Motors shut down Tarrytown's second shift, and laid off half the work force — 2,000 workers. Men on the second shift with high seniority "bumped" hundreds of workers on the first shift. To accommodate the new schedule, management had to rearrange jobs and work loads the entire length of the two miles of main conveyors, feeder conveyors, and work stations. A shock wave reverberated throughout the plant, not just among workers but supervisors as well. Some feared the convulsion would bring on an avalanche of '78s — work standards grievances — and all feared that the cutback was an early signal that Tarrytown was being targeted for permanent shutdown. After all, it was one of the oldest plants in General Motors and its past record of performance was not good.

However, the newly developing trust between management and the union had its effects. As the union president puts it, "Everyone got a decent transfer and there were surprisingly few grievances. We didn't get behind. We didn't have to catch up on a huge backlog."

What did suffer was the modest and fragile quality of work life experiment. It was all but abandoned. Many workers who had been part of it were laid off, and new workers "bumping in" had not been exposed to it. Also, a number of persons in the plant were not too disappointed to see it go. Some supervisors, seeing worker participation as a threat to their authority, made wisecracks such as "All they are doing is turning these jobs over to the union." Some committeemen felt threatened because the workers were going outside the regular political system and joining with representatives of management in solving problems.

In spite of the disruption of plant operations, the quality of work life team, the plant manager, and the union officials were determined not to give up. Reduced to a small group of 12 people during 1975, the team continued to work on water leaks and glass breakage problems. This group's success as well as that of some others convinced both parties that quality of work life had to continue despite a September 1975 deadline, after which management would no longer foot the bill on overtime.

During this period all parties had time to reflect on past successes as well as failures. The coordinators (one from the union and one from management) had learned a lesson. They had expected too much too soon: "We were frustrated at not seeing things move fast enough. We got in the trap of expecting 'instant QWL.' We thought that all you had to do was to design a package and sell it as you would sell a product."

Also, during this period, the grapevine was carrying a powerful message around the plant that something unusual was going on. The idea of involving workers in decisions spread and by midyear the molding groups were redesigning and setting up their own jobs. Other departments followed later.

At this time everyone agreed that if this program were to be expanded on a larger scale, it would require more careful planning. In 1975, a policy group made up of the plant manager, the production manager, the personnel manager, the union's top officers, and the two QWL coordinators was formed. The program was structured so that both the union and management could have an advisory group to administer the system and to evaluate the ideas coming up from the problem-solving teams. Everyone agreed that participation was to be entirely voluntary. No one was to be ordered or assigned to any group. Coordinators and others talked with all of the workers in the two departments.

A survey of interest was taken among the 600 workers in the two volunteering departments; 95% of these workers said they wanted in. Because of the large number that wanted to attend, pairs of volunteers from the ranks of the union and management had to be trained as trainers. Toward the middle of the year, a modified program was set up involving 27 off-time hours of instructional work for the 570 people. Four trainers were selected and trained to conduct this program, two from the union and two from management.

A second crisis occurred when the production schedule was increased to a line speed of 60 cars per hour. Total daily output would not be enough to require a second shift to bring back all the laid-off workers. Instead, the company asked that 300 laid-off workers be brought in and that the plant operate on an overtime schedule. Ordinarily the union would object strongly to working overtime when there were still well over 1,000 members out on the street. "But," as the union president puts it, "we sold the membership on the idea of agreeing to overtime and the criticism was minimal. We told them the survival of the plant was at stake."

## Full Capacity

Despite the upheavals at the plant, it seemed that the quality of work life program would survive. Then, a third blow was delivered. Just as 60 workers were completing their sessions, the company announced that Tarrytown was to return to a two-shift operation. For hundreds of those recalled to work, this was good news. Internally, however, it meant the line would have to go through the same musical chair game it had experienced 14 months earlier when the second shift was dropped.

Workers were shuffled around according to seniority and job classification. Shift preferences were granted according to length of service. With a faster line speed than before, the average worker had fewer operations to perform but those he did perform he had to do at a faster pace. In short, because of possible inequities in work loads, conditions were ripe for another wave of work standards grievances. Happily, the union and management were able to work out the work-load problems with a minimum of formal grievances.

But again the small, partially developed QWL program had to be put on ice. The number of recalled workers and newly hired employees was too great, and turnover was too high among the latter for the program to continue as it had been. Capitalizing on the mutual trust that had been slowly building up between them, management and the union agreed to set up an orientation program for newly hired employees — and there were hundreds of them. Such a program was seen as an opportunity to expose new workers to some of the information about plant operations, management functions, the union's role, and so forth. At one point, the union even suggested that the orientation be done at the union hall, but the idea was dropped.

The orientation program was successful. Some reduction in the ratio of "quits" among the "new hires" was observed. The union president did feel that "we had set a new tone for the new employee and created a better atmosphere in the plant."

## BRAVE NEW WORLD

Early the next year, 1977, Tarrytown made the "big commitment." The QWL effort was to be launched on a plant-wide scale involving approximately 3,800 workers and supervisors. Charles Katko, vice president for the division and UAW's top official, Irving Bluestone, gave strong signals of support. The plant manager retired in April and was replaced by the production manager. The transition was an easy one because the new manager not only knew every dimension of the program but also had become convinced of its importance.

The policy committee and the quality of work life coordinators went to work. In the spring of 1977, all the top staff personnel, department heads, and production superintendents went through a series of orientation sessions with the coordinators. By June, all middle managers and first-line supervisors (general foreman and foremen) were involved. Thus by the summer of 1977 more than 300 members of Tarrytown management knew about the QWL approach and about the plans for including 3,500 hourly employees. All union committeemen also went through the orientation sessions.

Also, during mid-1977, plans were underway to select and train those people who would eventually conduct the training sessions for the hourly employees. More than 250 workers expressed an interest in becoming trainers. After careful screening and interviewing, 11 were chosen. A similar process was carried out for supervisors, 11 of whom were subsequently selected as trainers, mostly from among foremen.

The 2 coordinators brought the 22 designated trainers together and exposed them to a variety of materials they would use in the training itself. The trainers conducted mock practice sessions which were videotaped so they could discuss their performance. The trainers also shared ideas on how to present information to the workers and on how to get workers to open up with their own ideas for changing their work environment. The latter is at the heart of the quality of work life concept.

The trainers themselves found excitement and challenge in the experience. People from the shop floor worked side by side with members of supervision as equals. At the end of the sessions, the trainers were brought together in the executive dining room for a wrap-up session. The coordinators report that "they were so charged up they were ready to conquer the world!"

## Plant-Wide Program

On September 13, 1977 the program was launched. Each week, 25 different workers (or 50 in all from both shifts) reported to the training rooms on Tuesdays, Wednesdays, and Thursdays, for nine hours a day. Those taking the sessions had to be replaced at their work stations by substitutes. Given an average hourly wage rate of more than $7 per attendee and per replacement (for over 3,000 persons), one can begin to get an idea of the magnitude of the costs. Also, for the extra hour above eight hours, the trainees were paid overtime wages.

What was the substance of the sessions themselves? The trainee's time was allocated to learning three things: first, about the concept of QWL; second, about the plant and the functions of management and the union; third, about problem-solving skills important in effective involvement.

At the outset, the trainers made it clear that the employees were not to use the sessions to solve grievances or to take up labor-management issues covered by the contract itself. The presentation covered a variety of subjects presented in many forms with a heavy stress on participation by the class from the start. The work groups were given a general statement of what quality of work life was all about. The union trainer presented materials illustrating UAW Vice President Bluestone's famous speech, and the management trainer presented a speech by GM's Landen stressing that hourly workers were the experts about their own jobs and had much to contribute.

The trainers used printed materials, diagrams, charts, and slides to describe products and model changes, how the plant was laid out, how the production system worked, and what the organizational structures of management and the union are. Time was spent covering safety matters, methods used to measure quality performance, efficiency, and so forth. The work groups were shown how and where they could get any information they wanted about their plant. Special films showed all parts of the plant with a particular worker "conducting the tour" for his part of the operation.

To develop effective problem-solving skills, the trainers presented simulated problems and then asked employees to go through a variety of some experiential exercises. The training content enabled the workers to diagnose themselves, their own behavior, how they appeared in competitive situations, how they handled two-way communications, and how they solved problems. By the final day "the groups themselves are carrying the ball," as the trainers put it, "with a minimum of guidance and direction from the two trainers."

Trainers took notes on the ideas generated in the sessions and at the end handed out a questionnaire to each participant. The notes and questionnaires were systematically fed back to the union and management coordinators, who in turn brought the recommendations to the policy committee. The primary mode of feedback to their foremen and fellow workers was by the workers themselves out on the shop floor.

## Continuing Effort

Seven weeks after the program began in September 1977, just over 350 workers (or 10% of the work force) had been through the training sessions. The program continued through 1978, and by mid-December more than 3,300 workers had taken part.

When all the employees had completed their sessions, the union and management immediately agreed to keep the system on a continuing basis. From late December 1978 through early February 1979, production operations at Tarrytown were closed down to prepare for the introduction of the all-new 1980X model. During the shutdown, a large number of workers were kept on to continue the process.

In preparation for the shift, managers and hourly personnel together evaluated hundreds of anticipated assembly processes. Workers made use of the enthusiasm and skills developed in the earlier problem sessions and talked directly with supervisors and technical people about the best ways of setting up various jobs on the line. What had been stimulated through a formal organized system of training and communication (for workers and supervisors alike) was now being "folded in" to the ongoing planning and implementation process on the floor itself.

In evaluating the formal program, the trainers repeatedly emphasized the difficulties they faced as well as the rewards. Many of the men and women from the shop floor were highly suspicious at the start of the sessions. Some old-timers harbored grudges against management going back for years. Young workers were skeptical. Some of the participants were confused at seeing a union trainer in front of the class with someone from management.

In the early period, the trainers were also nervous in their new roles. Few of them had ever had such an experience before. Many agreed that their impulse was to throw a lot of information at the worker trainee. The trainers found, however, that once the participants opened up, they "threw a lot at us." Although they understood intellectually that participation is the basic purpose of the QWL program, the trainers had to experience directly the outpouring of ideas, perceptions, and feelings of the participants to comprehend emotionally the dynamics of the involvement process.

But the trainers felt rewarded too. They describe example after example of the workers' reactions once they let down their guard. One skeptical worker, for example, burst out after the second day, ". . . You mean all this information about what's going on in the plant was available to us? Well, I'm going to use it." Another worker who had been scrapping with his foreman for years went directly to him after the sessions and said, "Listen, you and I have been butting our heads together for a long time. From now on I just want to be able to talk to you and have you talk to me." Another worker used his free relief time to drop in on new class sessions.

Other regular activities to keep management and the union informed about new developments parallel the training sessions. Currently, following the plant manager's regular staff meetings, the personnel director passes on critical information to the shop committee. The safety director meets weekly with each zone committeeman. Top union officials have monthly "rap sessions" with top management staff to discuss future developments, facility alterations, schedule changes, model changes, and other matters requiring advance planning. The chairman of Local 664 and his zone committeemen check in with the personnel director each morning at 7:00 A.M. and go over current or anticipated problems.

## AFTER THE DUST SETTLES

What are the measurable results of quality of work life at Tarrytown? Neither the managers nor union representatives want to say much. They argue that to focus on production records or grievance counts "gets to be a numbers game" and is contrary to the original purpose or philosophy of the quality of work life efforts. After all, in launching the program, the Tarrytown plant made no firm promises of "bottom line" results to division executives or anyone else. *Getting the process of worker involvement going was a primary goal with its own intrinsic rewards. The organizational benefits followed.*

There are, however, some substantial results from the $1.6 million QWL program. The production manager says, for example, "From a strictly production point of view—efficiency and costs—this entire experience has been absolutely positive, and we can't begin to measure the savings that have taken place because of the hundreds of small problems that were solved on the shop floor before they accumulated into big problems."

Although not confirmed by management, the union claims that Tarrytown went from one of the poorest plants in its quality performance (inspection counts or dealer complaints) to one of the best among the 18 plants in the division. It reports that absenteeism went from 7 1/4% to between 2% and 3%. In December 1978, at the end of the training sessions, there were only 32 grievances on the docket. Seven years earlier there had been upward of 2,000 grievances filed. Such substantial changes can hardly be explained by chance.

Does this report on Tarrytown sound unreal or euphoric? Here are the comments of the most powerful union officer in the plant, the chairman of Local 664:

"I'm still skeptical of the whole thing but at least I no longer believe that what's going on is a 'love-in' at Tarrytown. It's not a fancy gimmick to make people happy. And even though we have barely scratched the surface, I'm absolutely convinced we are on to something. We have a real and very different future. Those guys in the plant are beginning to participate and I mean really participate!"

By May 1979 the Tarrytown plant, with the production of a radically new line of cars, had come through one of the most difficult times in its history. Considering all the complex technical difficulties, the changeover was successful. Production was up to projected line speed. The relationship among management, union, and the workers remained positive in spite of unusual stress conditions generated by such a change.

As the production manager puts it, "Under these conditions, we used to fight the union, the worker, and the car itself. Now we've all joined together to fight the car." Not only were the hourly employees substantially involved in working out thousands of "bugs" in the operations, but plans were already under way to start up QWL orientation sessions with more than 400 new workers hired to meet increased production requirements.

Tarrytown, in short, has proved to itself at least that QWL works.

## Learning from Tarrytown

Although the Tarrytown story is, of course, unique, persons responsible for bringing about change in an organization might derive some useful generalizations and important messages from it. [See the observations below.]

---

### Quality of Work Life—Things to Consider

What generalization or principles might one derive from the Tarrytown story? The list below combines those of the participants themselves with my own observations about quality of work life experiments here and abroad. The list is not exhaustive. The first six are limited in general to organizations with collective bargaining agreements. The others have more universal applications.

1. For quality of work life to succeed, management must be wholly competent in running the business as a profit-making enterprise. When management lacks organizational competence and adequate technical expertise, no amount of good intentions to improve workers-union-management communication will succeed. Workers will not be willing to become involved knowing management lacks the competence to do anything about their ideas.

2. The union must be strong. The members must trust their leadership, and this trust must exist within the framework of a democratic "political" process.

3. In most instances, management has to be the first party to initiate change, to "hold out the olive branch."

4. Quality of work life should never be used by either party to circumvent the labor-management agreement. The rights, privileges, and obligations of both parties should remain inviolate. Dealing with grievances and disputes can be made easier through quality of work life efforts, but at no time should management give up its right to manage nor the union its right to protect its members on matters related to wages, hours, benefits, and general conditions of employment.

5. Top management and top union officials must make an explicit commitment to support quality of work life.

6. Even with agreement at high levels and a demonstrated concern on the part of rank-and-file employees, it is essential that middle management and front-line supervisors (and shop stewards) not only know what is taking place but also feel they have a say in the change process. Supervisors naturally feel threatened by any moves to give subordinates greater power in determining how work is to be performed. Union representatives can perceive unilateral work participation as a threat to their political position.

7. A quality of work life program is unlikely to succeed if management's intention is to increase productivity by speeding up the individual worker's work pace or, if it uses the program *as such,* to reduce the work force through layoffs. Workers will quickly see such actions as unfair exploitation. This is not to say that cost savings from better quality performance, lower absenteeism and turnover, and better production methods should not be an expected consequence of the effort.

8. A program should be voluntary for the participants.

9. Quality of work life should not be initiated with a detailed master plan. It should start on a limited scale focused on the solution of specific problems, however small. It should be flexible.

10. At each step in developing a program, all small bottlenecks or misunderstandings must be talked out and solved on the spot. If set aside simply to get on with the "important" plans, the little misunderstandings can later explode with enough force to destroy the entire program.

11. It is not enough to expose employees to the principles of effective interpersonal communication and problem-solving skills. There must be immediate opportunities available for them to use these skills in practical ways right in the job situation itself. Further follow-up action of some kind is necessary to serve as positive reenforcement to the employees.

12. Quality of work life efforts should not be thought of as a "program" with a finite ending. There must be a built-in momentum that is dynamic, ongoing, and that can continue regardless of changes in the personnel in the organization. Once employees come to believe

that they can participate and do in fact become involved in solving problems, the process gains a momentum of its own.

There is an implied warning here. Management may have the *formal* power to drop quality of work life efforts summarily. Union officers may have the *political* power to scuttle such efforts. Both would be acting at their peril for, under quality of work life, the workers will have gained a unique power to influence substantially the quality of their own lives at work. To them there is no turning back.

---

Bringing about change—any kind of change—is extraordinarily difficult in our modern organizations. It is challenge enough to introduce new machines, computers, management information systems, new organizational structures, and all the bureaucratic paraphernalia required to support our complex production systems. It is even more difficult to organize and stimulate people to accept innovations directed at greater efficiency. Perhaps most difficult of all, as one looks at the quality of work life process and Tarrytown as an example, is for managers, union officials, and even workers themselves to adjust to the idea that certain kinds of changes should be directed toward making life at work more meaningful and not necessarily toward some immediate objective measures of results.

Even when people become committed to this idea, starting the process is not easy. Witness, for example, how long it took to turn the Tarrytown ship around. Look at the roadblocks its people had to overcome: deep-seated antagonisms between management and labor and the impact of changes beyond the control of the organization itself—new facilities, new products, and personnel changes at all levels, especially among hourly workers. Just when the quality of work life efforts gained some momentum, an unanticipated event intervened and the program was stopped dead in its tracks—almost. Indeed, one gets the impression that the only constant was change itself.

Some observations are in order. Developing this climate for change takes extraordinary patience. It takes time. It calls for sustained commitment at all levels. In most of the efforts to change human behavior that I have observed directly, these characteristics are lacking. Managers and leaders are under pressure to change things overnight. They draw up a program, package it, press the authority button, set deadlines, then move. It all sounds so easy, so efficient, so American.

In changing the way Americans work, we have, as the chairman of Local 664 said, "barely scratched the surface." What went on at Tarrytown was only a beginning. The intrinsic nature of repetitive conveyor-paced jobs has not substantially changed. The commitment to quality of work life is strong at the local level and among some people at division and corporate levels, but it is not universal. Changes in management or new crises could threaten further developments. Nevertheless, a new atmosphere about change and the worker's role in it is clearly emerging. People feel they have some "say," some control over their work environment now and in the future.

The Tarrytown story may, however, reflect something important about quality of work life efforts springing up in many other places in the United States. Studies are showing that workers in our large, rationalized industries and businesses are seeking more control over and involvement in the forces affecting their work lives. Due in part to the rising levels of education, changing aspirations, and shifts in values, especially among young people, I believe we are witnessing a quiet revolution in what people expect from work, an expectation that goes beyond the economic and job security issues that led to labor unrest in an earlier day.[2]

In parts of Europe, the response to this quiet revolution is manifest in broad-scale political efforts on the part of labor and government to gain greater control over the management of the enterprise itself. In the United States, the response is different.[3] Workers or their unions have given no indications that they wish to take over basic management prerogatives. As the Tarrytown story illustrates, what they want is more pragmatic, more immediate, more localized—but no less important.

The challenge to those in positions of power is to become aware of the quiet revolution at the workplace and to find the means to respond intelligently to these forces for change. What management did at Tarrytown is but one example of the beginnings of an intelligent response.

## REFERENCE NOTES

1 Irving Bluestone, "A Changing View of Union-Management Relationships," *Vital Speeches*, December 11, 1976.

2 For recent confirmation based on survey data over a period of 25 years, see M. R. Cooper, et al., "Changing Employee Values: Deepening Discontent," HBR January–February 1979, p. 117.

3 For a fuller discussion of the differences between American and European responses to labor today, see Ted Mills's "Europe's Industrial Democracy: An American Response," HBR November–December 1978, p. 143.

## QUESTIONS

1. What was the relationship between management and labor in the late 1960s and early 1970s?

_____

_____

_____

2. How did Bluestone's view differ from the traditional management position about labor cooperation?

_____

_____

_____

3. When and where was the first major quality-of-work-life-program letter of agreement negotiated?

_____

_____

_____

4. What were some of the fears that supervisors and committeemen had about the program?

_____

_____

# Organizational Revitalization

Many years ago, in downtown Boston, a foreign visitor walked up to an American sailor and asked why the ships of his country were built to last only a short time. In the words of the foreign tourist,

> The sailor answered without hesitation that the art of navigation is making such rapid progress that the finest ship would become obsolete if it lasted beyond a few years. In these words, which fell accidentally from an uneducated man, I began to recognize the general and systematic idea upon which your great people direct all their concerns.

This shrewd observer of American morals and manners was Alexis de Tocqueville, and the year was 1835. In that brief exchange, he caught the central theme of our country, its preoccupation, its *obsession with change*. This central theme has persisted, but one thing is new since de Tocqueville's time — the *prevalence of newness*, the changing scale and scope of change itself, so that, as Oppenheimer said, ". . . the world alters as we walk in it, so that the years of man's life measure not some small growth, or rearrangement, or moderation of what was learned in childhood, but a great upheaval."

Numbers have a magic all their own. Take population. In 1789, when George Washington was inaugurated, American society comprised fewer than 4,000,000 people, of whom 750,000 were Negroes. Few people lived in cities; New York, then the capital, had a population of 33,000. In all, 200,000 people lived in what were then defined as "urban areas" — places with more than 2,500 inhabitants. By way of comparison, in the past 10 years, the population of Los Angeles increased by 2,375,000, almost equal the population of present-day Boston.

In July 1964, the population of the United States was about 192 million, and the United States Census Bureau estimates the population in 1975 will be between 226 and 235 million; by 1980 population will be between 246 and 260 million. World population was over 3 billion in 1964. If fertility remains at present levels until 1975 and then begins to decline, the population of the world will reach 4 billion in 1977, 5 billion by about 1990.

In 1960, when President Kennedy was elected, more than half of all Americans alive were over 33 years old, and most had received their

*Source:   Warren G. Bennis, "Organizational Revitalization,"* Trans-Action, *July-August 1965. Reprinted with permission from Alford P. Sloan Fellowship Program, Massachusetts Institute of Technology, Cambridge, MA 02139.*

formative experiences during the Great Depression. By 1970, only 10 years later, more than half of all Americans alive will be under 25 and will have been born after World War II. In one short decade, the mid-age of the United States will have dropped by a full 8 years — the sharpest such age drop recorded in history.

Observe the changes taking place in education. Thirty years ago, only one out of every eight Americans at work had been to high school. To-day four out of five attend high school. Thirty years ago, only 4 percent or less of the population attended college and today the figure is around 35 percent, in cities about 50 percent.

We are all aware of the momentous social change of the Scientific Revolution — moving like a juggernaut, transforming or ossifying every-thing in its path. But its magnitude, its scale, and its accelerating rate (to say nothing of its consequences) are truly staggering. . . .

"Everything nailed down is coming loose," an historian said recently, and it does seem that no exaggeration, no hyperbole, no outrage can realistically convey the extent and pace which modernization involves. It takes only a year or two for the exaggerations to come true. Nothing will remain in the next ten years — or there will be twice as much of it.

It is to our credit that the pseudo-horror stories and futuristic fantasies about accelerations of the rate change of obsolescence, technology, and science have failed to deter our compulsive desire to invent, to overthrow, and to upset inherited patterns and comfort in the security of the future.

We can all feel the impact of overwhelming numbers and social changes on the job, in the school, in the neighborhood, in our profes-sions, in our everyday lives. President Lyndon Johnson said recently, "We want change. We want progress. We want it both at home and abroad — and we aim to get it!" I think he has it.

*How will these changes taking place in our society influence human organizations?* First, it might be useful to describe the dominant form of human organization employed throughout the industrial world. We spend all of our working day in it and a great deal of our nonworking day. It is a unique and extremely durable social arrangement called "bureaucracy." I use this term "bureaucracy" not as a swear word about those "guys in Washington" or as a metaphor *à la* Kafka which conjures up an image of red tape or faceless and despairing masses standing in endless queues.

Bureaucracy, as I use the term, is a social invention, perfected during the industrial revolution to organize and direct the activities of the business firm. But it is also today the prevailing and supreme type of organization wherever people direct concerted effort toward the achievement of some goal. This holds for university systems, for hospitals, for large voluntary organizations, for governmental organizations, and so on.

Corsica, according to Gibbon, is much easier to deplore than to describe. The same holds true for bureaucracy. Basically, bureaucracy is a social invention which relies exclusively on the power to influence through rules, reason, and the law. Max Weber, the German sociologist who developed the theory of bureaucracy around the turn of the century, once described bureaucracy as a social machine:

> Bureaucracy is like a modern judge who is a vending machine into which the pleadings are inserted together with the fee and which then disgorges the judgment together with its reasons mechanically derived from the code.

The bureaucratic "machine model" Weber outlined was developed as a reaction against the personal subjugation, nepotism, cruelty, and capricious and subjective judgments which passed for managerial practices in the early days of the Industrial Revolution. The true hope for man, it was thought, lay in his ability to rationalize, to calculate, and to use his head as well as his hands and heart. Bureaucracy emerged out of the need for more predictability, order, and precision. It was an organization ideally suited to the values of the Victorian Empire.

Most students of organizations would say that the anatomy of bureaucracy consists of the following "organs":

- A division of labor based on functional specialization.
- A well-defined hierarchy of authority.
- A system of procedures and rules for dealing with all contingencies relating to work activities.
- Impersonality of interpersonal relations.
- Promotion and selection based on technical competence—the pyramidal arrangement we see on most organizational charts.

It is my premise that the bureaucratic form of organization is out of joint with contemporary realities, that new shapes, patterns, and models are emerging which promise drastic changes in the conduct of the corporation and of managerial practices in general. In the next 25 to 50 years, we should witness, and participate in, the end of bureaucracy as we know it and the rise of new social systems better suited to twentieth-century industrialization.

I think every age develops an organizational form appropriate to its genius. This is my personal vision of these coming events and of the potentialities of new forms of organization, beyond bureaucracy.

## SOCIAL CHANGES

I see two main reasons for the changes in organizational life. One has been implied earlier in terms of the changes taking place in society, commonly referred to as the population and knowledge explosions.

The other is more subtle and muted, perhaps less significant but for me, profoundly exciting. I have no easy name for it nor was it easy to designate. It has to do with man's historical quest for self-awareness, for using reason to achieve and stretch his potentialities—his possibilities. This deliberate self-analysis has spread to large and more complex social systems—to organizations. There has been a dramatic upsurge of this spirit of inquiry over the past two decades. At new depths and over a wider range of affairs, organizations are opening their operations to self-inquiry and analysis. This really involves two parallel shifts in values and outlooks, between the men who make history and the men who make knowledge. One change is the scientist's realization of his affinity with men of affairs and the other is the latter's receptivity and new-found respect for men of knowledge.

I am calling this new development organizational revitalization, a complex social process which involves a deliberate and self-conscious examination of organizational behavior and a collaborative relationship between managers and scientists to improve performance.

For many this new form of collaboration may be taken for granted. I have simply regarded reciprocity between the academician and the manager as inevitable and natural. But I can assure you that this development is unprecedented, that never before in history, in any society, has man in his organizational context so willingly searched, scrutinized, examined, inspected, or contemplated—for meaning, for purpose, for improvement.

This shift in outlook has taken a good deal of courage from both partners in this encounter. For the manager, he has had to shake off old prejudices about "eggheads" and "long-hair" intellectuals. More important, the manager has had to make himself and his organization vulnerable and receptive to external sources and to new, unexpected, even unwanted, information. The academician has had to shed some of his natural hesitancies. Scholarly conservatism is admirable except to hide behind, and for a long time caution was a defense against reality.

It might be useful to dwell a bit longer on the role of academic man and his growing involvement with social action, using the field of management education as a case in point. Until recently, the field of business was unknown to, or snubbed by, the academic establishment. There, management education and research were at best regarded with dark suspicion as if contact with the world of reality—particularly monetary reality—was equivalent to a dreadful form of pollution.

In fact, historically, academic man has taken one of two stances toward "The Establishment," any establishment: that of a rebellious critic or of a withdrawn snob. The stance of the rebel is currently popular. Witness the proliferation of such paperback titles as: *The Power Elite, The Lonely Crowd, The Organization Man, Hidden Persuaders, Tyranny of Testing, Mass Leisure, Exurbanites, Life and Death of Great American Cities, American Way of Death, Compulsory Mis-education, Status Seekers, Growing Up Absurd, Paper Economy, Silent Spring, Child Worshippers, Affluent Society,* and *Depleted Society.*

The withdrawn stance can still be observed in some of our American universities, but less so these days. However, it continues to be the prevailing attitude in many European universities. There, the universities seem intent on preserving the monastic ethos of their medieval origins, offering a false but lulling security to their inmates, and sapping the curriculum of virility and relevance. Max Beerbohm's whimsical and idyllic fantasy of Oxford, *Zuleika Dobson*, dramatizes this:

> It is the mild, miasmal air, not less than the grey beauty and the gravity of the buildings that has helped Oxford to produce, and foster, eternally her peculiar race of artist-scholars, scholar-artists. ". . .The buildings and their traditions keep astir in his mind whatsoever is gracious; the climate enfolding and enfeebling him, lulling him, keeps him careless of the sharp, harsh exigent realities of the outer world. These realities may be seen by him. . . . But they cannot fire him. Oxford is too damp for that."

"Adorable Dreamer," said Matthew Arnold, in his valedictory to Oxford.

> Adorable dreamer, whose heart has been so romantic! who has given thyself so prodigally, given thyself to sides and to heroes not mine, only never to the Philistine! . . . what teacher could ever so save us from that bondage to which we are all prone . . . the bondage of what binds us all, the narrow, the mundane, the merely practical.

The intellectual and the manager have only recently come out of hiding and recognized the enormous possibilities of joint ventures. Remember that the idea of the professional school is new, even in the case of the venerable threesome — law, medicine, and engineering — to say nothing of the recent upstarts like business and public administration. It is as new as the institutionalization of science itself, say, around fifty years. And even today, this change is not greeted with unmixed joy. Colin Clark, the economist, writing in a recent issue of the magazine *Encounter*, referred to the "dreadful suggestion that Oxford ought to have a business school."

It is probably true that in the United States we have had a more pragmatic attitude toward knowledge than anywhere else. Many observers have been impressed with the disdain European intellectuals seem to show for practical matters. Even in Russia, where one would least expect it, there is little interest in the "merely useful." Harrison Salisbury, the *New York Times* Soviet expert, was struck during his recent travels by the almost total absence of liaison between research and practical application. He saw only one agricultural experimental station on the American model. There professors were working in the fields and told him, "People call us Americans."

There may not be many American professors working in the fields, but they can be found, when not waiting in airports, almost everywhere else: in factories, in government, in less advanced countries, and more recently, in backward areas of our own country, in mental hospitals, in the State Department, in practically all the institutional crevices Ph.D. candidates can worm their way into. They are advising, counselling, researching, recruiting, interpreting, developing, consulting, training, and working for the widest variety of clients imaginable. This is not to say that the deep ambivalence which some Americans hold toward the intellectual has disappeared, but it does indicate that academic man has become more committed to action, in greater numbers, with more diligence, and with higher aspirations than at any other time in history.

Indeed, Fritz Machlup, the economist, has coined a new economic category called the "knowledge industry," which, he claims, accounts for 29 percent of the Gross National Product. And Clark Kerr, the President of the University of California, said not too long ago:

> What the railroads did for the second half of the last century and the automobile did for the first half of this century may be done for the second half of this century by the knowledge industry: that is, to serve as the focal point of national growth. And the university is at the center of the knowledge process.

## CHANGE IN PHILOSOPHY

I will now turn to my main theme and put the foregoing remarks about the reciprocity between action and knowledge into the perspective of changing organizations. Consider some of the relatively recent research and theory concerning the human side of enterprise which have made such a solid impact on management thinking and particularly upon the moral imperatives which guide managerial action. I will be deliberately sweeping in summarizing these changes as much to hide my surprise as to cover a lot of ground quickly. (I can be personal about this. I remember sitting in Douglas McGregor's class some 7 years ago when he first presented his new theories, and the sharp antagonism his Theory X and Theory Y analysis provoked. Today most take these ideas as self-evident.)

It seems to me that we have seen, over the past decade, *a fundamental change in the basic philosophy which underlies managerial behavior*, reflected most of all in the following three areas:

- A *new concept of Man*, based on increased knowledge of his complex and shifting needs, which replaces the oversimplified, innocent push-button idea of man.

- A *new concept of Power*, based on collaboration and reason, which replaces a model of power based on coercion and fear.

- A *new concept of Organizational Values*, based on humanistic-democratic ideals, which replaces the depersonalized mechanistic value system of bureaucracy.

## Human Problems Confronting Contemporary Organizations

| Integration | Bureaucratic Solutions | New Twentieth-Century Conditions |
|---|---|---|
| **Integration**<br>The problem of how to integrate individual needs and management goals. | No solution because of no problem. Individual vastly oversimplified, regarded as passive instrument or disregarded. | Emergence of human sciences and understanding of man's complexity. Rising aspirations. Humanistic-democratic ethos. |
| **Social Influence**<br>The problem of the distribution of power and sources of power and authority. | An explicit reliance on legal-rational power, but an implicit usage of coercive power. In any case, a confused, ambiguous, shifting complex of competence, coercion, and legal code. | Separation of management from ownership. Rise of trade unions and general education. Negative and unintended effects of authoritarian rule. |
| **Collaboration**<br>The problem of managing and resolving conflicts. | The "rule of hierarchy" to resolve conflicts between ranks and the "rule of coordination" to resolve conflict between horizontal groups. "Loyalty." | Specialization and professionalization and increased need for interdependence. Leadership too complex for one-man rule or omniscience. |
| **Adaptation**<br>The problem of responding appropriately to changes induced by the environment of the firm. | Environment stable, simple, and predictable; tasks routine. Adapting to change occurs in haphazard and adventitious ways. Unanticipated consequences abound. | External environment of firm more "turbulent," less predictable. Unprecedented rate of technological change. |
| **Revitalization**<br>The problem of growth and decay. | | Rapid changes in technologies, tasks, manpower, raw materials, norms and values of society, goals of enterprise and society all make constant attention to freedom of revision imperative. |

I do not want to overstate the case. I do not mean that these transformations of man, power, and organizational values are fully accepted or even understood, to say nothing of implemented, in day-to-day affairs. These changes may be light years away from actual adoption. I do mean that they have gained wide intellectual acceptance in enlightened management quarters, that they have caused a terrific amount of rethinking and searching behavior on the part of many organizations, and that they have been used as a basis for policy formulation by many large-scale organizations.

All the changes affecting organizations, both from the behavioral sciences and trends in our society, are summarized in the table. These problems (or predicaments) emerge basically from twentieth-century changes, primarily the growth of science and education, the separation of power from property, the correlated emergence of the professional manager, and other kinds of changes. The bureaucratic mechanism, so capable of coordinating men and power in a stable society of routine tasks, cannot cope with contemporary realities. The table shows five major categories, which I visualize as the core tasks confronting the manager in coordinating the human side of enterprise.

The problem of *integration* grows out of our "consensual society," where personal attachments play a great part, where the individual is appreciated, and where there is concern for his well-being, not just in a veterinary-hygiene sense, but as a moral, integrated personality.

The problem of *social influence* is essentially the problem of power, and leadership studies and practices reveal not only an ethical component but an *effectiveness component:* People tend to work more efficiently and with more commitment when they have a part in determining their own fate and a stake in problem solving.

The problem of *collaboration* grows out of the same social processes of conflict, stereotyping, and centrifugal forces, which inhere in and divide nations and communities. They also employ the same furtive, often fruitless, always crippling mechanisms of conflict resolution: avoidance or suppression, annihilation of the weaker party by the stronger, sterile compromises, and unstable collusions and coalitions. Particularly as organizations become more complex, they fragment and divide, building tribal patterns and symbolic codes which often work to exclude others (secrets and noxious jargon, for example) and on occasion to exploit difference from inward, and always fragile, harmony. Some large organizations, in fact, can be understood only through an analysis of their cabals, cliques, and satellites, their tactics resembling a sophisticated form of guerrilla warfare, and a venture into adjacent spheres of interest is taken under cover of darkness and fear of ambush.

The university, for example, is a wondrous place for these highly advanced battle techniques, far overshadowing the business field in the use of subterfuge and sabotage. Quite often a university becomes a loose collection of competing departments, schools, and institutes, largely noncommunicating because of the multiplicity of specialist jargons and interests and held together chiefly, as Robert Hutchins once said, by a central heating system or, as Clark Kerr amended, by questions of what to do about the parking problem.

The real *coup de grâce* to bureaucracy has come as much from our turbulent environment as from its incorrect assumptions about human behavior. The *pyramidal structure of bureaucracy*, where power was concentrated at the top — perhaps by one person or a group who had the knowledge and resources to control the entire enterprise — seemed perfect to "run a railroad." And undoubtedly, for tasks like building railroads — the routinized tasks of the nineteenth and early twentieth centuries — bureaucracy was and is an eminently suitable social arrangement.

Nowadays, primarily because of the growth of science, technology, and research and development activities, the organizational environment of the firm is rapidly changing. Instead of a placid and predictable environment, today it is turbulent. There is a deepening interdependence among the economic and other facets of society. This means that economic organizations are increasingly enmeshed in legislation and public policy. Put more simply, it means that government will be in almost everything more of the time. It might also mean (and this is radical) that maximizing cooperation rather than competition between firms — particularly if their fates are correlated — may become a reality.

Finally, the problem of *revitalization:* Alfred North Whitehead sets the problem neatly before us: "The art of free society consists first in the maintenance of the symbolic code, and secondly, in the fearlessness of revision. . . . Those societies which cannot combine reverence to their symbols with freedom of revision must ultimately decay."

Organizations, as well as societies, must be concerned with those social conditions that engender buoyancy, resilience, and a fearlessness of revision. Growth and decay emerge as the penultimate problem in contemporary society where the environment is turbulent and uncertain.

*Forecast of the future.* A forecast falls somewhere between a prediction and a prophecy. It lacks the divine guidance of the latter and the empirical foundation of the former. On thin empirical ice, I want to set forth some of the conditions that I believe will dictate organizational life in the next twenty-five to fifty years.

## THE YEARS TO COME

Those factors already mentioned in the environment will continue in force and increase. Rapid technological change and diversification will lead to interpenetration of the government — its legal and economic policies — with business. Partnerships between business and government will be typical. Because of the immensity and expense of the projects, there will be fewer identical units competing for the same buyers and sellers. The three main features of the environment will be *interdependence* rather than competition, *turbulence* rather than steadiness, and *large-scale* rather than small-scale enterprises.

## THE KNOWLEDGE INDUSTRY

The most distinctive characteristic of our society is, and will be become even more so, its *education*. Peter Drucker calls us the "educated society," and for good reason: Within 15 years, two-thirds of our population living in metropolitan areas will have attended college. Adult education is growing even faster. It is now almost routine for the experienced physician, engineer, and executive to go back to school for advanced training every two or three years. Some fifty universities, in addition to a dozen large corporations, offer advanced management courses to successful men in the middle and upper ranks of business. Before World War II, only two such programs existed, both new, and struggling to get students.

All of this education is not just "nice," but necessary. For, as Secretary of Labor Wirtz recently pointed out, computers can do the work of most high school graduates — cheaper and more effectively. Fifty years ago, education used to be regarded as "nonwork" and intellectuals on the payroll (and many staff workers) were considered "overhead." Today the survival of the firm depends more than ever before on the proper exploitation of brain power.

## THE WORKING ATMOSPHERE

One other characteristic of the population which will aid our understanding of organizations of the future is increasing *job mobility*. The lowered expense and ease of transportation, coupled with the real needs of a dynamic environment, will change drastically the idea of "owning" a job—or "having roots," for that matter. Participants will be shifted from job to job and even employer to employer with little concern for roots and homestead.

The increased level of education and mobility will change our *work values*. People will be more intellectually committed to their jobs and will probably require more involvement, participation, and autonomy in their work.

Also, people will tend to be more "other directed"; taking cues for their norms and values from their immediate environment more than from tradition. We will tend to rely more heavily on temporary social arrangements, on our immediate and constantly changing colleagues. We will tend to be more concerned and involved with relationships rather than with relatives.

The tasks of the firm will be more technical, complicated, and unprogrammed. They will rely more on the intellect than muscle. And they will be too complicated for one person to comprehend, to say nothing of control. Essentially, they will call for the collaboration of specialists in a project or team form of organization.

## A STRUCTURE OF GOALS

There will be a *complication of goals*. Business will increasingly concern itself with its adaptive or innovative-creative capacity. In addition, meta-goals will have to be articulated and developed, that is, *supra-goals* which shape and provide the foundation for the goal structure. For example, one meta-goal might be a system for detecting new and changing goals; another could be a system for deciding priorities among goals.

## ORGANIZATIONAL STRUCTURE

Finally, there will be *more conflict and contradiction among diverse standards of organizational effectiveness*, just as in hospitals and universities today there is conflict between teaching and research. The reason for this is the increased number of professionals involved, who tend to identify more with the goals of their profession than with those of their immediate employer. University professors can be used as a case in point. More and more of their income comes from outside sources, such as foundations and consultant work. They tend not to be good "company men" because they divide their loyalty between their professional values and organizational goals.

*The social structure of organizations* of the future will have some unique characteristics. The key word will be "temporary"; there will be adaptive, rapidly changing temporary systems. These will be "task forces" organized around problems-to-be-solved by groups of relative strangers who represent a diverse set of professional skills. The groups will be arranged on an organic rather than mechanical mode; they will evolve in response to a problem rather than to programmed role expectations. The "executive" thus becomes a coordinator or "linking pin" between various task forces. He must be a man who can speak the diverse languages of research, with skills to relay information and to mediate between groups. People will be differentiated not vertically according to rank and status but flexibly and functionally according to skill and professional training.

## CREATIVE SYSTEMS

Adaptive, problem-solving, temporary systems of diverse specialists, linked together by coordinating and task-evaluating specialists in an organic flux — this is the organizational form that will gradually replace bureaucracy as we know it. I call this an *organic-adaptive structure*.

The organic-adaptive structure should increase *motivation* and thereby effectiveness because it enhances satisfactions intrinsic to the task. There is a harmony between the educated individual's need for meaningful, satisfactory, and creative tasks and a flexible organizational structure.

There will, however, also be reduced commitment to work groups, for these groups, as I already mentioned, will be transient and changing. While skills in human interaction will become more important, due to the growing needs for collaboration in complex tasks, there will be a concomitant reduction in group cohesiveness. It is possible to predict that, in the organic-adaptive system, people will have to learn to develop quick, intense relationships on the job and learn to bear the loss of more enduring work relationships. Because of the added ambiguity of roles, more time will have to be spent on the continual rediscovery of the appropriate organizational mix.

In general, I do not agree with those who emphasize a New Utopianism, in which leisure, not work, becomes the emotional-creative sphere of life. Jobs should become more rather than less involving; man is a problem-solving animal and the tasks of the future guarantee a full agenda of problems. In addition, the adaptive process itself may become captivating to many.

At the same time, the future described is not necessarily a "happy" one. Coping with rapid change, living in temporary work systems, quickly developing meaningful relations — and then breaking them — all augur social strains and psychological tensions. Learning how to live with ambiguity, to identify with the adaptive process, to make a virtue out of contingency, and to be self-directing will be the task of education, the goal of maturity, and the achievement of the successful manager. To be a wife in this era will become a profession of providing stability and continuity.

In these new organizations, participants will be called on to use their minds more than at any other time in history. Fantasy, imagination, and creativity will be legitimate in ways that today seem strange. Social structures will no longer be instruments of psychic repression but will increasingly promote play and freedom on behalf of curiosity and thought.

Bureaucracy was a monumental discovery for harnessing the muscle power of the Industrial Revolution. In today's world, it is a lifeless crutch that is no longer useful. For we now require structures of freedom to permit the expression of play and imagination and to exploit the new pleasure of work.

One final word: While I forecast the structure and value coordinates for organizations of the future and contend that they are inevitable, it should not bar any of us from giving a little push here and there to the inevitable. And while the French moralist may be right in saying that there are no delightful marriages, just good ones, it is possible that, if managers and scientists continue to get their heads together in organizational revitalization, they might develop delightful organizations—just possibly.

I started with a quote from de Tocqueville and I think it would be fitting to end with one:

> I am tempted to believe that what we call necessary institutions are often no more than institutions to which we have grown accustomed. In matters of social constitution the field of possibilities is much more extensive than men living in their various societies are ready to imagine.

## QUESTIONS

1. What social changes do you see affecting organizations in America today? Are you in favor of them?

———————————————————————————————

———————————————————————————————

———————————————————————————————

———————————————————————————————

———————————————————————————————

**2.** Discuss the "knowledge explosion" and employee education as these factors influence life in American business.

_____

_____

_____

_____

_____

# Four-Star Management

In the clear skies over southern Nevada, a major air battle is raging. Fifteen Russian MiGs are swarming like high-tech hornets as Air Force fighters close in at twice the speed of sound. One of the MiGs lets fly an air-to-air missile, sending an F-15 Eagle banking into a nine-G evasion turn. Another F-15, locking its sights on an MiG, launches a Sidewinder missile and blows the enemy out of the air. Moments later, a handful of A-10 Thunderbolts, cruising in at low altitude, open fire on a column of Soviet tanks as four F-16 Falcons suddenly appear from behind a mountain to bomb a Soviet troop formation.

The Russian troops are only simulated, of course, as are the missiles, bombs, and bullets. The planes, however, are real. At nearby Nellis Air Force Base, several controllers in a darkened room are watching the battle unfold on huge screens, the world's biggest and most expensive video game. It is something straight out of James Bond—and, as we'll see, straight out of Tom Peters as well.

This is one of the Air Force's Red Flag training exercises, a mock war that rages year-round over several million acres of Nevada desert. On one side are the men and planes of the Tactical Air Command (TAC), which is charged with defending American interests in the skies anywhere in the world. On the other, squadrons of F-5 Tigers sporting Warsaw Pact paint jobs, flown by American pilots who have been specially trained in Soviet air tactics.

On this day, the good guys win. But it wasn't always that way. A decade ago, when Red Flag was just beginning, the Tactical Air Command was in a sorry state. At any one time, half of the planes in its $25-billion fleet were not battle ready and more than 220 airplanes were classified as "hangar queens"—grounded at least three weeks for lack of spare parts or maintenance. Because of equipment problems, TAC pilots—trained at a cost of $1 million each—lacked the flying time necessary to keep their skills sharp, and the best of them were deserting the Air Force in droves. So, too, were mechanics and technicians, frustrated in their jobs and disappointed by the deplorable living conditions at almost every TAC installation. Perhaps worst of all was the soaring

*Source: Jay Finegan. Reprinted with permission,* INC. *magazine, January 1987. Copyright © 1987 by INC. Publishing Company, 38 Commercial Wharf, Boston, MA 02110.*

accident rate that resulted in tragic deaths, unnecessary loss of expensive airplanes, and embarrassment for the service.

Into this mess in 1978 stepped General W. L. (Bill) Creech. As the new commander sized up his domain from TAC headquarters at Langley Air Force Base, in Virginia, it looked to him like a potential national security disaster. "The U.S. military was coming apart," is how he remembers it. "It was worse than you think."

This is the remarkable story of how, in six and a half years, Creech turned his command into one of the bright stars of the defense firmament. TAC fighters today are in superb condition, its pilots fully trained, its installations sparkling. The number of hangar queens has declined from 200 to just a handful. Reenlistment rates are way up. And a dramatic reduction in the crash rate has saved dozens of lives and billions of dollars' worth of airplanes.

Perhaps most remarkable, Creech was able to work his magic with no more money, no more planes, and no more personnel than were available when he started. Creech's strategy was to force a bottoms-up management style on an organization that had always been strictly top-down — pushing responsibility and authority down into the tiniest crevices of his command. And so stunning was his execution that the Pentagon has now begun to apply his techniques throughout the U.S. military. Says one Defense Department official, "It's probably our biggest success since MacArthur's Inchon landing."

Any chief executive officer would have been daunted by the challenge of simply running so sprawling an operation, let alone reviving it. At the time that Creech settled into his post, he was in charge of 115,000 full-time employees working at 150 installations around the world — plus another 65,000 men and women trained and on call. The assets under his control were valued at more than $40 billion, including some 3,800 aircraft — more than twice as many as all U.S. airlines combined. He had a discretionary budget of $1.4 billion, with billions more reserved for fuel and spare parts.

Creech was no stranger to TAC. By 1978, he had already spent nearly 30 years in the Air Force, a career that took in the first jet-age dogfights of the Korean war, a military position with the United Nations, and wing commands in Europe. But perhaps most crucial to his views on managing TAC was a stint he had put in at the Pentagon during the days of Defense Secretary Robert McNamara.

The watchword of the McNamara regime was centralization, for which there was a dual imperative. Politically, the Kennedy administration came into office as suspicious of the military as the military was of the new president and his advisers. McNamara's assignment was to curb interservice rivalry and bring all of the services under greater civilian control. In addition, as the former president of Ford Motor Co., McNamara was a disciple of the management gurus of the day who preached that centralization was synonymous with efficiency. While his whiz kids fashioned new military strategies for the various services, battalions of cost analysts and systems planners cranked out new rules and regulations that reached into every facet of military life. Commanders in the field sensed that they had been stripped of much of their autonomy. Decision making was jealously guarded within the Pentagon.

"The thrust was on saving money and people." Creech says. "It overlooked the requirement to do a good job. A lot of these guys, when you started talking about spirit and teamwork and cooperation, their eyes glazed over. They just couldn't relate to that."

By the time Creech put on his fourth star and took command of TAC, Robert McNamara was long gone from Defense, but his dogma of centralized management and command had become inviolate within the Pentagon. Only it wasn't working — not at TAC, anyway. Granted, some duplication had been eliminated, along with some jobs. But the cost had been high: the American military command had been robbed of much of its vigor. Innovation and initiative were discouraged, and people were dehumanized, thought of as mere costs of production, like so many bullets or mess kits.

It was not that Creech was unwilling to use quantitative means by which to judge TAC's performance. On the contrary, taking stock of the crucial measurement of production — the number of training sorties flown — Creech found that TAC had been losing ground at the rate of 8% each year since 1969. And to deal with the problem, he proposed nothing less than a radical restructuring of his command, one that would send authority down the ranks along with responsibility for meeting clear and simple goals.

Pentagon planners were appalled at the thought. Creech, they argued, would wind up adding thousands of new jobs and spending millions of new dollars. They were uneasy with the notion that one command might be different from all others. And although they didn't quite come out and say it, they were suspicious that authority could be intelligently exercised by the likes of career military men.

"They were legion, the people against me," recalls Creech. "You couldn't single anyone out. The villian wasn't any particular person, but the whole system. It was all the staffers down below — these faceless regulation writers and approvers. I was going against the grain of the Pentagon culture. The system bristled."

Creech had an early ally, however, in Air Force Chief of Staff General David C. Jones. Jones's support would not assure success for the decentralization campaign, but it did give Creech the kind of bureaucratic altitude he needed to escape the flak from the doubters within the Pentagon.

A $27-million F-15 is a beautiful piece of design and engineering, but without spare parts and skilled mechanics, it soon becomes a relatively useless hunk of metal.

In 1978, when Creech took command, the procedures for getting a fighter fixed might just as well have been devised by a British labor-union steward. Consider the case of a jet grounded for a minor electrical malfunction.

The first man on the scene would be a general aircraft mechanic, known as a crew chief. The chief, after making his initial inspection, would put a call into Job Control, the centralized unit for each base. Job Control, in turn, would call the electrical shop, which would dispatch a man out to the flight line to work on the problem. On arriving, however, the electrician might well discover that an entire panel would have to be removed before he could really get to the problem, requiring yet another technician. There would be another round of calls to Job Control and the electrical shop. Then — perhaps after a stop at the post office and the coffee shop — the panel remover would finally arrive on the flight line, only to find that he needed a spare part. So somebody would put in a call to the base's central supply depot, which stocked everything from jet engines to toilet paper, to see if one was available. Three more hours might pass before the part was trucked out by somebody else from the warehouse to the flight line. Meanwhile, the jet and its pilot probably would have missed their scheduled sortie.

Time, however, was only half the problem. Quality was the other half. The electrical shop, like the other specialized units for hydraulics, ejection seats, radar, navigation systems, and the like, would invariably dispatch its lowest-ranking people for routine calls. That left the senior sergeants, with their 15 to 25 years of experience, back at their comfortable offices, pushing paper or maybe just reading the paper. And without their direct supervision, much of the work done on the flight line was of the quick-fix variety — or worse.

"We were all aware that a human being was strapping into that jet, but there was a lot of sloppy work done to get it into the air," says Technical Sergeant Ruben Saldana, an F-15 crew chief at Langley and a TAC man before, during, and after the Creech command. "And if it missed its sortie, it was no big deal."

The pilots, too, were less than enthralled. "Used to be you could take an airplane off, but your radar wasn't working or the inertial navigation system didn't work," says Lieutenant Colonel Burr Crittenden, an F-16 squadron commander at Nellis. "So even when we did fly, the sorties were often low quality."

It all added up to a lackluster fighter force, beset with apathy, sagging morale, and horrifying statistics. Only 20% of "broken" planes were getting repaired in a typical eight-hour shift. Pilots who needed a minimum of 15 hours of flying time a month were getting 10 or less. The average plane, which had flown 23 sorties a month in 1969, was flying only 11 by 1978. And for every 100,000 hours flown, seven planes were crashing. Investigators blamed many of the crashes on faulty maintenance.

"One reason we were doing so poorly is because we were so good at centralization," says Creech. "It was a highly matrixed system, where the functional specialists only loosely worked for the person in charge of getting the job done. The supervisor was just a voice on the radio. Nobody really cared."

Creech's first move was to structure his command around a smaller and more manageable unit of organization—the squadron, which consists of 24 planes, rather than the wing, which is three times the size. Starting on a trial basis at a few installations, he created squadron repair teams, drawing technicians from each of the maintenance disciplines. The team would work only on their own squadron's aircraft. And instead of operating out of rear-area dispatching locations, Creech ordered them to move right down to the flight lines.

Almost immediately, there was an undercurrent of opposition from some of the senior sergeants, the princes of the maintenance realm, who had to abandon their cushy offices and move with their men to the flight lines. Worse still, the sergeant who once had supervised 60 electricians was now supervising 20. Many felt demoted or diminished.

"We didn't care for it," says one of these so-called supersergeants, who asked not to be named. "Here was this crazy general coming in and splintering an operation we'd spent years putting together."

Creech had anticipated some hostility, but in this instance a military culture worked in his favor: in the Air Force, there are severe penalties for insubordination. "I'm not saying everyone thought this change was great," he says. "But slowly they were won over. In the centralized system, we were top-heavy in management. We were keeping beautiful track of what we were doing. But in our system, sergeants were sergeants. They were in charge of people, not paper. And they had to make those people produce. If they didn't, they were out."

The idea was to give each operational squadron and its companion maintenance team a common identity, purpose, and spirit. The maintenance people, who had been faceless cogs in a 2,000-person wing operation, found themselves sporting the prestigious flight squadron patches on their fatigues. They now belonged to the Buccaneers or the Black Falcons. They began wearing squadron baseball caps.

With the crew chiefs, the general practitioners of the maintenance staffs, this sense of identity was further reinforced. Where before they had worked on any jet in the wing, now they were assigned airplanes of their very own. They painted their names on the sides, just as pilots did. And all of a sudden, a 23-year-old buck sergeant making $15,000 a year was in charge—yes, in charge—of a $27-million jet.

"It was exactly what we needed," remembers Sergeant Tony M. Brunner, a young F-15 crew chief at Nellis. "It makes you feel important to be in charge of something. There's got to be more to what we do here than a paycheck."

The crew chiefs took to their new responsibilities with a passion, doing whatever was necessary to make their jets the best. They went everywhere with them—on deployments, through inspections, to the wash racks. And they kept a sharp eye on the technicians—in military parlance, "kicking ass and taking names." Excellence became an obsession. When Creech went to visit some crew chiefs to find out how they liked the new arrangement, a sergeant summed it up nicely. "General," he said, "when was the last time you washed a rental car?"

The pilots couldn't help but notice the change in attitude. "Crew chiefs now come in sometimes on days off to buff up the planes," says Lieutenant Colonel Paul V. Hester, a former F-15 squadron commander at Langley. "When we get back from a sortie, they are standing at attention, saluting, holding the forms. That's not anything they're directed to do. That's pride in their airplanes. They want us to feel that pride when we fly."

It was not long before a strong comradery grew up between pilots and their crew chiefs. They talked electronics, they talked football, and they went drinking together after work. At the same time, squadrons began to build strong identities. Squadron colors were painted once again on the tail wings of aircraft, a time-honored tradition that had been outlawed under centralization. And pretty soon one squadron was working overtime to beat the other two squadrons in a wing, on everything from pilot performance to quality of maintenance.

What Creech did best, perhaps, was to remind even the lowest-level employees that their jobs were directly tied into TAC's central mission: flying and fighting. Wing commanders were ordered to resume active flying, and to emphasize the point, they were encouraged to wear flight suits when visiting Langley. For their part, squadron maintenance officers were routinely summoned to headquarters for three days of classroom work and inspiration from the top brass.

"We didn't send captains in to brief them," recalls General Jerry Rogers, Creech's logistics chief. "We did it ourselves. And on the third day, General Creech himself came in and spent half a day with them. They had to figure that if he does that, then he thinks maintaining airplanes is pretty important."

TAC's new spirit was soon reflected in the statistics. In Creech's first year as TAC's commander, the sortie rate shot up 11%, and another 11% in the second year. By 1980, the average fighter was in the air 24 hours a month, up from 17 in 1978. Some 60% of the planes were now rated mission capable, up from half.

Creech, however, was just beginning to decentralize his command and improve the sortie rate. Moving beyond maintenance, there was also the question of the sorties themselves—how they were planned and scheduled. In the past, a handful of officers at wing headquarters had plotted schedules out in detail, squadron by squadron, a year at a time—16,000 sorties. Each squadron was given not only its quota, but also detailed instructions on how and when the sorties should be run.

In Creech's decentralized TAC, squadron commanders were given a sortie goal and set free to design their own flying schedules. And they were given some added incentive to meet their targets: if a squadron met its monthly goal early, Creech decreed, then the entire squadron, from pilots to maintenance techs, could take an extra three-day weekend.

Mind you, meeting these goals wasn't easy. These were highly sophisticated jets with hundreds of components that often require repair or replacement. And the training hops were no snaps for fliers, either.

An F-16 pilot, for instance, had to master precision bombing, air-to-air combat with complicated missiles systems, and the delicate maneuvers required for tactical nuclear strikes, should they ever be required. Still, the incentive plan worked splendidly. Virtually every squadron in TAC now averages 10 extra three-day weekends a year.

By the early 1980s, the TAC turnaround was attracting plenty of attention at the Pentagon. "There were people who would say, 'You're fudging the numbers. It looks too good,' " General Rogers recalls. The pattern was repeated many times: they'd try something and gather enough evidence that it worked. Then, to make it official policy, they'd have to write a regulation and send it to the Pentagon for approval. "That was a vehicle for endless bickering about details," Creech recalls. "There was a good bit of hostility and foot-dragging." But with the help of the successive Air Force Chiefs of Staff, Creech most often prevailed. And, slowly, the converts to decentralization grew in number.

Creech and Rogers weren't shy about inviting Pentagon officials to see their new program in action. At one important outing in 1980, for instance, they took members of the Pentagon's vaunted Program Analysis and Evaluation Office (PA&E) — prim proponents of centralization — along on the first training deployment of F-15s to Europe. Eighteen fighters screamed into Bremgarten, a Luftwaffe base in southwest Germany, and four hours later all of them were loaded for combat. The next day, those same jets flew 75 sorties, nearly 4 apiece.

"Under the old system, we couldn't have dreamed of that kind of launch rate," says Rogers. "The PA&E folks had been very suspicious of our statistics, but that made believers of them. They went back and became evangelists for us in budget battles and such. It was really a watershed."

By the time, of course, centralization was under attack everywhere, as newer management theories began to emphasize motivation, competition, delegation, and employee ownership — all concepts Creech had used. And as stories began to surface about $600 toilet seats and $200 wrenches — the stuff of centralized procurement — the Pentagon searched to demonstrate that it was changing with the times. Creech's decentralization efforts became part of the official program. And the general found there was plenty more decentralizing to do.

He started with spare parts. An F-15 crew chief who needed a new tire for his jet, as an example, at that time had to phone in his request to the base warehouse and wait hours for delivery. Moving a part through the system required 243 entries on 13 forms, involving 22 people and 16 man-hours for administration and record keeping. It was cumbersome, frustrating, and worst of all, slow.

"We had lost focus on why we existed — to support aircraft and the maintenance guys," says Colonel Donald W. Hamilton, TAC's director of supply at Langley. "We'd grown too bureaucratic."

In 1981, Creech decided to break up the warehouse system and move aircraft parts from the storage areas at the rear of the base right up to flight line. Not that there was always a convenient place for parts stores big enough to stock 10,000 different items. But with scraps of wood and leftover cans of paint and underutilized shelving, folks made do.

What serious money Creech had, he spent for minicomputers that let crew chiefs and their technicians know exactly what parts were available, and let supply specialists know what parts needed to be reordered. Now, all a crew chief had to do was climb off a jet and walk a few yards to a terminal to find out if a part was available. A push of a button ordered the part to be set aside. Then it was only a short walk down to the parts store with a simplified order form to have the part in hand. More often than not, it was waiting on the counter by the time he arrived. Total time lapsed: about 15 minutes. Today it's down to 8.

At the same time, Creech mounted a crusade he considered equally critical to the rebuilding of TAC. On the theory that quality begets quality, he ordered a top-to-bottom sprucing up of every TAC facility, ranging from airplane hangars to barracks to mess halls. Once the Reagan defense dollars began to flow, that crusade took on a momentum of its own. But long before, Creech had begun by ordering that nearly everything within his domain receive a fresh coat of paint, from airplanes to cars to buildings. Nothing was spared. TAC even went so far as to paint the backs of stop signs.

"I could paint all of TAC for the price of one F-15," he says. "My philosophy is that if equipment is shabby looking, it affects your pride in your organization and your performance. You can't preach to a young man that an airplane can be shabby on the outside but has to be spic-and-span on the inside. You either have a climate of professionalism, or one of deterioration and decay. You can't segment it. Only on TV do you have these Black Sheep squadrons. Good outfits look sharp and act sharp. The great pilots — the Chuck Yeagers — are not sloppy people."

Fresh paint gave way to murals and lounges and comfortable furniture in flight-line facilities, and then to new barrack complexes with carpeted rooms and semiprivate baths. And while pilots had formation flybys to show their stuff to the public and the brass, squadron vehicle fleets held annual "roll-bys" displaying their gleaming trucks and vans.

It was all part of General Creech's emphasis on respect and recognition for his people. "Pride is the fuel of human accomplishment," he preached to his command. And competition was the spark plug. To drive home the point, annual awards banquets, complete with citations and trophies, were held at every wing, to recognize the year's best maintenance and supply specialists.

By the time General Creech left TAC, 85% of his airplanes were rated as mission capable, and jets were averaging 21 sorties a month, with 29 hours in the air. In wartime, TAC was capable of launching 6,000 sorties a day, double what it had been when he arrived at Langley. In peacetime, the crash rate had dropped from one for every 13,000 flying hours to one for every 50,000 — and crashes traced to faulty maintenance nearly vanished.

TAC, under Creech, had gone from the Air Force's worst command to its best. For much of the time, it had been a battle, and heads had rolled. The lazy and the incompetent, who had found numerous hiding places in a centralized structure, were smoked out when maintenence operations moved to the flight line and squadrons were held accountable for their performance. Some had to leave. But many more decided to stay. In 1983, two-thirds of the first-term mechanics decided to reenlist, or nearly double the rate of 1977, the year before Creech took command. Second-termer retention rates went from 68% to 85% over the same period. And some of the older technicians found they liked Creech's program so much that they recalled retirement papers to see it through.

TAC commanding officers thrived under the new system. Of the 148 wing commanders who served under Creech, only about 3% were relieved for poor performance—fewer than under any of Creech's three predecessors. "It was not a ruthless system," Creech emphasizes. "You just don't get results by going around chopping people's heads off."

Even in retirement, Creech's philosophy sets the tone for Air Force management. General Larry D. Welch, now the Air Force Chief of Staff, served in staff positions under Creech. He later went on to head up the Strategic Air Command, the nation's nuclear strike force, where decentralization also became a battle cry.

Even the Pentagon has got the religion. A recent Pentagon directive gives commanders new authority to abolish regulations, streamline procedures, and do whatever they think best to enhance mission accomplishment. "People doing the job day in and day out know better how to do it than some guy who is sitting behind a desk," asserts William H. Taft IV, deputy secretary of defense.

As for Creech, now 59, he continues to spread the gospel to leaders of industry and government as a lecturer, consultant, and corporate board member.

In his travels, Creech remarks how common it is for executives to think of decentralization and delegation as loss of control and abdication of command. If anything, he says, just the opposite is true: "When I left TAC, I had more control over it than my predecessors. I'd created leaders and helpers at all those various levels. Without that kind of network below you, you're a leader in name only.

"It's not really that hard to run a large organization," the general explains. "You just have to think small about how to achieve your goals. There's a very finite limit to how much leadership you can exercise at the very top. You can't micromanage—people resent that. Things are achieved by individuals, by collections of twos and fives and twenties, not collections of 115,000. And that's as true in industry as it is in the military."

# QUESTIONS

1. Evaluate General Creech's management practices. List points of agreement and disagreement with his leadership philosophy and the actions he took.

   _____

   _____

   _____

2. Cite another case in which an effective leader improved the morale and performance of an organization or work group. What policies and techniques were used?

   _____

   _____

   _____

# A Business and Its Beliefs:
# The Ideas That Helped Build IBM

## INTRODUCTION

One may speculate at length as to the cause of the decline or fall of a corporation. Technology, changing tastes, and changing fashions all play a part. But the fact remains that some companies manage to flourish while others in the same industry may falter or fail. Normally we ascribe these differences to such things as business competence, market judgment, and the quality of leadership in a corporation. Each one of these is a vital factor. No one can dispute their importance. But I question whether they in themselves are decisive.

I believe the real difference between success and failure in a corporation can often be traced to the question of how well the organization brings out the great energies and talents of its people. What does it do to help these people find common cause with each other? How does it keep them pointed in the right direction despite the many rivalries and differences which may exist among the many changes which take place from one generation to another?

This, then, is my thesis: I firmly believe that any organization, in order to survive and achieve success, must have a sound set of beliefs on which it premises all its policies and actions.

Next, I believe that the single most important factor in corporate success is the leaders' faithful adherence to those beliefs.

And finally, I believe that if an organization is to meet the challenges of a changing world, it must be prepared to change everything about itself except those beliefs as it moves through corporate life.

## HELPING PEOPLE GROW

The beliefs that mold great organizations frequently grow out of the character, the experiences, and the convictions of a single person. More

*Source: Excerpts from Thomas J. Watson, Jr.*, A Business and Its Beliefs: The Ideas That Helped Build IBM. *Copyright © 1963, McGraw-Hill Book Company. Reprinted with permission.*

than most companies, IBM is the reflection of one individual — my father, T. J. Watson.

Father joined the company at forty, a point at which most businessmen, thinking they were middle-aged, might not feel able to start a new career. He had, by that time, a firm grip on most of the beliefs he felt were necessary to succeed in business. He held to them so strongly that he was sometimes exasperating. But the depth of his belief was directly related to the success of our company.

My father was the son of an upstate New York farmer. He grew up in an ordinary but happy home where the means, and perhaps the wants, were modest and the moral environment strict. The important values, as he learned them, were to do every job well, to treat all people with dignity and respect, to be neatly dressed, to be clean and forthright, to be eternally optimistic, and above all, to be loyal.

There was nothing very unusual about this. It was a normal upbringing in rural nineteenth-century America. Whereas most men took the lessons of childhood for granted, however, and either lived by them or quietly forgot them, my father had the compulsion to work hard at them all his life. As far as he was concerned, those values were the rules of life — to be preserved at all costs, to be commended to others, and to be followed conscientiously in one's business life.

## BELIEF I: RESPECT FOR THE INDIVIDUAL

I want to begin with what I think is the most important: our respect for the individual. This is a simple concept, but in IBM it occupies a major portion of management time. We devote more effort to it than to anything else.

This belief was bone-deep in my father. Some people who start out in modest circumstances have a certain contempt for the average man when they are able to rise above him. Others, by the time they become leaders, have built up a unique respect for the average man and a sympathy for his problems. They recognize that in a modern industrial nation the less fortunate often are victims of forces not wholly within their own control. This attitude forms the basis for many of the decisions they make having to do with people. T. J. Watson was in the latter category. He had known hard times, hard work, and unemployment himself, and he always had understanding for the problems of the working man. Moreover, he recognized that the greatest of these problems was job security.

In 1914, having been fired as sales manager of the National Cash Register Company following a series of clashes with Mr. Patterson, my father was brought in to run the Computing-Tabulating-Recording Company, a loose alliance of three small companies. It was the organization that was to become IBM ten years later.

C-T-R was a demoralized organization. Many of the people there resented the newcomer who had been brought into the organization and quarreled among themselves. It was a situation that presented him with an early test of his belief in job security.

Despite the questionable condition of the company, no one was fired. T. J. Watson did not move in and shake up the organization. Instead he set out to buff and polish the people who were already there to make a success of what he had.

That decision in 1914 led to the IBM policy on job security, which has meant a great deal to our employees. From it has come our policy to build from within. We go to great lengths to develop our people, to retrain them when job requirements change, and to give them another chance if we find them experiencing difficulties in their jobs.

This does not mean that a job at IBM is a lifetime ticket or that we do not occasionally let people go — we do, but only after we have made a genuine effort to help them improve. Nor does it mean that people do not leave us — they do. But policies like these, we have found, help us to win the goodwill of most of our people.

Among plant people, where job security is ordinarily a matter of major concern, IBM's ability to avoid layoffs and work interruptions has encouraged our people to respond with loyalty and with diligence on the job. Over the years we have been willing to take chances and strain our resources rather than resort to layoffs. For almost a quarter of a century now, no one has lost an hour's time in layoffs from IBM, in spite of recessions and major product shifts.

Steady employment, however, is only one part of good human relations, an area where IBM inherited much from John Patterson. In many ways Patterson was a typical nineteenth-century businessman. He deplored competition and went to great lengths to overcome it. On the other hand, while most businessmen were fighting off the demands of their workers, Patterson made great strides in employee welfare.

He was decades ahead of his time. Early in his career he had learned a hard lesson when indifferent workmen produced $50,000 worth of defective machines and almost ruined his company. Patterson's response was to build modern factories with improved facilities for his people. He provided showers on company premises and company time, dining rooms serving meals at cost, entertainment, schools, clubs, libraries, and parks. Other businessmen were shocked at Patterson's notions. But he said they were investments which would pay off — and they did. T. J. Watson observed Patterson's practices carefully and carried many of them with him to IBM.

In the early days, C-T-R was working so close to the line that there was no money available to duplicate Patterson's handsome factory buildings and his generous benefit program. Father used showmanship instead. He staged band concerts and picnics and made scores of speeches. Almost every kind of fanfare was tried to create enthusiasm. The more substantial things — above-average wages and benefits — came later.

Along with wages and job security, we have always thought it equally important that the company respect the dignity of its employees. People, as I have said, occupy more IBM management time than our products.

As businessmen we think in terms of profit, but people continue to rank first.

Our early emphasis on human relations was motivated not by altruism but by a simple belief that if we respected our people and helped them to respect themselves, the company would make the most profit.

Our management also recognized that the individual has his own problems, ambitions, abilities, frustrations, and goals. We wanted to be certain that no one got lost in the organization and, most of all, that no individual became a victim of any manager's unfairness or personal whim. In this regard, we developed what we call our "Open Door" policy. This is a key element in our employee relations.

The Open Door grew out of T. J. Watson's close and frequent association with individuals in the plant and field offices. It became a natural thing for them to bring their problems to him, and in time this was established as a regular procedure. My father encouraged this in his visits. He spoke of it in his telephone broadcasts to offices and plants. If a man was not getting along, or if he thought he was being treated unfairly by his manager, he was told to go to the plant or branch manager. If that did not work, he was then invited to come and lay his case before my father.

Hundreds of employees literally did just that. Many would take the day off from our plant in Endicott, New York, and come to my father's office in New York City to talk about their problems. More often than not, he favored the complaining employee—sometimes, I'm sure, more than he should have. But he built up a lasting relationship with a great many employees, and they helped him to keep in touch with what was going on in the company. At the time of his death in 1956, most of our then 57,000 employees thought of T. J. Watson as a friend they could count on.

The Open Door exists today as it did then. I'm sure that a policy of this kind makes many a traditional manager's blood run cold. He probably sees it as a challenge to his authority or, worse yet, as a sharp sword hanging over his head. But the fact remains that in IBM it has been remarkably effective, primarily because by its mere existence it exercises a moderating influence on management. Whenever a manager makes a decision affecting one of his people, he knows that he may be held accountable to higher management for the fairness of that decision.

Our management has long believed that sharp contrast between the blue- and the white-collar people in a business is to be avoided. For many years IBM benefits were the same for all employees with a given amount of service, regardless of rank or position. Insurance and vacation programs to this day relate to service. Other benefits, such as medical care, are the same for all.

In our retirement plan, however, we now recognize salary as well as length of service.

Years ago all piecework was eliminated in our plants. First-line managers in the plants did not keep data on the production of parts because we did not want their evaluation of workers to be directly related to units produced. The IBM employee was compensated on the basis of his manager's judgment of overall contribution to the business.

Obviously some of these practices caused inefficiencies. Yet on the whole, they contributed in a major way to the morale of the hourly rated man.

Naturally the key factor in the maintenance of good human relations is the individual manager, and when my father first went on the road for The National Cash Register Company, he learned a lesson in management that he made a permanent part of IBM. Right after he joined "The Cash," as it was known, he spent several weeks calling on prospects without making a single sale. His manager had him on the carpet, and after treating him pretty roughly, said, "Young man, I'll go out with you when you call on your prospects, and if we fall down, we'll fall down together." They went out together and made several sales. After that, having learned a little more about how to sell and after having recaptured his confidence, T. J. Watson found the job a great deal easier. The episode made a tremendous impression on him.

Today this same approach is expected of all IBM managers. The manager must know how to work with his people, how to help them, and how to train them. For example, if a salesman is having difficulty, we insist that his branch manager or even his district manager make a number of calls with him to help him improve.

Another consideration in human relations that has meant a great deal is the continual opportunity for advancement. Because we have grown so rapidly, we have created a great many opportunities for promotion. No matter how great the temptation to go outside for managers, we have almost always filled these new jobs from within; no more than a small percentage of our people have come into the company at other than the lowest level in their specialty. We have hired a few top scientists, lawyers, and other specialists, but with those exceptions all our executives came up from the bottom. This has been a great factor in maintaining morale.

You cannot always make as many promotions in a plant as you can elsewhere, but we have found that there are other things you can do to keep morale high. One technique is job enlargement. People running a nearly automatic machine tool all day making hundreds of the same item may have very little feeling of personal accomplishment. In IBM we fight this problem whenever practical by teaching our people to do their own set-up work when they change from one operation to another. In some cases, they make up unit assemblies. In others, they do their own inspecting. We try to rotate the very boring jobs to break monotony. This helps a person to keep his sense of dignity, accomplishment, and involvement.

Cause and effect are often impossible to match up, but I have always been convinced that without our attitude toward human relations we would have fallen short of our business goals.

Some say that when an organization tries to get too close to its people and makes a lot of the "team" idea, the individual gets swallowed up, loses his identity, and becomes a carbon copy of his fellow employees. So far as I can see, this is not true to any serious degree in our large organizations today. Corporate people may not necessarily be more independent than others, but neither do I believe that they are any less.

I suspect we have our fair quota of security-minded men who are careful never to rock the boat. At the same time, I suspect there are some college professors who are absent-minded, some scientists who are eccentric, and some military men who are martinets. But just as these stereotypes do not apply to the general run of people in those occupations, the stereotype of the "organization man" does not apply to all forms of corporate life.

IBM has more than 125,000 employees. A substantial number of them, many of whom I could pick out by name, are highly individualistic men and women. They value their social and intellectual freedom, and I question whether they would surrender it at any price. Admittedly, they may like their jobs and the security and salaries that go along with them. But I know of few who would not put on their hats and slam the door if they felt the organization had intruded so heavily on them that they no longer owned themselves. Business may have its share of hypocrites, but I am sure that big business has no more than any other group.

Early in 1961, in talking to our sales force, I attempted to size up the then-new Kennedy administration as I saw it. It was not a political talk. I urged no views on them. It was an optimistic assessment, nothing more. But at the close of the meeting, a number of salesmen came up front. They would listen to what I had to say about business, they said, but they didn't want to hear about the new administration in a company meeting.

On my return to New York, I found a few letters in the same vein. "Lay off," they seemed to say. "You're stepping on our toes in something that's none of your business."

At first I was a bit annoyed at having been misunderstood. But when I thought about it I was pleased, for they had made it quite clear they wore no man's collar and they weren't at all hesitant to tell me so. From what I have read of organization men, that is not the way they are supposed to act.

It is interesting to contemplate the possible nature of individual achievement in the absence of large organizations. It probably would be of a different order. The challenges in a large organization are great, and achievement, really, is the successful response to challenge. Men who have accomplished great deeds in large organizations might have done less if they had been challenged with less, and they would have realized less of their potential and their individuality.

In IBM we frequently refer to our need for "wild ducks." The moral is drawn from a story by the Danish philosopher Sören Kierkegaard. He told of a man on the coast of Zealand who liked to watch the wild ducks fly south in great flocks each fall. Out of charity, he took to putting feed for them in a nearby pond. After a while, some of the ducks no longer bothered to fly south; they wintered in Denmark on what he fed them.

In time they flew less and less. When the wild ducks returned, the others would circle up to greet them but then head back to their feeding grounds on the pond. After three or four years they grew so lazy and fat that they found difficulty in flying at all.

Kierkegaard drew his point — you can make wild ducks tame, but you can never make tame ducks wild again. One might also add that the duck who is tamed will never go anywhere anymore.

We are convinced that any business needs its wild ducks. And at IBM we try not to tame them.

## BELIEF II: PROVIDE THE BEST CUSTOMER SERVICE

Years ago we ran an ad that said simply and in bold type, "IBM Means Service." I have often thought it our very best ad. It stated clearly just exactly what we stand for. It also is a succinct expression of our second basic corporate belief. We want to give the best customer service of any company in the world.

We recognize that service is the key element in what is, I hope, our good reputation. T. J. Watson realized early the great importance of reputation. When he was eighteen, he drove a horse and buggy across northern New York state, selling pianos and sewing machines. His customers were farmers and, like farmers everywhere at the time, they seldom had much cash. To make a sale he frequently took animals or farm equipment in trade, later selling them off in Painted Post, his home base. He had two years of good training in how to get along with people, how to make a fair trade and leave people happy. As he drove his team through the countryside, he saw at once the value of the golden rule in business, for many people would buy his goods on the basis of what satisfied customers had to say about his products.

We found that good service to the customer requires the cooperation of all parts of the business. I think this was brought home to us years ago when we centered many of our activities on our plant in Endicott. Sales and customer engineering schools were located there, as were our sales conventions in the 1940s. Customer executives and administrative personnel also visited and studied at Endicott. This arrangement brought together all our people, as well as our customers, and made it possible for us to give the latter better service as we learned more about their problems.

In a business like ours, a reputation for service is one of the company's principal assets. Many operations performed by our machines are vital to the customer's business. Lengthy breakdowns could be ruinous. Furthermore, most of what we call "sales" in IBM are really rentals. IBM's contracts have always offered not machines for rent but machine services, that is, the equipment itself and the continuing advice and counsel of IBM's staff.

In time, good service became almost a reflex in IBM, and Father loved to show what the company could do. In 1942 an official of the War Production Board gave him a perfect excuse to do it. The WPB man called him late on the afternoon of Good Friday to place an order for 150 machines, challenging him to deliver the equipment to Washington, D.C., by the following Monday. Father said he would have the machines there on time. On Saturday morning, he and his staff phoned IBM offices all over the country and instructed them to get some 150 machines on the road Easter weekend. Just to make sure his caller got the point, Father instructed his staff to wire the WPB man at his office or home the minute each truck started on its way to Washington, giving the time of departure and expected arrival. He made arrangements with police and Army officials to escort the trucks, which were to be driven around the clock. Customer engineers were brought in and a miniature factory was set up in Georgetown to handle the reception and installation of the equipment. There were sleepless people in IBM — and in WPB — that weekend.

These are not small things. The relationship between the man and the customer, their mutual trust, the importance of reputation, the idea of putting the customer first, always — all these things, if carried out with real conviction by a company, can make a great deal of difference in its destiny.

## BELIEF III: PERFORMANCE EXCELLENCE

The third IBM belief is really the force that makes the other two effective. We believe that an organization should pursue all tasks with the idea that they can be accomplished in a superior fashion. IBM expects and demands excellent performance from its people in whatever they do.

I suppose a belief of this kind conjures up a mania for perfection and all the psychological horrors that go with it. Admittedly, a perfectionist is seldom a comfortable personality. An environment which calls for perfection is not likely to be easy. But aiming for it is always a goad to progress.

In addition to this persistent striving for perfection, we believe an organization will stand out only if it is willing to take on seemingly impossible tasks. The men who set out to do what others say cannot be done are the ones who make the discoveries, produce the inventions, and move the world ahead.

T. J. Watson used to tell our people, "It is better to aim at perfection and miss it than it is to aim at imperfection and hit it."

As a result of this insistence on perfection and the way we went at almost impossible tasks, there soon developed within the company what might best be called a *tone*. It was a blend of optimism, enthusiasm, excitement, and pace. The company was always on the move, constantly changing, always striving for something better. Evidences of it were everywhere — new products, new branch offices, sales contests, slogans. Better to do something — even the wrong thing — than to do nothing at all.

Believing in success can help to make it happen. Back in 1924, when things like butcher scales and time clocks were still mainstays of our business, we had the temerity to change our name from the Computing-Tabulating-Recording Company to the International Business Machines Corporation. We constantly acted as though we were much bigger, much more sophisticated, much more successful than any current balance sheet might bear out.

As I have already pointed out, part of this tone was optimism, of course, and in this my father excelled. One day during the depression of the thirties, my father met one of his major competitors in an art gallery. IBM was not doing particularly well but was managing to equal its previous year's income. The other fellow was having more difficulty.

He said to my father, "Tom, I hear you're still hiring salesmen in spite of the depression, and I just can't see how that's a prudent thing for your business."

My father said, "Well, Bill, you know when a man gets about my age, he always does something foolish. Some men play too much poker, and others bet on horse races and one thing and another. My hobby is hiring salesmen."

We had an "IBM day" at the World's Fair in 1939, and the next year we brought 10,000 of our people to the fair at company expense. People realized they were working for an unusual individual and an unusual company that was capable of doing unusual things.

By the 1930s our sales conventions had become spectacular affairs. Salesmen, on awakening, would find newspapers under their doors carrying a complete account of the previous day's events. Our overseas salesmen attended our conventions at that time, and when they went to their seats, they found small headphones with which they could hear the speeches in their native tongue.

When General Eisenhower, then president of Columbia University, went to Endicott to address a Hundred Percent Club meeting in July 1948, T. J. Watson persuaded him to spend an extra hour and talk to the plant people. Within the same hour the people were let off their jobs and a platform was constructed in the street outside the main plant. As the general and my father climbed the steps, the carpenters hammered in the last nails. "My gosh," one worker was heard to say, "what a business."

In a way, no one knew quite what to expect next. It may not have been management according to the book, but it seemed to keep us on our toes. Things were always being done in a highly vigorous fashion, with little regard for how much energy was being expended but with great regard for the quality of the result and for the impression it would make on people.

In 1934 we told the sales force that as soon as the company's profits were doubled the annual convention would be held in Europe. All salesmen making their quotas would qualify for the trip. The year of doubled profits came in 1941, but Hitler had other plans for Europe, and the idea of the trip was swallowed up by the war. Then in 1961 one of our old-timers, a salesman who had qualified for that trip, wrote to remind me that the pledge had never been fulfilled. I knew that I had to make good on the promise and was glad of the opportunity. So in the summer of 1962, 197 salesmen who had qualified for that trip traveled to Europe with their wives to keep the date that had been interrupted.

The trip provided an interchange between American and European salesmen with, we hope, mutual benefits. In addition, it proved to be a great morale booster on both sides of the ocean.

Looking back on it now, I can see that many of the things we did in the formative years were anything but scientific. But what we learned, I believe, is that there are times in an organization when an instinct for leadership and drama are many times more important than following the book on good management procedure.

What T. J. Watson did, probably more than anything else, was to set the tone for IBM. This was created in large part by the beliefs he brought to the company, for with them he brought vigor and great excitement. But it was also colored by his own good sense of what would be most appropriate for the time and the situation. When things were difficult and the sledding was uphill, he could be very optimistic. But when things looked good and our future began to clear up, he was forever cautioning us against becoming complacent. I suspect this is a necessity for any leader—to be a balanced wheel, a leavener.

Certainly no one can argue with the results. From 1914 to 1946 our company's profits grew thirty-eight times. By the end of World War II, IBM's management had developed a deep belief in the policies upon which we had built out business: respect for the individual, major attention to service, and drive for superiority in all things.

It is interesting to note that we didn't have quite the clear sailing that some people seem to think we had in our industry. When Dr. Herman Hollerith was developing the original electrically sensed punched card, there was another engineer with him in the Census Bureau by the name of James Powers. Powers took out patents on a mechanically sensed punched card that gave about the same results as ours.

The Powers patents have been in the hands of reputable companies for as long as the Hollerith patents have been in ours. In fact, holders of those patents have produced a number of firsts in our industry—including the first printing tabulating machine and the first alphabetic printer. Each time we are second best in a new machine announcement, we take it as a personal affront and redouble our efforts to be more responsive to customers' needs.

Occasionally we have failed to respond with vigor, and when this has happened we have always lost ground. When we lost ground to others in those areas in which we have competence, we did so because we forgot to strive for superiority. This is easy to do when you are generally successful. "Well, you can't win them all," you just say, "and the overall picture is good." This is the first step toward failure. We've taken it once or twice, but fortunately we've never failed to correct our mistakes before they became a habit.

During the period prior to 1946, it was quite easy for us to make everyone understand how interested we were in the well-being of our people. For one thing, we had relatively few of them. For another, we added to them slowly. When a man joined the company he would, in time, learn of its traditions from his manager and others with whom he worked.

But with the rapid changes that began to take place as a result of technology and growth in the years following 1946, we found it harder to convince the individual employee that we still looked upon him as the most important asset in the corporation.

Prior to 1946, our sales growth rate averaged more than 12 percent a year. During the early 1950s, we grew at the rate of 24 percent a year. If the company's beliefs were to count for anything, we would have to make it very clear to new employees what IBM stood for.

Naturally, we had recourse to all the usual company communications. But the key to helping our people understand lay with the individual managers. Unfortunately, most of our managers in the middle and later 1950s had been with the company a very short time, and it was difficult for them to explain our traditional philosophies.

We attacked the problem by setting up two management schools — one for junior executives, and another, two years later, for line managers. These schools were not only to teach general management but — most important — to give our managers a feeling for IBM's outlook and its beliefs. After a time we found that the schools tended to put too much emphasis on management and not enough on the beliefs. This, we felt, was putting the cart before the horse, so we changed the curriculum. We felt it was vital that our managers be well grounded in our beliefs. Otherwise, we might begin to get management views at odds with the company's outlook. If this were to happen, it might possibly slow down our growth and change our basic approach to the management of our company.

On the question of fair treatment, I'm reminded of the lesson we learned about the transfers of our people in the field. With nearly two hundred branch offices and rapid company growth, a certain amount of moving was inevitable. But when people began to say that IBM stood for "I've Been Moved," we naturally looked into what we were doing in that area.

We found that many of these moves were really being made for the convenience of the company rather than for the benefit of the employee. This called for a new set of requirements, the principal one of which made it mandatory that a person moved on individual reassignment be given a substantial increase in responsibility and pay. This change resulted in relatively fewer moves. To make certain we were fair to those being moved, we introduced an improved program to minimize the individual's out-of-pocket moving costs.

In all good human relations, communication plays a very important part. People can be directed, but they respond best when they understand what they are supposed to do and why. Until there is understanding, there is no real basis for motivation. I believe management must seek consent.

Our problems here have been pressing. From 1946 through 1962, IBM's worldwide population increased by more than 10,000 people. We are more spread out than ever. Growth has brought with it thousands of new managers. Despite our efforts to contain them, there are many levels of management. We have had to face the problem of how to implant and keep alive in these people a real feeling for the traditions and beliefs of the business:

- how to keep people pulling together despite their natural diversity in interests;
- how to shorten the distance between the man at the bench and his division manager, the president, or the board chairman;
- how to maintain the "small-company attitude" that meant so much to us when we were growing up.

"Small-company attitude" is a term we frequently use. We encourage this attitude in every way we can. We want our people to feel that they understand one another, that they have some knowledge of each other's problems and goals. And we want them to feel that they always have access to management, that no one is so far down in the chain of command that he cannot be kept aware of what is going on.

In IBM today there are eight levels of management between the man at the bench and the president or the board chairman. There are seven levels above the salesman. This is more than we like, but we try to keep it down to that. And we do a number of things to help shorten the distance.

Some are conventional. For example, we have a question-and-answer program that draws some 300 inquiries or complaints a month, and few pull their punches. We have a suggestion award program that brings in more than 100,000 entries a year; annual employee appraisals and frequent attitude surveys; and eighteen plant, division, and company news publications.

Others are more unusual. One is a newsletter called *Management Briefing*. A few years ago we surveyed a group of managers and found we were falling far short of keeping them well informed. Today *Management Briefing* goes regularly to more than 10,000 managers — the majority of whom many companies would call "foremen."

*Management Briefing* provides our managers with background information on company announcements and activities. It explains the "why" behind policies, and it covers actual case studies — or object lessons — in management to help us avoid making the same mistakes twice.

For communications to executives on very important matters, we began three years ago to issue "President's Letters" — they are now called "Executive Letters." On the average we publish fewer than a dozen a year, and we use them to explain basic IBM policies when we feel that such explanation is in order.

One of our most unique customs is the IBM Family Dinner. At least once every two years in every one of our branch offices around the country, our people — along with their husbands or wives — are asked to dinner with an officer of the corporation to learn what is going on. In telling his story, he shows a half-hour filmed report on what the company has done in the past year. These Family Dinners keep our executives on the go, but they give us an occasion to get together informally, and they help keep our small-company attitude alive.

We also write letters of congratulations on promotions and jobs well done. And when our people get sick or lose a member of their family, we remember them with notes of sympathy or condolence.

When I have an important announcement to make, I do it by a telephone broadcast to all our domestic employees. I believe it means more to them when they hear these announcements directly from me. There are seldom more than one or two a year; we save them for things that personally affect most of our people.

But before leaving this whole question of attitudes and communication, there is one point about which I have some real concern. It has to do with the cautious attitude of so many young men in middle management today. They seem reluctant to stick their necks out or to bet on a hunch.

This is not always because they lack nerve. Sometimes they make the mistake of thinking that top management places a greater premium on following form than on anything else. I wish we could stir them up a bit and encourage a little more recklessness among this group of decision makers. Every time we've moved ahead in IBM, it was because someone was willing to take a chance, put his head on the block, and try something new.

## WHAT GROWTH AND CHANGE HAVE TAUGHT US

Our job, and that of each division of IBM, is to help customers solve their problems through the use of data processing systems and other information handling equipment. There is a close relationship between all of the parts of our product line. Any major technological move or marketing decision in any division is bound to have a direct effect on other segments of the business.

This means that decisions are being made constantly, all the way down the line, on matters that involve two or more divisions. One might suppose that burdensome machinery would have to be set up throughout the business to settle the thousands of small differences that could be expected to arise among the divisions.

To date this has not been necessary. No matter what division they may be in, basically all of our managers are company oriented. They think primarily in terms of what is good for IBM rather than what may be good for a particular division. This may be because many of them were with IBM long before we became a divisional organization. Many of our higher executives have incentive plans in addition to their salaries. But the plans are based on overall IBM performance rather than that of any single division. The arrangement, we believe, has helped to keep everyone pulling together.

Much of this we owe to the company's beliefs. Our people so thoroughly understand the need to give superior service that their concern for the well-being of the customer often overrides whatever differences of opinion there might be among them. Of course I do not mean that we have no differences. It is my responsibility, as it is the president's and that of the corporate management committee, to resolve the major ones. By and large, it hasn't been too bad.

As I said earlier, at the time of reorganization, we suddenly found that we had need for a great many more staff experts and specialists than were on our rolls. In nearly every case we "made" these experts simply by naming a man to a job. We had some failures, but on the whole our method worked pretty well. The reason, I think, is that these young and relatively inexperienced executives knew three things as well as they knew their own names:

- they knew that any decisions they might make and any actions they might take had to be right for our people;

- they knew that the main aim of our business is service, to help the customer solve his problems, no matter how many problems this may create for us;

- they knew that we will not settle for anything less than a superior effort in everything we do.

In other words, they understood our basic beliefs, and this understanding enabled them to move into unfamiliar jobs and to overcome the shortcomings they may have had in technical skills. This emphasis on beliefs is not meant to downgrade the importance of technical skill. But from the time of our divisional reorganization we have found that an ingrained understanding of the beliefs of IBM, far more than technical skill, has made it possible for our people to make the company successful.

In looking back on the history of a company, one can't help but reflect on what the organization has learned from its years in business. In thinking specifically of the period since the war when IBM faced the twin challenges of great technological change and growth, I would say that we've come out with five key lessons. They may not be applicable to all companies. All I can do is attest to the great value these five lessons have had for us.

1. There is simply no substitute for good human relations and for the high morale they bring. It takes good people to do the jobs necessary to reach your profit goals. But good people alone are not enough. No matter how good your people may be, if they don't really like the business, if they don't feel totally involved in it, or if they don't think they're being treated fairly, it's awfully hard to get a business off the ground. Good human relations are easy to talk about. The real lesson, I think, is that you must work at them all the time and make sure your managers are working with you.

2. There are two things an organization must increase far out of proportion to its growth rate if that organization is to overcome the problems of change. The first of these is communication, upward and downward. The second is education and retraining.

3. Complacency is the most natural and insidious disease of large corporations. It can be overcome if management will set the right tone and pace and if its lines of communication are in working order.

4. Everyone — particularly in a company such as IBM — must place company interest above that of a division or department. In an interdependent organization, a community of effort is imperative. Cooperation must outrank self-interest, and an understanding of the company's particular approach to things is more important than technical ability.

5. And the final and most important lesson: Beliefs must always come before policies, practices, and goals. The latter must always be altered if they are seen to violate fundamental beliefs. The only sacred cow in an organization should be its basic philosophy of doing business.

The British economist Walter Bagehot once wrote, "Strong beliefs win strong men and then make them stronger." To this I would add, "And as men become stronger, so do the organizations to which they belong."

## QUESTIONS

1. Do you know of a company with a set of beliefs that guides employees in their work? Are these beliefs positive and constructive or negative and harmful? Are these beliefs stated or implied? How were the beliefs begun; how are they perpetuated?

_____

_____

_____

2. Critique the author's thesis that a company must be willing to change everything about itself — products, equipment, supplies, and methods — but not its basic beliefs.

_____

_____

_____

3. Discuss the social and historical factors that underpin IBM's three corporate principles — respect for the individual, customer service, and performance with excellence.

_____

_____

_____

4. If you were the owner or manager of a business, what specific policies and practices would you use to (a) demonstrate respect for the individual employee, (b) provide the best customer service possible, and (c) perform every job with excellence?

_____

_____

_____

# CASES

# Making Eight Is a Hassle

"My case is hardly unique," commented Jack Whitney. "But perhaps in telling it other people like myself will avoid the same trap. We've all heard this story many times, but it bears repeating. Engineers and the companies that employ them just don't seem to need constant reminders about this problem.

"When I was released from the service, I was looking forward to finally getting a chance to be a real engineer. I guess you could have said I was gung-ho. You see, I had spent a total of six years in college earning a master's degree in electrical engineering. Starting my engineering career had to be postponed for almost five years after graduation while I repaid Uncle Sam for financing my education, but now I was ready to go.

"I took a job with a large shipyard in Virginia that had several contracts to build Navy warships. I had almost four years of sea duty as a missile fire control and systems officer and felt I could apply my education and experience to building those ships and their missile systems. It was a rude shock to me when I was assigned to anti-submarine systems about which I knew very little. It was worse to realize a few weeks later that I wasn't expected to know or, for that matter, to do very much. I read more than one novel and many magazines just to have something to fill the hours. I was not alone in my frustration either. Numerous other engineers referred to their time-filling activities as 'making eight.' To compound the aggravation, we were occasionally required to put in overtime because 'the project is behind.' Talk about waste, a master's degree in automatic control systems engineering, four years of experience on the Navy's newest missile systems, and I was reduced to checking plans from some jerk in Washington who probably had never seen the inside of a college or a ship.

"It really got to me. I was coming home from work frustrated and discouraged. I've never been particularly easy to get along with, but my wife said I was becoming even more of a grouch. I had to do something!

"More education wasn't the answer. An engineer friend in the same company took a year's leave of absence without pay, went back to the University of Virginia, and earned a master's in electronics. When he came

Source:  *Reprinted with permission, Andrew J. DuBrin*, Casebook of Organizational Behavior, *copyright © 1977, Pergamon Press. (This case was prepared and written by Gerald J. Soltas.)*

back to work, he got his old desk, his old job, and his old salary. We held another going-away party for him two months later.

"About the time I had been with the yard a year, I started sending out my resume and talking to employment agencies. In 1970–71, however, things were not exactly rosy for engineers. Once, out of 75 resumes I mailed, I received not one reply. Not so much as a 'thanks, but no thanks' letter. Just nothing. I even tried to get back into the Navy. You can imagine how desperate I was becoming. Then, to make matters worse, I was pulled from my projects on anti-submarine warfare and placed in a submarine development group. Just so you won't get the wrong idea, I was doing excellent work according to my supervisors and had already been promoted, at very little increase in salary, incidentally, to Senior Design Engineer, a move which usually took six to eight years for an engineer just out of college.

"In the submarine development group, I was further from my missile backgound and was only pretending to be an engineer. I was assigned to write various chapters in a training and maintenance manual dealing with systems which had already been designed and constructed. I specifically remember the first chapter I wrote was on the ship's entertainment system. Talk about useless!

"That was the last straw! I doubled and redoubled my job hunting efforts. Finally, one of the companies I had interviewed in college eight years before responded with what seemed to be a perfect opportunity at a decent increase in pay, at least enough to cover the cost of living difference between here and Virginia. At this point, however, pay was secondary in my mind. I was going to seed in that job and would have taken almost anything that offered the chance of a challenge.

"I have been at my new job almost two years now and it is everything I had hoped for. I have more projects now than I have time for. The challenge is stimulating; I have to dig and push, but I get more done, enjoy it more, and come home refreshed instead of depressed. Don't get me wrong, I still have problems and there are days when almost nothing goes right, but I have never once wished I had my old job back."

## QUESTIONS

1. What type of job would be satisfying to you?

_____

_____

_____

2. Have you ever experienced low job satisfaction? Describe.

_____

_____

_____

**3.** What should employees and managers do to solve morale problems?

_____

_____

_____

# The Coffee Break

You are the personnel director of a large company. While there has been no written policy regarding coffee breaks, they are a long-established tradition, and all employees avail themselves of the privilege each morning and afternoon of the workday. In fact, company management has allowed a vending machine company to place their machines in several locations throughout the building in which the company is located. As a result, employees take coffee breaks, usually 10 minutes long, at any time of the day they desire.

In general, this approach has not caused too much difficulty in work accomplishment, but in one department, in the opinion of its supervisor, the work has suffered. There was socializing around desks while the coffee was consumed; telephones went unanswered, and work came to a halt. In some instances, the employees in that department took breaks longer than 10 minutes, and this too upset work patterns.

Because of this, the supervisor, Mr. Kobe, issued a memorandum to all employees under his jurisdiction. In it he reaffirmed the tradition of the coffee break, but he restricted it to 10:15 to 10:25 in the morning and 3:15 to 3:25 in the afternoon. He also requested all employees to be back at their desks at the end of each break.

When the memo was received, many of the employees reacted negatively. Indignation ran high, and two employees were designated as spokesmen to come to you with their grievance without first going to their supervisor.

*Source: William J. McLarney and William M. Berliner*, Management Training: Cases and Principles, *5th ed. (Homewood, Ill.: Richard D. Irwin, Inc., 1970). Reprinted with permission.*

## QUESTIONS

1. If you were a supervisor, how would you handle questions about employee breaks?

   _____

   _____

   _____

2. If you had a complaint about your manager, what would you do to solve the problem?

   _____

   _____

   _____

# The Disappointed OD Practitioner

*Brent Garwood, a behavioral science consultant and college professor, was contacted by the Plastics Division of a manufacturing corporation to analyze the problems the manufacturing supervision seemed to be experiencing. Division management wanted Brent to make some recommendations about the type of training the supervisors should receive in order to be more effective in their work. Professor Garwood noted that an analysis of training needs alone would not represent a valid prescription for any organization's problems. Usually other problems underlie training needs.*

*Brent conducted a series of organization analysis sessions with all the Plastics Division supervisors (about 50 men and 10 women) to obtain a clear perspective about company problems. The 60 supervisors were divided into five groups. The sessions were loosely structured. Brent acted as note taker and discussion leader, while group members talked about company problems. Participants were told that (a) top management would receive a general report of the findings; (b) no supervisor would be identified in the report; (c) some form of feedback on the sessions would be provided to participants. Toward the conclusion of the second session, with each group, Brent summarized the main problems and concerns he felt the group had identified. Group members were encouraged to critique any of the consultant's perceptions of their comments.*

*At least one member in every group cautioned Brent that the company would probably not use whatever findings he uncovered.*

*Several supervisors commented that attitude surveys had been conducted twice in the last several years. In both instances, nothing constructive was done with the findings. Brent reassured the supervisors that the company seemed serious about using the results of this organization analysis. Furthermore, he would urge management to take immediate corrective action on some of the more pressing problems.*

*Brent conducted his organization analysis sessions on Friday mornings for several months, each meeting lasting about three hours. Two sessions were held with each group. Group participation in the meetings was widespread and intensive. Brent was optimistic that these organization development (OD) sessions would be a force for constructive change in the Plastics*

*Source: Reprinted with permission, Andrew J. DuBrin, Casebook of Organizational Behavior, copyright © 1977, Pergamon Press.*

*Division. Two weeks after the last OD session was conducted, Brent submitted a written report to management (as they had requested). A copy of the report is presented next.*

> To:       Martin Griffin and John H. Baldwin
> From:     Brent Garwood
> Subject:  Report on Organization Analysis Sessions with Plastics
>           Division Production Supervisors

## BACKGROUND

Summarized in this report are findings gathered in 18 organization analysis sessions conducted by me with approximately 60 Plastics Division supervisors and superintendents. (Statements made in this report about supervisors also apply to superintendents.) Fifteen categories are used to summarize the findings. Some overlap exists among many of the categories. Not every problem cited in the report occurs in every department; however, there was high consistency among the nine supervisory groups about the nature of problems facing them. None of the problems cited have been verified by an objective investigation of my own. I base my conclusions upon the perceptions and attitudes of the program participants. One exception is that I received a thorough plant tour.

Recommendations to management made by me later in the report are based upon my own opinion about what is feasible and practicable. Management may be aware of an underlying problem on a given issue that would make a recommendation by a consultant (or supervisor) unfeasible.

## PROBLEM AREAS

### Turnover and Absenteeism

A major problem facing supervisors is the high rate of turnover and absenteeism among low seniority hourly personnel. One supervisor noted, for example, that "110 employees in the coating department left in one year." Supervisors seem to have a feeling of futility in coping with these problems. Often factors beyond their control—such as modest wages, difficult working conditions, and high welfare and unemployment benefits—encourage turnover. Even government regulations, it was noted, such as OSHA standards about wearing masks and heavy clothing, have a negative influence upon longevity and coming to work regularly.

### Communications to Supervisors

Almost unanimously, supervisors felt that communications about important matters are too infrequent to allow them to perform their best. Some specific examples include: (a) operating instructions for new products are given at the last moment, causing confusion; (b) often four different people or groups elicit information from the supervisors on the same problem, such as an order inquiry; (c) some departments receive master scheduling forms with almost no explanation; (d) communications between supervisors on different shifts are impoverished; (e) quality specifications are infrequently communicated to supervisors, resulting in needless rejects of finished parts. On the positive side, several experienced supervisors noted that communications have improved in the last year.

### Demands Placed upon Supervisors

In general, supervisors feel they are spread too thin (too many responsibilities in terms of the time available). Various problems cited include receiving insufficient recognition, having no formal job description, too many forms to complete, no time for proper training of subordinates, and very tight schedules. One supervisor reported humorously: "Management treats us like mushrooms. We're kept in the dark and fed horse manure."

### Wages

No other problem area received as much attention in the team building sessions. Supervisors felt that their wages are low in comparison to supervisors in comparable companies and also in comparison to their own subordinates. Many supervisors noted that a competent hourly employee on incentive and overtime earns more than most supervisors. Secretiveness about salary ranges is an area of high concern, including how one might qualify for the maximum pay. Asked about what would be a fair wage for company supervisors, some opinion was expressed that $1 more per hour would be adequate. A major complaint expressed was that supervisors should receive time and one-half rather than time and one-quarter for overtime work.

### Benefits

A number of minor irritations were expressed in this area. In general, supervisors think that their benefits should be better than those of their subordinates. Supervisors believe that their benefits exceed hourly workers' only in the areas of sick pay and life insurance. Two specific complaints were: (a) employees who work four out of eight Saturdays prior to shutdown receive one day of bonus pay, while supervisors do not; (b) supervisors, unlike hourly employees, are told when to take a floating holiday.

### Prestige

A variety of factors appear to be responsible for the low prestige of supervisors, including issues covered at other points in this report. Comments such as these illustrate the feelings of low prestige observed: "Very few people would take a supervisor's job." "A supervisor is the 'whipping boy' around here." "A supervisor is a fire hydrant." "The workers feel we are messengers." "Face it, life is better as a setup man." "Maintenance personnel have more power than we do."

### Job Security

An important underlying theme is that the job security of Plastic Division supervisors is threatened. They wonder if the local division will continue to operate much longer. They react strongly to the early retirement of other salaried employees, feeling that some people are released because of chronological age and not poor job performance. Concern is also evident about the possibility of being replaced by younger employees with more formal education.

### Manufacturing Service Personnel

Considerable intergroup conflict exists between manufacturing service personnel and line supervisors. From the supervisor's viewpoint, many of these people are inexperienced about procedures. It is thought that engineers take supervisors' ideas and later receive credit for them. Supervisors note that one of the reasons master scheduling has not yet lived up to expectations is that inexperienced people are providing the basic input.

### Budgeting

Supervisors, in general, feel that the type of budgets they are preparing are of limited value. According to their perception, unstable marketing forecasts necessitate frequent changes, budgets are imposed upon them from above with little real input of their own, and they are prepared haphazardly. Also noted was that proper instruction in budget preparation was missing.

### Caliber of Newly Hired Hourly Employees

A root cause of many of the supervisors' problems — in their analysis — is the low caliber of newly hired hourly employees. Opinion was expressed that the more qualified members of the labor pool gravitate to higher paying companies. The "youth culture" and "decline of the work ethic" undoubtedly contribute heavily to the problems of hiring well motivated, dependable people. A genuine concern was expressed that the prospect of replacing competent, dedicated, senior employees as they retire appears remote. Superintendents note that the new work force contains very few prospects for supervisory positions.

### Machinery

With few exceptions, the opinion was expressed that much of the Plastic Division equipment is antiquated. Case examples were cited of purchasing equipment that was already obsolete and the impossibility of purchasing parts to repair some of the equipment. "We're expected to perform miracles with scrap iron" is a typical sentiment. It was noted that supervisors and perhaps operators should be involved in decisions about new equipment purchases. The lack of preventive maintenance was cited as a major reason for many equipment problems.

### General Working Conditions

A variety of general working conditions were cited as substandard. Included among these are a building that was last painted in 1927, leaky faucets, leaky roofs, cramped and crowded working areas and aisles, an incentive system that encourages high scrap rates, and a poor security system that is unable to cope with vandalism in the parking lot. Many supervisors said that the reluctance to erect new buildings combined with the growth in business created the space problem. Among poor working conditions mentioned were poor ventilation and excessive temperatures in a few areas.

### Training of Employees

The high turnover rate combined with the heavy demands of the supervisor's job contribute to inadequate training of hourly employees (which in turn creates even more problems for the supervisors). Few experienced employees are available to train newer employees, and supervisors are so busy with paperwork, projects with engineering, etc., that not enough time is left to work with employees.

### Worker Morale

A variety of factors, such as low wage rates and poor physical working conditions, contribute to low morale among many members of the work force. A low morale work force, in turn, creates more pressures upon the supervisor. Some opinion was expressed that older workers would like to see a return of the "division newsletter" and the suggestion system. A system of profit sharing was cited as an important way of raising morale for all levels of manufacturing personnel.

### Miscellaneous Problem Areas

Various concerns were expressed that perhaps do not deserve the status of a separate category. These are: (a) Too much competition rather than cooperation among departments. An instance was cited of some people shipping their scrap to other departments. (b) The corporation makes public statements of prosperity while internally manufacturing is pressed for cost cutting measures. (c) The difficulty in getting constructive suggestions implemented. (d) The complex order entry system that results in delays, creating pressures on supervisors to rush production schedules. (e) Minor areas of neglect such as providing shoes and protective clothing for "dirty" jobs.

# RECOMMENDATIONS FOR TRAINING

Several program topics will be suggested here for training for supervisors and superintendents. All courses should be workshop-seminar in format. Details about the conduct and content of these programs can be worked out between representatives of the Plastics Division and the Center for Management Studies. All of the suggestions focus upon job-related issues, and, from my observations, would be well received by manufacturing personnel.

## Motivating Younger Employees

A program of this nature must receive top priority. It should emphasize coping with the "new breed" of young people in terms of their value system and work motivation. A major emphasis would be placed upon the problems of absenteeism, turnover, and lack of concern for company objectives.

## Budgeting

Some emphasis should be given to both budget preparation and interpretation. Brief information about budgets in general combined with an explanation of company budgeting is recommended. A representative of company management should conduct most of this program.

## Team Building Sessions

Group discussions should be held by supervisors and superintendents on the one hand and manufacturing service personnel on the other. These meetings will bring to the surface some of the conflicts between the two groups and also lead to a resolution of some differences and to improved communications. I, or any other organization development specialist, might conduct these sessions.

## Safety

A brief reminder and perhaps some new information on this perennial topic will be well received by supervisors. The current safety manager would be the seminar leader of choice. (He is well liked by your people.)

## Interpretation of Company Policy

Supervisors need some clarification about their job responsibilities, the extent of their authority, interpretation of plant regulations, and the union contract. Only a member of company management is qualified to conduct this program. A union official should be invited to the contract interpretation session.

## New Supervisor Orientation

Training for new supervisors should include a more extensive on-the-job orientation. Perhaps visits to work areas other than their own would be helpful. An orientation "refresher," about six months to one year after assuming supervisory responsibilities, is also recommended.

### Industrial Broadening

Many supervisors suggested they would welcome visits to vendor and customer plants. Among its many values, this will help supervisors explain the proper function (and use) of many of the Plastics Division products.

## RECOMMENDATIONS FOR MANAGEMENT ACTION

1. Immediately review the wage and benefit schedules for supervisors and superintendents. Without improvement in this area, very little else management might do can improve morale.

2. Provide supervisors more lead time (if possible) on new instructions, and make a concentrated effort to increase the flow of communications to supervisors and superintendents.

3. Provide a frank discussion of the future of the Plastics Division to supervisors and superintendents.

4. Provide more verbal encouragement and praise for good performance.

5. Hire as many four-year and two-year college students as the union contract allows for hourly production work during summers and throughout the year. Supervisors seem to agree that the motivation and output of these workers is better than that of full-time permanent employees. College students are often available for part-time shift work throughout the year.

6. Conduct periodic "Executive Rap Sessions" with supervisors, superintendents, and hourly employees. In these sessions a member of top management holds an informal discussion with a few people down the line about problem areas and concerns. Such sessions are vastly superior to "tours of the ship" in obtaining upward communication.

7. Immediately make several urgently needed repairs, such as to leaky roofs or peeling paint. Investigate the true status of the widely perceived "obsolete equipment."

8. Review the training program for manufacturing service personnel. Perhaps they in fact need more "hands on" production experience.

9. In general, take appropriate action on problems cited in this report.

10. Conduct a group feedback session on this report. Ideally, I should meet with about one half of the group at a time, accompanied

by a member of top management. He could then discuss with supervisors what plans management might have to remedy some of the valid problem areas uncovered by this report. (The group feedback will be conducted in such a manner as to reflect favorably upon Plastics Division top management.)

## EFFECTIVENESS OF THE PROGRAM

Without the group feedback session mentioned above, and without some constructive action on management's part in regard to a few valid problem areas, this program will fail to achieve its most important objective — improvement of organizational effectiveness. However, the objectives of providing an interesting experience for participants, improving communications among plant supervision, and identifying training needs have all been met (in my opinion).

*Brent Garwood describes the follow-up action taken to this report in these words: "Two, three, four weeks, and still no reaction from the company. I phoned them and was informed by the Division President's secretary that Mr. Baldwin (the coordinator of the program) would be sending me a written reply shortly. The letter did arrive three days later, and it was a shocking disappointment. John Baldwin wrote me a curt note stating that the company found my observations interesting and that they would be in touch with me should the need arise. They completely ignored my comments about the importance of feedback and management action. The basic purpose of organization development was perverted. Instead of using my findings to bring about constructive change, the company was just collecting information. My program was aborted, and my professional integrity was sacrificed. I felt I owed something more than a company sponsored rap session and some free doughnuts and coffee to the participants. OD work can be very frustrating."*

## QUESTIONS

1. If you were in Brent Garwood's position, what would you do differently?

   _____

   _____

   _____

2. If you were in top management's position, what would you do differently?

_____

_____

_____

3. What is your view on using consultants to help solve quality-of-work-life problems?

_____

_____

_____

# Phil Hancock Tries Changing the World
## . . . a Little Bit at a Time

Phil Hancock is the personnel director for Sta-Brite Enterprises, a digital light manufacturing firm located in Houston, Texas. Sta-Brite has grown from 25 employees in 1976 to its current level of 250 employees. Sta-Brite's success is attributable to a good product, an efficient work force, a high product demand, an attractive price, and an effective sales force. Sta-Brite is a subsidiary of a moderate sized, five-division organization headquartered in Toledo, Ohio. Phil Hancock joined Sta-Brite eight months ago. Among Phil's many reasons for joining the company was his desire to work in a firm where he felt he could make some changes in organizational climate and help the firm grow.

Phil's boss, Edward Zewadski, gave him a semifree rein to begin taking actions Phil thinks will improve the organization. Ed does not like to define people's roles but rather prefers to let them "reach their own level." This bothers Phil a little. He would prefer to know exactly what he could do.

After being with the firm for three months, Phil feels he recognizes the major personnel problems that exist and is ready to take action on them. As Phil sits contemplating his objectives and his plans to reach those objectives, he makes the following notations:

*My Objectives:*    To improve managerial relations with subordinates at all levels; to improve teamwork in management, especially at top management levels.

*My Plan:*    Initially gain support; hire a consultant to begin the training; perhaps carry on the training with company personnel later.

*People:*    Ed Zewadski, president. Ed wants to make changes, wants to improve the company, wants to improve the situation. He works for a corporation president who is very authoritarian. Ed himself is much more reasonable in action but is limited in exactly what he can do to change how people are treated. He has little expertise in management systems. He sponsors an annual employee survey, and company actions in response to the survey results have kept the company from being unionized. He has been with the firm since it began and is an accountant by profession.

Walt Frazier, sales manager. Sales are the key to this company's success and Walt is a good manager. He has been with the firm for three years. The company's sales force has ten members, all working on a regional basis and concentrated in the heavy electronics areas. Walt is not one to rock the boat and would probably not support changes in managerial style. Salesmen have had no company sales training.

Tony Gabarro, chief engineer. Tony is not people-oriented; his primary concern is getting the work out. The twenty engineers who work for him are generally left alone to "do their own thing," but not infrequently, Tony has personnel problems. Tony is content with the status quo and not inclined to favor changes.

Sid "Rusty" Morgan, plant manager. A salty old veteran, deep down inside he is easygoing and understanding. With the company for all five years, he has made many important changes that have increased the plant's efficiency. He does not know how to train his subordinates to be more people-oriented. He would support a training program, although perhaps reluctantly.

Terri Hamilton, office manager. A very passive person, Terry is in charge of the office clerical staff, mostly women. She would support efforts for improved management style, a closer feeling of teamwork.

*Work Force:* Mostly women because of the high degree of manual dexterity required. Approximately half of the work force are Spanish-speaking Americans.

*First-line Supervision:* Mostly women, except in quality control; virtually none has management training.

*Middle Management:* Six men and two women; none has management training. Their performance is adequate.

*The Current Climate:* Not as much teamwork as would be desirable. Management systems such as Management by Objectives, Results, and Rewards (MBORR) need to be instituted. Communication between top management and first-line employees is weak. Employees are seldom brought into decision making. Self-evaluation by top management could improve this situation, as could employee development programs.

Phil looked at the information before him. The firm had the money to begin a program of management training. His personal goal was to increase positive attitudes within the organization, and he believed that training by an outside management consultant would help accomplish this. But he felt he had to have a well-conceived plan before he began.

Phil was a devout Christian. He was a lay minister in his church and actively participated in religious events in the community. Much of his philosophy about people carried over from his personal feelings. He wanted to see people happy at work. He felt it was very important to move the organization in a certain direction. . . . His thoughts turned to the firm's future. "What if the company continues to grow? We just purchased thirty additional acres for expansion. What changes might occur? What changes would need to occur?"

## QUESTIONS

1. Describe the characteristics of a good organizational climate.

   _____

   _____

   _____

2. If you were a personnel director, how would you go about creating a positive organizational climate?

   _____

   _____

   _____

# APPLICATIONS

# The Joe Bailey Problem

On the following page (Exercise page 1) is a problem that you, a supervisor, are having with Joe Bailey, one of your employees. Your effectiveness in solving this problem will influence the morale and performance of your entire work group. Instead of reading each page in sequence (1, 2, 3, 4, etc.), decide on page 1 what action you will take—*then turn to the page indicated under that choice.* Other action choices will refer you to other pages, back and forth, until you have completed the exercise.

Record each page you turn to on the "path record" below.

## Path Record

| Action Number | Page Number | Action Number | Page Number |
|:---:|:---:|:---:|:---:|
| 1 | _____ | 16 | _____ |
| 2 | _____ | 17 | _____ |
| 3 | _____ | 18 | _____ |
| 4 | _____ | 19 | _____ |
| 5 | _____ | 20 | _____ |
| 6 | _____ | 21 | _____ |
| 7 | _____ | 22 | _____ |
| 8 | _____ | 23 | _____ |
| 9 | _____ | 24 | _____ |
| 10 | _____ | 25 | _____ |
| 11 | _____ | 26 | _____ |
| 12 | _____ | 27 | _____ |
| 13 | _____ | 28 | _____ |
| 14 | _____ | 29 | _____ |
| 15 | _____ | 30 | _____ |

*Source: Terry Almond and Naomi Miller, Northern Kentucky University, 1982, based upon GTE Personnel Training, Southern Illinois University, 1980.*

| Action Number | Page Number | Action Number | Page Number |
|---|---|---|---|
| 31 | _____ | 37 | _____ |
| 32 | _____ | 38 | _____ |
| 33 | _____ | 39 | _____ |
| 34 | _____ | 40 | _____ |
| 35 | _____ | 41 | _____ |
| 36 | _____ | 42 | _____ |

*Question:* How many actions did it take you to solve the Joe Bailey problem?

## STATEMENT OF THE PROBLEM

You are a first-line supervisor. You have a work group of 12 employees.

Joe Bailey is one of your subordinates, and he has been with you for months. (He has been with the company for six years.)

Joe is absent today (Monday). You know that he has been absent quite a bit, but when you note today's absence in your attendance record, you are surprised to see that he has been absent for three of the past four Mondays. This has no doubt interfered with productivity and has been part of the reason why your group is behind schedule. You have had to work people overtime on Saturdays and Sundays for the last two months to try to catch up. You note that, on occasion, Joe Bailey has been among those selected to work.

You feel that some action must be taken about Joe Bailey. Which of the following five steps will you take first?

*Select the first step you will take and turn to the page number indicated.*

A. Call Joe aside on his return and have a talk with him.

Turn to page 9.

B. Ask some of Joe's co-workers if they know what Joe's problem might be.

Turn to page 4.

C. Ask the supervisor of the work group in which Joe previously worked what his record was there.

Turn to page 7.

D. Discuss the matter with your supervisor.

Turn to page 11.

E. Transfer Joe at the next opportunity.

Turn to page 34.

*You are not following instructions!* You were not instructed to turn to this page.

*Remember* — you are not to read the pages in sequence. Instead, you will skip around according to the action you decide to take.

Turn back to page 1, select the first step you will take to solve Joe Bailey's problem, and turn to the page number indicated.

You asked the employees who laughed to tell you what they saw. They are embarrassed, but one of the more outspoken says: "We were just laughing at a joke Fred told at lunchtime. It didn't have anything to do with you or Joe."

*What will you do now?*

Turn to page 24 and select another answer.

You have decided to ask others in the work group if they know what Joe's problem might be. You wonder if he has a drinking problem, a family problem, a real illness, or what.

You talk to three of the employees playing cards at lunchtime. They seem hesitant to talk, but one finally admits that another employee reported seeing Joe and some blonde woman speeding in a car early this morning. They looked like they were heading for the state line. He reported that Joe "could have been drunk — anyway, the guy said he looked like it."

*What will be your approach now?*
Turn to page 1.

You have decided to keep calling Joe's home at regular intervals during the day.

Late that afternoon, the same woman who phoned to say that Joe was ill answers the phone, still sounding strange. She says that Joe is not there. When you ask where Joe is, she begins crying. After a few minutes of this, Joe comes on the phone and asks who you are. When you tell him, he says, "I can't talk to you right now; goodbye," and hangs up the phone.

*Tuesday morning when Joe comes to work, how will you approach him?*

Turn to page 9.

You have asked Joe if he has really been ill. Joe says: "Now look, I know the contract! It provides for five weeks of paid absent time due to sickness, and I haven't used near that much!"

*What will be your general approach to Joe?*

A.  Explain to Joe that you can require proof of illness before sick leave is allowed—that you are in charge, and he should respect this fact.

    Turn to page 13.

B.  Tell him that his personal problems are his business, but that production is your business. Tell him he must "shape up or ship out."

    Turn to page 24.

C.  Say: "I didn't mean it that way, Joe, and I'm sorry you have been having so much trouble. But I'm concerned about how your absences have been affecting your work."

    Turn to page 28.

D.  Tell Joe he is fired.

    Turn to page 25.

E.  Transfer Joe at the first opportunity.

    Turn to page 34.

You have decided to ask Joe's previous supervisor about his experiences with Joe. He says:

"Joe Bailey? Why, I know Joe very well. I think a lot of him, too. He was one of my best employees, and I was sorry to see him go. If it hadn't been an upgrade for him, I would have tried to keep him.

"How is Joe doing, anyway? I hear he married a woman with two teenage kids. Boy, that's really getting a ready-made family."

*Turn back to page 1 to decide on your next step.*

You have decided to call Joe over to a more private place and ask him what is on his mind. He is reluctant to discuss it at first, then he blurts out:

"You know very well what's wrong. Everything seems to be screwed up! At first it was just at home, but now you're picking on me, too. It's enough to drive a man to drink! The least you could do would be to get off my back, and keep off!"

*How will you respond now?*

A. Remind him that you are the one in charge of the work group and of him, that you are just doing your duty, and that he should have more respect for this fact.

Turn to page 13.

B. Suggest that he go back to work and cool off and you will talk to him later.

Turn to page 19.

C. Warn him that if there are any more such comments from him, you will see that he is severely dealt with.

Turn to page 20.

D. Tell him you think it might help if the two of you discussed it. You don't wish to intrude, but you are concerned about his absences.

Turn to page 28.

E. Tell Joe he is fired for insubordination.

Turn to page 25.

F. Transfer Joe at the first opportunity.

Turn to page 34.

*In discussing Joe's absences, which general approach will you take with him?*

A. Explain to him the importance of good attendance to the production record of the work group. Point out to him what would happen if everyone were absent on Monday. Urge him to try to do better.

Turn to page 10.

B. Tell him that his personal problems are his business, but that production is your business. Tell him that he must "shape up or ship out."

Turn to page 24.

C. Wait until Joe brings up the matter of his absences, so as not to embarrass him.

Turn to page 16.

D. Ask him what difficulty he is having.

Turn to page 12.

E. Be friendly, but tell him that you are going to place a warning letter in his personnel folder stating that he must improve during the following month.

Turn to page 17.

F. Tell him that he is fired.
Turn to page 25.

Joe says, "I'll try to do better."

However, the following Monday he is absent again, and someone phones in to say that he is ill. She says she is Joe's wife. She sounds strange—as if she has been drinking.

*What will you do now?*

A. Telephone his home to verify his illness.
Turn to page 14.

B. Send some flowers to his home with a "get well soon" card.
Turn to page 27.

C. Ask others in the crew if they know what Joe's problem might be (if you have not done this before).
Turn to page 4.

D. Wait until Joe's return to deal with him.
Turn to page 26.

E. Contact a social worker to get some help with this problem.
Turn to page 40.

You have decided to discuss the problem with your supervisor before taking any further action. He says:

"No, I don't know Bailey, but I do know how far behind we are on our schedule! We just had a staff meeting on it, and brother, I don't want to go through another meeting like that one! It was embarrassing. So for Pete's sake, get some life into your people. It looks like we will have to schedule weekend overtime again, and that is really driving up costs. Go to it, and give it everything you've got!"

*Turn back to page 1 to decide on your next step.*

You have asked Joe what difficulty he is having. Joe says, "Well, it's rather personal, and I would rather not talk about it, if you don't mind."

*What general approach will you follow now?*

A. Tell Joe he is fired.

Turn to page 25.

B. Ask Joe if he has really been ill for the last three out of four Mondays.

Turn to page 6.

C. Tell him that his personal problems are his business, but that production is your business. Tell him that he must "shape up or ship out."

Turn to page 24.

D. Be friendly, but explain that you are going to place a warning letter in his personnel folder stating that he must improve during the following month.

Turn to page 17.

E. Say something like: "Joe, I don't want to butt in where I'm not wanted; but at the same time, you must see how your Monday absences are affecting your work. I'm concerned about this, and I know you are too."

Turn to page 28.

You have told Joe that you are in charge and that he should have more respect for this fact. Joe says: "Well, one thing I have respect for is myself! Too much respect to keep on with this outfit. I quit!"

Joe then heads for the exit with tears in his eyes.

*How do you feel at this point?*

A. That you might have handled the situation differently somewhere along the line? Would you like a chance to retrace your steps to see what could be done differently?

   If so, go back to page 9.

B. That you did what any supervisor would do to correct employees, keep them in line, and make sure they know who is the boss?

   If so, the exercise is over for you.

You telephone Joe's home to verify his illness. No one answers.

*Now will you:*

A.  Keep calling at regular intervals during the day?
    Turn to page 5.

B.  Ask a secretary to keep calling?
    Turn to page 21.

C.  Wait to handle it when Joe returns?
    Turn to page 26.

You have responded to Joe, "You have talked about it with your wife?"
Joe says: "Yes, but she is so wrapped up in her two kids that she won't listen. I knew I would have problems when I married her, but I didn't expect this."

*What general approach will you follow now?*

A. Say: "I'm glad you realize the seriousness of this, and I hope you can make her see it, too. Joe, I hope you will try to do better."
   Turn to page 10.

B. Say, "It's pretty tough being married to a woman with kids, I guess."
   Turn to page 33.

C. Say nothing, but continue to listen.
   Turn to page 18.

You decided to wait until Joe brought up the matter of his absence. He did not. However, he was present each day for the next two weeks; then he missed Monday and Tuesday of the following week, and he is absent today (Monday).

*When (and if) he comes in tomorrow, what approach will you take with him?*

Turn to page 9.

You have placed a warning letter in Joe's personnel folder telling him that he must improve during the following month.

Joe is absent the first two Mondays in the next month.

*At this point, what will you do?*

A. Warn Joe what will happen if he is absent again on either of the next two Mondays.

Turn to page 35.

B. Wait to see if Joe is absent during the remainder of the month.

Turn to page 37.

C. Transfer him at the first opportunity.

Turn to page 34.

D. Tell Joe that you don't wish to intrude on his personal problems, but you are concerned about how his absences continue to affect his work.

Turn to page 28.

E. Express to Joe your hope that he will be able to improve this month. Then, wait to see if he is absent during the remainder of the month.

Turn to page 37.

You have decided to say nothing, but to continue to listen. Joe continues:

"Martha, my wife, has a teenage daughter who has been married, but is breaking up, I guess. Also, Martha's boy, who is two years younger, is supposed to be living with us, but he has run away twice in the past two months. Everything seems to happen on weekends!

"First, the daughter comes home mad at her husband, then the husband follows and they have a scene. Sometimes they make up and go back to their house, and sometimes not.

"Then the boy takes off, and the police phone me to come and get him. Sunday night at midnight I had to drive to the next state to get him out of jail. I didn't get back till late last night.

"All of these things are very upsetting to Martha. In addition, her health hasn't been the best. The doctor has her on some sort of medication now. She has been so upset and ill on several Mondays that I have been afraid to leave her. But I know it is causing you problems on the job. I hope I can get it worked out soon."

*What will be your general approach?*

A. Explain to Joe that you understand what he is dealing with, and tell him that you suggest you wait two weeks to see how things look then.

Turn to page 22.

B. Tell him that his personal problems are his business, but that production is your business. Tell him that he must "shape up or ship out."

Turn to page 24.

C. Suggest that Joe take his problem to his family doctor or minister.

Turn to page 41.

D. Explain that you are going to place a warning letter in his personnel folder stating that he must improve during the following month.

Turn to page 17.

After the situation involving Joe and the other employees, things seem calm for the next several days, except for some loud laughter in Joe's area when you are not nearby.

*You must schedule overtime work for two-thirds of your work group on the following Saturday and Sunday. Will you:*

A. Exclude Joe from overtime work, but say nothing about it to him directly?

Turn to page 30.

B. Exclude Joe from overtime work, but tell him if he "shapes up" he will be included in the future?

Turn to page 32.

C. Tell Joe that you are scheduling him for overtime, but ask him to pitch in and be on your team to get the production out, and stress the importance of every employee doing his part?

Turn to page 10.

D. Call Joe in and explain that you have wondered what to do to help him improve his attendance because it is affecting his work, and you don't want to schedule him for overtime if this will complicate the problem he is having?

Turn to page 28.

You have warned Joe that if he makes any more such comments, he will be severely dealt with. Joe says: "That's what I mean by everybody being on my back. Well, I don't have to take it from you! I quit!"

Joe then heads for the exit with tears in his eyes.

*At this point, how do you feel?*

A. That you might have handled the situation differently somewhere along the line? Would you like a chance to retrace your steps to see what could be done differently?

   If so, go back to page 9.

B. That you did what any supervisor would do to correct employees, keep them in line, and make sure they know who is the boss?

   If so the exercise is over for you.

You have asked a secretary to keep calling Joe's home. At 3:00 p.m., she phones to say that there has been no answer.

*When Joe returns on Tuesday morning, what will be your approach to him?*

Turn to page 9 and select an approach.

Now that Joe has explained the problems causing his Monday absences, let's think about the situation.

Although taking six action choices was the best performance possible in this exercise, and the best path record was 1, 9, 12, 28, 18, and 22, there is no clear-cut answer to the problem given here—nor is there, usually, in real life. A leader is constantly dealing with people—subordinates, fellow supervisors, bosses—regarding problems such as these. The leader's attitude and approach to taking action will often determine how problems are resolved and will often have a great impact on both employee morale and performance.

Joe Bailey's problem raises some interesting questions:

1. Is it easier to handle an employee's problem once you know what it is?

2. Do you feel that a company should be understanding toward employees when they have personal problems?

3. Does merely talking about a problem sometimes help?

4. Are you familiar with where (in your company or community) an employee could be referred for help with personal, health, and social problems?

**End of Joe Bailey Problem**

The union steward says: "Well, Joe's story sounded pretty wild to me. Why don't you talk it over with him, and let's see how it comes out. I see no reason to be there."

*Turn to page 8 for your talk with Joe.*

After your comment to Joe, he doesn't say anything, but goes directly to work.

That afternoon, one of the employees tells you that Joe has been telling everyone how unfairly you have treated him. Later the same afternoon as you pass Joe, you catch a glimpse of a gesture he makes behind your back. Three other employees on your crew laugh. When you turn around, Joe is back at work.

*What will you do?*

A. Do nothing; continue on your rounds, but keep your eye on Joe.
   Turn to page 19.

B. Ask the employees who laughed to tell you what they saw.
   Turn to page 3.

C. Warn Joe that he had better stick to work and forget about making comments and gestures toward you. Then, continue walking.
   Turn to page 19.

D. Call Joe over to a more private place and ask him what is on his mind.
   Turn to page 8.

E. Tell Joe that he is fired.
   Turn to page 25.

You have fired Joe.

Do you feel that, not having given Joe any previous warning, you can make this stick? Chances are you can't. But at any rate, here are some questions for you.

1. Would firing Joe cause any problems with others in the work group?

2. Were you responsive to Joe's feelings?

3. Is there nothing more to know about Joe?

If you answered yes to any of these questions, you may be admitting that you have something to learn about supervising people. If so, turn to the previous page and take another choice.

If you answered no to all three questions, there is evidently no doubt in your mind that the way you operate is the correct way. This exercise can teach you no more.

*You are finished with the exercise.*

You have decided to wait until Joe's return to deal with him.
Turn to page 9 and select your approach to Joe when he returns.

You have decided to send some flowers to Joe's home with a "get well soon" card.

Tuesday, when Joe returns, he does not mention the flowers.

*What will be your approach to Joe now?*

Turn to page 9 and select your next step.

You have told Joe that you didn't want to intrude, but you wanted to express your concern over how his absences were affecting his work. Joe says: "I know you are concerned, and I have been, too. I'm sorry it's happening, but I just can't help it. I've told my wife that I might lose my job if it keeps up."

*What general approach will you follow now?*

A. Say: "I'm glad you realize the seriousness of this, and I hope you can make your wife see it, too. Joe, I know you will try to do better."

Turn to page 10.

B. Say, "You have talked about it with your wife?"

Turn to page 15.

C. Say nothing, but continue to listen.

Turn to page 18.

D. Impress Joe with the seriousness of his behavior and warn him that he must improve or take the consequences.

Turn to page 35.

You have removed the warning letter from Joe's file and told him that you hope he will keep up the good record he has started.

Joe may or may not be absent on future Mondays — if he is, then that is another problem.

Did you ever wonder exactly what Joe's problem was? Other paths led to his telling his story. Perhaps you would like to hear him describe it, too.

If so, turn to page 18. Then, turn to page 22 and consider the questions there.

You have decided to exclude Joe from overtime work, and say nothing to him directly, but inform the other employees that you wish them to work.

Turn to page 36.

Since Joe has been present each Monday for the remainder of the month, you have told him to "keep up the good work." Joe says, "I'm certainly trying."

Joe is in attendance for the next three weeks, including the overtime work you assigned.

*At the end of this time, what will you do?*

A. Do nothing.

   Turn to page 39.

B. Tell Joe that you are removing the letter from his file and express the hope that he will be able to keep up the good record he has started.

   Turn to page 29.

You have decided to exclude Joe from overtime work next weekend but tell him that if he "shapes up," he will be included in the future. Joe says nothing, but goes back to work.

Turn to page 36.

Exercise page 33

You have remarked to Joe how tough it must be to be married to a woman with kids. Joe says, "Boy, I'll say!" and clams up.

*What general approach will you follow now?*

A. Say: "I'm glad you realize the seriousness of this, and I hope you can make your wife see it, too. Joe, I hope you will try to do better."
Turn to page 10.

B. Say nothing, but continue to listen.
Turn to page 18.

*Morale,* Applications • The Joe Bailey Problem      279

You have transferred Joe at the first opportunity, and that eliminated your problem. But what about the company you work for? Did you really fulfill your responsibility as a supervisor?

*Return to your previous page and make another decision.*

You reminded Joe what would happen if he was absent again on Monday. Joe was there the next Monday.

On the following Monday, you notice Joe at lunch sitting by himself, looking flushed and ill. When you ask him what the trouble is, Joe says he feels quite sick. You advise him to see his family doctor and then go home. You receive word that Joe had a fever of 103 degrees and was dangerously ill with influenza.

Joe reportedly told the nurse that he was afraid you would have him fired if he had stayed home ill. Joe is absent for six days.

*When Joe returns, how will you approach him?*

A. Tell him that despite his illness, the warning letter is still in effect because of his Monday absences, and he must improve.

   Turn to page 24.

B. Tell him that you are "wiping the slate clean" and hope he has no more trouble in the future.

   Turn to page 10.

C. Say that you are sorry he was ill and that you don't want to intrude, but ask him if the difficulty he was having with the Monday absences seems to be cleared up.

   Turn to page 28.

D. Say nothing to Joe.

   Turn to page 36.

That afternoon, the union steward tells you that Joe has brought a grievance against you and that he charges you with persecuting him.

*Will you:*

A. Tell the steward that the charges are ridiculous and dare him to put them in writing suitable to go up the line and into arbitration?

Turn to page 38.

B. Tell the steward the situation, say that you wish to talk to Joe about it, and tell the steward that he also can be present if he and Joe wish?

Turn to page 23.

You have waited to see if Joe is absent during the remainder of the month. He is not.

*At this point, what action will you take?*

A. Do nothing.
   Turn to page 39.

B. Tell Joe to keep up the good work.
   Turn to page 31.

C. Tell Joe that you are removing the letter from his file and express the hope that he will be able to keep up the good record he has started.
   Turn to page 29.

You have dared the steward to put the charges into writing. The next day he comes in with a lengthy statement of charges containing not only Joe's remarks, but testimony from quite a few others in your work group. After a few minutes, you clearly see that nothing is to be gained by discussing the statement, so you sign it and kick it upstairs.

So there it is. You may win the final arbitration on the basis of Joe's absenteeism, but it will be a long road between here and there, and it certainly won't help your relations with your employees. And you must still deal with Joe.

*At this point, how do you feel?*

A. That you might have handled the situation differently? Would you like a chance to retrace your steps to see what could be done differently?

If so, go back to page 9.

B. That you did what any supervisor would do to correct employees, keep them in line, and make sure they know who is the boss?

If so, the exercise is over for you.

You have decided to do nothing if Joe is not absent during the remainder of the month.

Why not? Joe seems to be trying to do what you wish him to. One principle of developing subordinates it to recognize and thus reinforce good behavior.

Turn back to your previous page and reward Joe.

You have contacted a social worker to get some help with Joe's problem. The social worker is unable to help because you are unable to explain what the problem is. You have also received a bill for $50.00 for the social worker's services.

You then decide to discuss the matter with Joe.

Turn to page 9 and select your approach.

You have suggested that Joe take his problem to his family doctor or minister. Joe says, "Well, we are not really churchgoers, and we don't have a regular doctor."

Turn back to page 18 and select another route.

At no place in this exercise were you instructed to turn to this page. Return to your previous page to get back on the track.

# Organizational Norms Questionnaire

## Introduction

Norms of behavior influence employee morale and productivity in every organization. Norms can be supportive or harmful to the organization. This questionnaire identifies norms of behavior in ten important categories:

1. organizational/personal pride;
2. performance/excellence;
3. teamwork/communication;
4. leadership/supervision;
5. profitability/cost effectiveness;
6. colleague/associate relations;
7. customer/client relations;
8. innovativeness/creativity;
9. training/development;
10. candor/openness.

## Directions

You are asked to predict what most employees in your organization would think or do if another employee behaved in a particular manner. For example, the first item reads:

> If an employee in your organization were to criticize the organization and the people in it . . . most other employees would:

To complete this statement, choose one of the following alternatives:

A. strongly agree with or encourage it;

B. agree with or encourage it;

C. have or express no opinion;

*Source: Reprinted from John E. Jones and J. William Pfeiffer (eds.),* The 1977 Annual Handbook for Group Facilitators *(San Diego, Calif.: University Associates, Inc., 1977). Used with permission.*

D. disagree with or discourage it;

E. strongly disagree with or discourage it.

Choose the alternative that you think would be the most common response of most employees, and place the corresponding letter in the blank space following each item. Complete all 42 statements in the same manner.

**If an Employee in Your Organization Were to:**

**Most Other Employees Would:**

1. Criticize the organization and the people in it . . . _____

2. Try to improve things, even though the operation is running smoothly . . . _____

3. Listen to others and try to get their opinions . . . _____

4. Think of going to a supervisor with a problem . . . _____

5. Look on himself or herself as being responsible for reducing costs . . . _____

6. Take advantage of another employee . . . _____

7. Keep a customer or client waiting in order to look after matters of personal convenience . . . _____

8. Suggest a new idea or approach for doing things . . . _____

9. Actively look for ways to expand his or her knowledge in order to be able to do a better job . . . _____

10. Talk freely and openly about the organization and its problems . . . _____

11. Show genuine concern for the problems that face the organization and make suggestions for solving them . . . _____

12. Suggest that employees should do only enough to get by . . . _____

13. Go out of his or her way to help other members of the work group . . . _____

14. Look on the supervisor as a source of help and development . . . _____

15. Purposely misuse equipment or privileges . . . _____

16. Express concern for the well-being of other members of the organization . . . _____

17. Attempt to find new and better ways to serve the customer or client . . . _____

18. Attempt an experiment in order to do things better . . . _____

19. Show enthusiasm for going to an organization-sponsored training and development program . . . _____

20. Suggest confronting the boss about a mistake or something in the boss's style that is creating problems . . . _____

21. Look on the job as being merely a paycheck . . . _____

22. Say that there is no point in trying harder, as no one else does . . . _____

23. Work alone, rather than work with others to try to get things done . . . _____

24. Look on the supervisor as someone to talk with openly and freely . . . _____

25. Look on making a profit as someone else's problem . . . _____

26. Make an effort to get to know co-workers . . . _____

27. See the customer or client as a burden or obstruction to getting the job done . . . _____

28. Criticize another employee who is trying to improve things . . . _____

29. Mention that she or he is planning to attend a recently announced organization-sponsored training program . . . _____

30. Talk openly about problems facing the work group, including personalities or interpersonal problems . . . _____

31. Talk about work with satisfaction . . . _____

32. Set very high personal standards of performance . . . _____

33. Try to make the work group operate more as a team . . . _____

34. Look on the supervisor as the one who sets the goals and standards of performance for the work group . . . _____

35. Evaluate expenditures in terms of the benefits they will provide for the organization . . . _____

36. Always try to treat the customer or client as well as possible . . . _____

37. Think of going to the boss with an idea or suggestion . . . _____

38. Go to the boss to talk about what training one should have in order to do a better job . . . _____

39. Be perfectly honest in answering this questionnaire . . . _____

40. Work harder than what is considered to be the normal pace . . . _____

41. Look after oneself before the other members of the work group . . . _____

42. Do his or her job even when the supervisor is not around . . . _____

## Scoring

On the ten scales below, circle the value that corresponds to the response you gave for each item on the Organizational Norms Questionnaire. Total your scores for each of the ten categories, and follow the mathematical formulas. The results are your final percentage scores.

### I. Organizational/Personal Pride

| Item | Response | | | | |
|---|---|---|---|---|---|
| | A | B | C | D | E |
| 1 | −2 | −1 | 0 | +1 | +2 |
| 11 | +2 | +1 | 0 | −1 | −2 |
| 21 | −2 | −1 | 0 | +1 | +2 |
| 31 | +2 | +1 | 0 | −1 | −2 |

Total Score _____ ÷ 8 × 100 = _____ Final % Score

## II. Performance/Excellence

| Item | Response | | | | |
|------|------|------|------|------|------|
| | A | B | C | D | E |
| 2 | +2 | +1 | 0 | −1 | −2 |
| 12 | −2 | −1 | 0 | +1 | +2 |
| 22 | −2 | −1 | 0 | +1 | +2 |
| 32 | +2 | +1 | 0 | −1 | −2 |
| 40 | +2 | +1 | 0 | −1 | −2 |

Total Score _____ ÷ 10 × 100 = _____ Final % Score

## III. Teamwork/Communication

| Item | Response | | | | |
|------|------|------|------|------|------|
| | A | B | C | D | E |
| 3 | +2 | +1 | 0 | −1 | −2 |
| 13 | +2 | +1 | 0 | −1 | −2 |
| 23 | −2 | −1 | 0 | +1 | +2 |
| 33 | +2 | +1 | 0 | −1 | −2 |
| 41 | −2 | −1 | 0 | +1 | +2 |

Total Score _____ ÷ 10 × 100 = _____ Final % Score

## IV. Leadership/Supervision

| Item | Response | | | | |
|------|------|------|------|------|------|
| | A | B | C | D | E |
| 4 | +2 | +1 | 0 | −1 | −2 |
| 14 | +2 | +1 | 0 | −1 | −2 |
| 24 | +2 | +1 | 0 | −1 | −2 |
| 34 | +2 | +1 | 0 | −1 | −2 |
| 42 | +2 | +1 | 0 | −1 | −2 |

Total Score _____ ÷ 10 × 100 = _____ Final % Score

## V. Profitability/Cost Effectiveness

| Item | Response | | | | |
|------|------|------|------|------|------|
| | A | B | C | D | E |
| 5 | +2 | +1 | 0 | −1 | −2 |
| 15 | −2 | −1 | 0 | +1 | +2 |
| 25 | −2 | −1 | 0 | +1 | +2 |
| 35 | +2 | +1 | 0 | −1 | −2 |

Total Score _____ ÷ 8 × 100 = _____ Final % Score

## VI. Colleague/Associate Relations

| Item | Response | | | | |
|------|------|------|------|------|------|
| | A | B | C | D | E |
| 6 | −2 | −1 | 0 | +1 | +2 |
| 16 | +2 | +1 | 0 | −1 | −2 |
| 26 | +2 | +1 | 0 | −1 | −2 |

Total Score _____ ÷ 6 × 100 = _____ Final % Score

## VII. Customer/Client Relations

| Item | Response | | | | |
|------|------|------|------|------|------|
| | A | B | C | D | E |
| 7 | −2 | −1 | 0 | +1 | +2 |
| 17 | +2 | +1 | 0 | −1 | −2 |
| 27 | −2 | −1 | 0 | +1 | +2 |
| 36 | +2 | +1 | 0 | −1 | −2 |

Total Score _____ ÷ 8 × 100 = _____ Final % Score

## VIII. Innovativeness/Creativity

| Item | Response | | | | |
|------|------|------|------|------|------|
| | A | B | C | D | E |
| 8 | +2 | +1 | 0 | −1 | −2 |
| 18 | +2 | +1 | 0 | −1 | −2 |
| 28 | −2 | −1 | 0 | +1 | +2 |
| 37 | +2 | +1 | 0 | −1 | −2 |

Total Score _____ ÷ 8 × 100 = _____ Final % Score

## IX. Training/Development

| Item | Response | | | | |
|------|------|------|------|------|------|
| | A | B | C | D | E |
| 9 | +2 | +1 | 0 | −1 | −2 |
| 19 | +2 | +1 | 0 | −1 | −2 |
| 29 | +2 | +1 | 0 | −1 | −2 |
| 38 | +2 | +1 | 0 | −1 | −2 |

Total Score _____ ÷ 8 × 100 = _____ Final % Score

## X.   Candor/Openness

| Item | | | Response | | |
|------|------|------|------|------|------|
| | **A** | **B** | **C** | **D** | **E** |
| 10 | +2 | +1 | 0 | −1 | −2 |
| 20 | +2 | +1 | 0 | −1 | −2 |
| 30 | +2 | +1 | 0 | −1 | −2 |
| 39 | +2 | +1 | 0 | −1 | −2 |

Total Score _____ ÷ 8 × 100 = _____ Final % Score

## Instructions

For each of the ten categories, enter your final percentage score from the score sheet, and then plot that percentage by placing an X on the following graph at the appropriate point. (Negative percentages are plotted to the left of the center line; positive percentages are plotted to the right.) Next, connect the X's you have plotted with straight lines. The result is a profile of organizational norms (see page 296).

## Interpretation

The higher the percentage for each category on the Organizational Norms Questionnaire, the more effective the organization is and the more satisfied employees would be expected to be. The following is a description of each category:

I.    *Organizational/personal pride.* High scores in this area represent a concern for the health of the organization, its vitality, and its success. The work itself is rewarding, and problems are looked on as challenges rather than as causes for apathy or defeat.

II.   *Performance/excellence.* Favorable ratings in this area represent striving for personal and organizational excellence. High standards of performance are the norm.

III.  *Teamwork/communication.* Organizations in which members share information and help one another usually experience high morale and productivity, while organizations with restricted communications and less cohesive groups typically experience failure.

IV.   *Leadership/supervision.* Leadership refers to technical skill, consideration of employee problems, and strength of character. Without effective leadership, a group or organization will not be successful.

V.    *Profitability/cost effectiveness.* Employees must be aware of economic factors relating to organizational success. A lack of concern for company property and expenses often indicates poor morale.

## Profile of Organizational Norms

| Categories | Final score | Graph |
|---|---|---|
| | | −100%   −50%   0%   +50%   +100% |
| I. Organizational/ personal pride | | |
| II. Performance/ excellence | | |
| III. Teamwork/ communication | | |
| IV. Leadership/ supervision | | |
| V. Profitability/ cost effectiveness | | |
| VI. Colleague/ associate relations | | |
| VII. Customer/ client relations | | |
| VIII. Innovativeness/ creativity | | |
| IX. Training/ development | | |
| X. Candor/openness | | |
| | | Negative          Positive |

VI.  *Colleague/associate relations.* People need social interaction and a sense of belonging. Unless conditions in the organization satisfy these needs, reduced commitment and poor job performance can result.

VII.  *Customer/client relations.* The behavior of each representative of the organization reflects on the integrity and professionalism of the entire organization. A poor attitude or misconduct by one employee may result in a poor reputation for all employees.

VIII. *Innovativeness/creativity*. Employees who exercise creativity show interest in their work. The distinction should be made between a grumpy complainer and an employee who is trying to develop better methods for the benefit of the organization.

IX. *Training/development*. Training and development for all levels and classifications of employees is important for organizational effectiveness and employee satisfaction. Training builds skills, relationships, and commitment.

X. *Candor/openness*. A high score in this area represents honest and free-flowing communications. Such openness is necessary if an organization is to accomplish its performance objectives as well as meet the social and psychological needs of its employees.

The Organizational Norms Questionnaire can be used for team building and organizational development. For team building, group profiles can be developed to diagnose problems and make improvements. For organizational development, a profile can be developed showing the overall strengths and weaknesses of the organization in the ten categories. This profile can be used as a basis for maintaining or improving overall effectiveness. Consider the following figure for a historical and humorous appreciation of the importance of organizational effectiveness (see page 298).

## The Importance of Organizational Effectiveness

*Disorganization—* Perhaps the earliest recognition of the importance of organizational effectiveness is found in the Bible. The Book of Exodus, Chapter 18, tells how "Moses sat to judge the people: and the people stood by Moses from the morning unto the evening." Moses' father-in-law, Jethro, saw this and told him: "The thing thou doest is not good. Thou wilt surely wear away, both thou, and this people that is with thee: for the thing is too heavy for thee; thou art not able to perform it alone." At that time the Israeli organization chart was as follows:

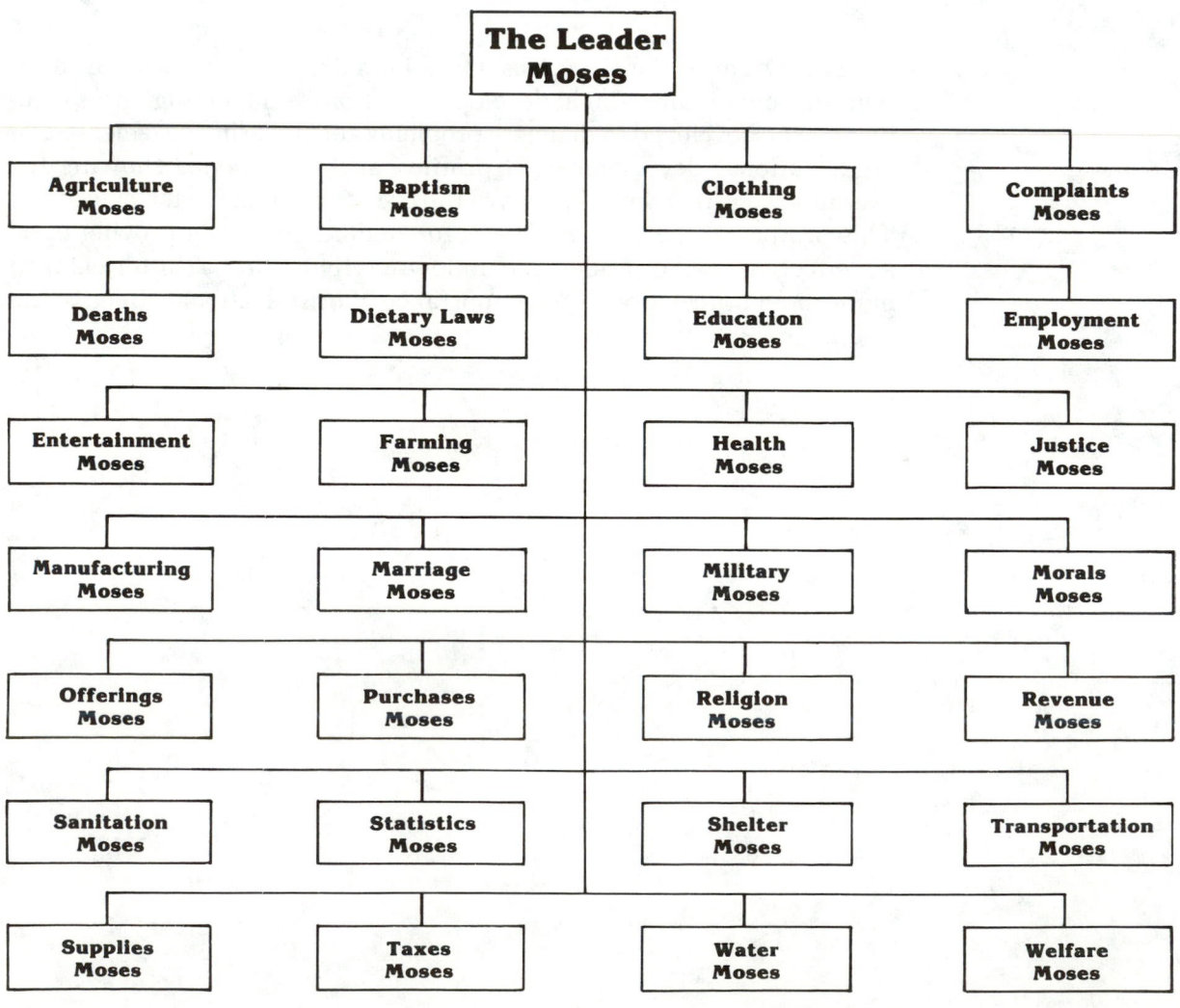

*Organization*—The subordinate rulers, Jethro advised, could judge "every small matter" and bring the great matters to Moses. Up to this point, the Israelites had spent 39 years on a journey that had taken them only about halfway to the Promised Land. After the reorganization took place, the remaining half of the journey was completed in less than a year. The new organization chart looked like this:

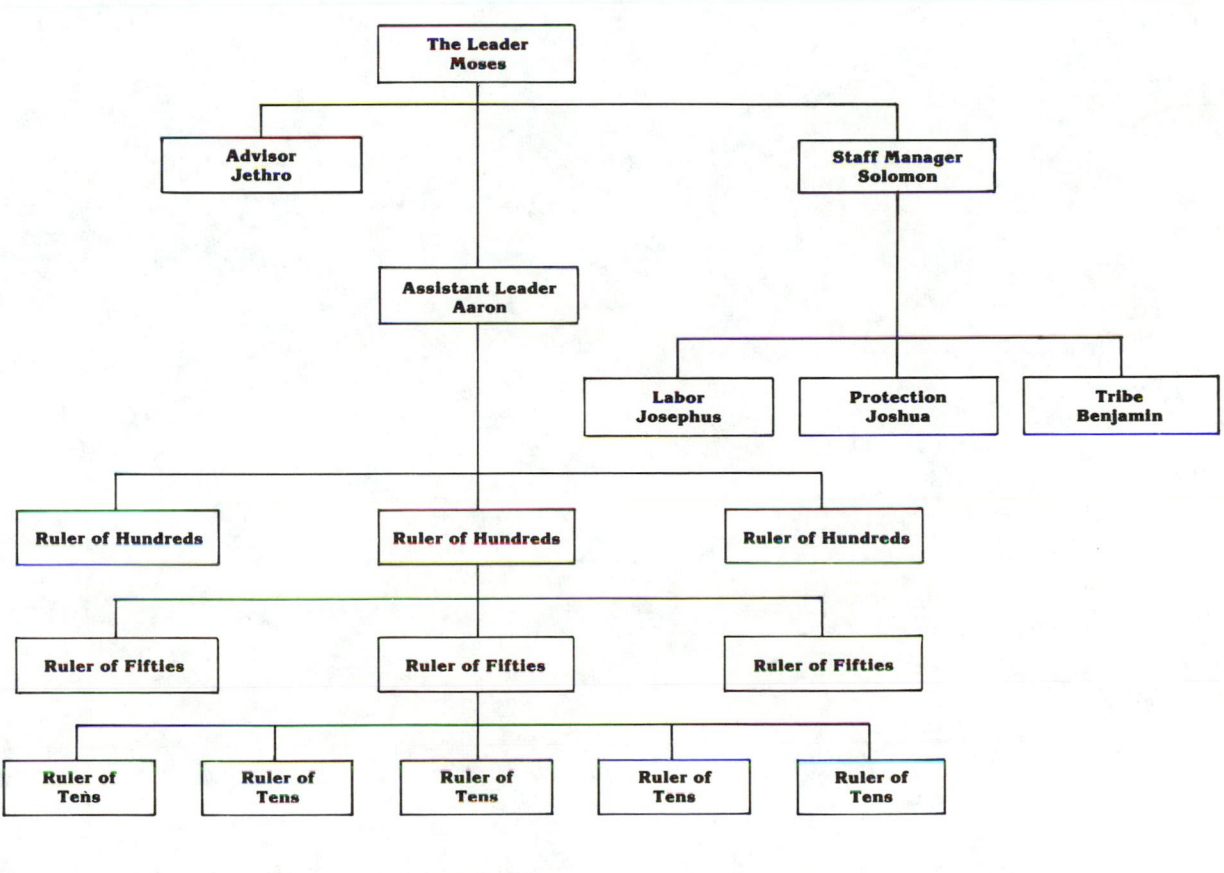

*Source:* *Ernest Dale*, Management: Theory and Practice, *3d ed. (New York:* McGraw-Hill, Inc.). *Copyright © 1973; reprinted with permission.*

# Management Effectiveness Audit

## Introduction

Figure 1 on page 302 shows the five normal phases of an organization's life. Each phase includes a period of evolution, when growth takes place, and a period of revolution, when crisis threatens the continued development and possibly the existence of the organization.

The following is a description of the typical periods of growth and crisis for each of the five phases:

- *Phase 1: Creativity.* In its earliest stage, an organization's activities are usually centered around the development of products and markets. Top management's energy is devoted to these ends rather than to overall management of the operation. Communication between managers and subordinates is frequent and informal. Organization members may work long hours for low pay in anticipation of future benefits. Growth through creativity characterizes this stage.

  As the company grows through this stage, it becomes increasingly difficult to handle the rapidly swelling staff by old, informal methods. Leaders become more and more overworked and harried by administrative details. A crisis in leadership leads to the first revolution. Founders, frequently incapable of or unwilling to change managerial styles, may have to step aside in favor of managers who can focus the organization's activities.

- *Phase 2: Direction.* Under strong and capable organizers, a period of sustained growth may be anticipated. A functional structure is introduced, separating production from marketing and leading to more specialization. Accounting systems, incentives, budgets, and work standards are adopted. Communications become more formal as management becomes more divided between upper level policy makers and lower level functional specialists. This stage is one of growth through direction.

*Source:* *James A. F. Stoner,* Management, *copyright © 1978, pp. 336–38.*
*Reprinted by permission of Prentice-Hall, Englewood Cliffs, New Jersey.*

## FIGURE 1

Five Phases of Organizational
Development

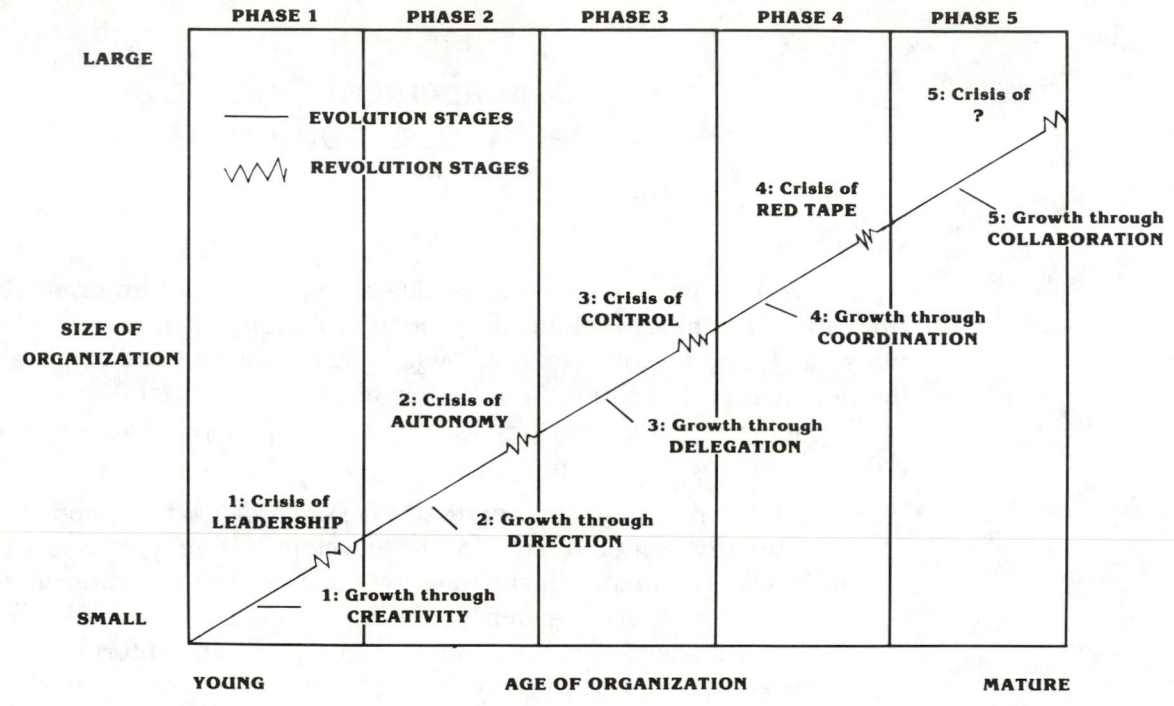

Lower level managers, however, become increasingly frustrated and demand more autonomy and room to exercise their own initiative. With upper level managers reluctant to give up authority, a new revolutionary period is at hand — the crisis of autonomy.

• *Phase 3: Delegation.* The successful company will install an effective decentralization program in answer to the crisis of autonomy in Phase 2. Greater responsibility is given to lower level managers. Top executives stay out of day-to-day operations, often concentrating on acquiring new units for the organization. Communication from the top is less frequent. This period is called growth through delegation.

Decentralized managers are able to penetrate new markets, respond faster to customers, and develop new products. Eventually, however, top managers may attempt to return to a centralized structure because of a sense of loss of control. This attempt brings on the Phase 3 revolution, the crisis of control. The company must find a new solution to coordination problems.

- *Phase 4: Coordination.* The evolutionary period in Phase 4 is characterized by the installation of formal systems for achieving coordination under the initiation and administration of top management. Decentralized units may be merged into product groups, each of which is expected to show satisfactory return on invested capital. Central staff personnel are added to initiate, control, and review programs for line managers.

  These changes encourage more efficient use of company resources, and field managers learn to justify their actions more carefully to headquarters. Tension gradually builds, however, between line and staff and between headquarters and the field. In addition, a red-tape crisis develops as rules and regulations begin to interfere with problem-solving activities.

- *Phase 5: Collaboration.* In response to Phase 4 problems, a more flexible and behavioral approach to management becomes necessary. Groups and interdivisional teams are created to perform tasks and solve problems. Headquarters' staff is reduced, and the remaining staff experts join field teams as consultants. Managers are trained in behavioral skills so that they can improve employee performance. The successful organization experiences growth through collaboration during this period. Many companies today are in this stage of evolution. What the next revolutionary phase will bring is speculative.

  Revolution may center around the psychological saturation of employees who become emotionally and physically exhausted by the intensity of teamwork and the heavy pressure for innovative solutions. There may also be pressure for labor representation on management boards, as already exists in many European countries.

At each phase of an organization's development, effective management can resolve crises and maximize growth. Use the questionnaire on pages 304-310 to evaluate the management effectiveness of your organization. After you have completed the questionaire, return to the following section for scoring and interpretation.

# MANAGEMENT EFFECTIVENESS AUDIT

## Directions

Complete this questionnaire to evaluate the management processes—planning, organizing, leading, and controlling—as they are generally practiced in your organization. In rating each item, circle the number on the scale that represents your evaluation (1 through 5, with 5 representing the highest rating). Each item should be rated independently without looking back to previous ratings. When you are unable to rate an item, indicate why in the space provided under "Unable to Rate." When you have a comment or recommendation regarding an item, write this in the space provided under "Comments or Recommendations."

### *Planning*

| | | Rating Scale | | Unable to Rate (Explain Why) | Comments or Recommendations |
|---|---|---|---|---|---|
| 1. Who participates in formulating plans for the organization? | Plans formed by few at the top | 1  2  3  4  5 | Broad participation in developing plans | _____ | _____ |
| | | | | | _____ |
| 2. Are plans clear and easy to understand? | Confusing, conflicting | 1  2  3  4  5 | Clear, exact | _____ | _____ |
| | | | | | _____ |
| 3. Are plans valued and shared by all responsible for their accomplishment? | Indifferent, little interest | 1  2  3  4  5 | Involvement, identification | _____ | _____ |
| | | | | | _____ |

4. Are plans reasonable in light of available physical facilities, supplies, and equipment?

| | Not reasonable | 1 | 2 | 3 | 4 | 5 | Fully reasonable | _____ | _____ |
|---|---|---|---|---|---|---|---|---|---|
| | | | | | | | | | _____ |

5. Are plans realistic in consideration of the number and training of employees?

| | Not realistic | 1 | 2 | 3 | 4 | 5 | Very realistic | _____ | _____ |
|---|---|---|---|---|---|---|---|---|---|
| | | | | | | | | | _____ |

6. Are plans based on appropriate market or target-service group forecasting?

| | Not appropriate | 1 | 2 | 3 | 4 | 5 | Very appropriate | _____ | _____ |
|---|---|---|---|---|---|---|---|---|---|
| | | | | | | | | | _____ |

7. Are policies formulated to serve as guidelines in accomplishment of plans?

| | No policy formation | 1 | 2 | 3 | 4 | 5 | Policies well defined | _____ | _____ |
|---|---|---|---|---|---|---|---|---|---|
| | | | | | | | | | _____ |

8. Are operating procedures developed so that plans can be attained?

| | Poorly developed, inappropriate | 1 | 2 | 3 | 4 | 5 | Effective for implementation | _____ | _____ |
|---|---|---|---|---|---|---|---|---|---|
| | | | | | | | | | _____ |

9. Are performance standards specified, including time limits, quantities, and qualities?

| | Standards indefinite, not defined | 1 | 2 | 3 | 4 | 5 | Performance standards determined | _____ | _____ |
|---|---|---|---|---|---|---|---|---|---|
| | | | | | | | | | _____ |

| | Rating Scale | Unable to Rate (Explain Why) | Comments or Recommendations |
|---|---|---|---|
| **10.** Are responsibilities divided among individuals and groups in such a way as to assure the most effective attainment of the organization's goals? | There are either overlaps or gaps in responsibilities  1 2 3 4 5  There are neither overlaps nor gaps in responsibilities | _____ | _____ |
| **11.** Are communications open, accurate, and timely between individuals and work groups? | Lacking, insincere  1 2 3 4 5  Open, authentic | _____ | _____ |
| **12.** Do employees trust each other? | Everyone for themselves  1 2 3 4 5  Genuine teamwork | _____ | _____ |
| **13.** Do employees respect each other? | Serious lack of respect  1 2 3 4 5  High respect | _____ | _____ |
| **14.** Is either consideration of people's feelings or doing a job according to procedures overemphasized? | Overemphasis of one or the other harms morale and productivity  1 2 3 4 5  There is a balance between consideration of people's feelings and managing according to plans and procedures | _____ | _____ |

# Directing

| | | Rating Scale | | Unable to Rate (Explain Why) | Comments or Recommendations |
|---|---|---|---|---|---|
| **15.** Are subordinates expected to respect leaders, even when actions do not merit respect? | Respect demanded, even when not earned | 1   2   3   4   5 | Respect expected only when earned | _____ | _____ _____ |
| **16.** Are subordinates free to work at their own pace and style as long as the job is accomplished? | No room for creativity; conforming behavior required | 1   2   3   4   5 | Individualized approach to work; respect for differences | _____ | _____ _____ |
| **17.** Do leaders give subordinates approval and praise for work, thus reinforcing performance? | Approval or praise never occurs | 1   2   3   4   5 | Approval and praise are common | _____ | _____ _____ |
| **18.** Do leaders keep subordinates informed on a regular basis? | Followers not kept up to date on plans or activities | 1   2   3   4   5 | Every effort made by leaders to keep followers up to date on what is happening | _____ | _____ _____ |

| | | Rating Scale | | Unable to Rate (Explain Why) | Comments or Recommendations |
|---|---|---|---|---|---|
| 19. Is competition between individuals and work groups encouraged to such an extent that cooperation suffers? | Competition weakens cooperation between members | 1  2  3  4  5 | Cooperation is emphasized and competition is used where appropriate | _____ | _____ _____ |
| 20. How free do subordinates feel to talk with leaders? | Reluctant; poor communications | 1  2  3  4  5 | Fully free to talk with leaders | _____ | _____ _____ |
| 21. Are employees' ideas sought, given full consideration, and used if worthy? | Leaders disregard employees' ideas | 1  2  3  4  5 | Leaders value employees' ideas | _____ | _____ _____ |
| 22. How much cooperation exists between followers and leaders? | Cooperation is nonexistent | 1  2  3  4  5 | Strong spirit of teamwork exists between leaders and followers | _____ | _____ _____ |
| 23. How concerned are leaders with problems faced by subordinates? | Leaders are not concerned with employees' problems | 1  2  3  4  5 | Leaders are genuinely concerned with employees' problems | _____ | _____ _____ |
| 24. How tolerant are leaders toward different types of subordinates? | Restrictive; pressure for conformity | 1  2  3  4  5 | Free; respect for differences | _____ | _____ _____ |

# Controlling

|  | | Rating Scale | | Unable to Rate (Explain Why) | Comments or Recommendations |
|---|---|---|---|---|---|
| 25. Are there workable procedures for evaluating performance? | No workable procedures | 1 2 3 4 5 | Very workable procedures | _____ | _____ |
|  | | | | | _____ |
| 26. Is control emphasized to such an extent that personal initiative is discouraged? | Control is over-emphasized, discouraging personal initiative | 1 2 3 4 5 | Controls are constructively used; no detraction from personal initiative | _____ | _____ |
|  | | | | | _____ |
| 27. Are corrective actions implemented when performance does not meet standards? | Corrective actions are not implemented appropriately | 1 2 3 4 5 | Corrective actions are implemented appropriately | _____ | _____ |
|  | | | | | _____ |
| 28. What are reporting, comparing, and corrective procedures used for? | Policing and punishment | 1 2 3 4 5 | Guidance and problem solving | _____ | _____ |
|  | | | | | _____ |

## Scoring and Interpretation

Total the scores received for each section of the Management Effectiveness Audit, and follow the formula below. The result is the percentage of managerial effectiveness for your organization.

### Planning

Total score _____ ÷ 45 × 100 = _____ % Effectiveness

### Organizing

Total score _____ ÷ 20 × 100 = _____ % Effectiveness

### Directing (Leadership)

Total score _____ ÷ 55 × 100 = _____ % Effectiveness

### Controlling

Total score _____ ÷ 20 × 100 = _____ % Effectiveness

The higher the percentage of effectiveness in all four management processes, the greater the success the organization can expect to experience during each phase of development — creativity, direction, delegation, coordination, and collaboration. Effective management practices attract and keep the best employees, and this results in the best quality of work and the best quality of work life.

# In Search of Excellence

The following questionnaire is based on the best-seller *In Search of Excellence: Lessons from America's Best-Run Companies* by Thomas J. Peters and Robert H. Waterman, Jr. This questionnaire is designed to evaluate an organization's current strengths and weaknesses. With this information, project teams, led by champions, can then create strategies and commitments to improve.

## IN SEARCH OF EXCELLENCE
### (Rating the Eight Attributes)

### Directions

Listed below are eight attributes and their characteristics common among excellent companies. Rate your organization on each characteristic using the following scale:

5 — This characteristic is *always* present.
4 — This characteristic is present *most of the time*.
3 — This characteristic is *sometimes* present.
2 — This characteristic is *rarely* present.
1 — This characteristic is *never* present.

Total the scores of the characteristics for each attribute. Then, divide by the number of characteristics under that particular attribute. This will give you an overall rating for each attribute.

#### I. Risk and Experimentation
#### (A Bias for Action)

1. _____ Concrete action is taken early.

2. _____ Prototypes are provided for customers; they can experiment.

3. _____ Risk taking is supported by a tolerance for failure (within limits, of course).

4. _____ Physical layout and tools, such as conference rooms, blackboards, and flip charts, invite interaction, impromptu problem solving, and "good-news-story swapping."

*Source:   Tim Baker and Teresa Waterman, Northern Kentucky University, 1984.*

5. _____ Resources are willingly shifted as required to get the job done.

6. _____ Small teams of volunteers solve problems or develop new products and then dissolve.

7. _____ A freewheeling informality prevails, and the "glue" is a common purpose.

8. _____ "One-page-only" memos, five-page new product proposals, and an aversion to planning documents and reports create an action-oriented environment.

_____ Total

_____ Divide the total by 8.

Mark your score on the scale below.

| 1 | 2 | 3 | 4 | 5 |
|---|---|---|---|---|
| 1.5 | 2.5 | 3.5 | 4.5 | |

There is *not* a bias toward action.

There *is* a bias toward action. (Things get done.)

## II. Customers Are Full Partners
### (Closeness to the Customer)

1. _____ Quality and service are the number one priority.

2. _____ Proposals are cost justifiable from the customer's standpoint.

3. _____ Salespeople and service representatives put themselves in the customer's shoes.

4. _____ "Satisfaction guaranteed" is the sales and service philosophy.

5. _____ Senior managers know and care about customers.

6. _____ Customers participate in experiments with prototypes.

7. _____ Inventions and improvement ideas come from the customer.

_____ Total

_____ Divide the total by 7.

Mark your score on the scale below.

| 1 | 2 | 3 | 4 | 5 |
|---|---|---|---|---|
| 1.5 | 2.5 | 3.5 | 4.5 | |

Customers receive little consideration.

Customers are treated as full partners.

### III. Innovation Through Entrepreneurship
### (Autonomy and Entrepreneurship)

1. _____ Self-initiated, self-directed experimentation is encouraged.

2. _____ The creative fanatic is tolerated.

3. _____ People who have the know-how, energy, daring, and staying power to implement ideas (the champions) are rewarded positively.

4. _____ Rewards and a share of success are provided.

5. _____ Support systems exist to get the job done.

6. _____ The burden of proof is transferred to those who want to prove that an idea will *not* work.

_____ Total

_____ Divide the total by 6.

Mark your score on the scale below.

| 1 | 2 | 3 | 4 | 5 |
|---|---|---|---|---|
| 1.5 | 2.5 | 3.5 | 4.5 | |

Innovation is
*not* encouraged.

Innovation *is* encouraged
within the organization.

### IV. Motivating People to Choose Productivity
### (Productivity Through People)

1. _____ Respect for the individual is the number one operating philosophy.

2. _____ There is a dedication to training people.

3. _____ Reasonable, clear expectations are established for each person.

4. _____ Lots of feedback and celebrating are done.

5. _____ There is a great deal of positive reinforcement.

6. _____ There is an everyday commitment to helping people become winners.

7. _____ People are treated as adults.

_____ Total

_____ Divide the total by 7.

Mark your score on the scale below.

| 1 | 2 | 3 | 4 | 5 |
|---|---|---|---|---|
| 1.5 | 2.5 | 3.5 | 4.5 | |

There is a lack of motivation within the
organization.

People are motivated to
be productive.

## V. Shaping a Powerful Value System
### (Hands-On, Value-Driven Approach)

1. \_\_\_\_\_ There is a simple, clear, compelling description of what the organization stands for.

2. \_\_\_\_\_ People do not have to change their value systems when they go home.

3. \_\_\_\_\_ Goals of the organization are not only financial.

4. \_\_\_\_\_ Leadership does not concentrate on sheer survival.

5. \_\_\_\_\_ Managers walk around and reinforce shared values "on the floor," "with the people."

6. \_\_\_\_\_ Leaders are masters of two ends of the spectrum — abstract visioning and mundane details.

\_\_\_\_\_ Total

\_\_\_\_\_ Divide the total by 6.

Mark your score on the scale below.

| 1 | | 2 | | 3 | | 4 | | 5 |
|---|---|---|---|---|---|---|---|---|
| | 1.5 | | 2.5 | | 3.5 | | 4.5 | |

A powerful value system to guide behavior is lacking.

A meaningful value system operates throughout the organization.

## VI. Staying in the Business You Know
### (Sticking to the Knitting)

1. \_\_\_\_\_ The majority of attention, energy, and resources is focused on the mainstream business.

2. \_\_\_\_\_ Cultures and value systems of new ventures and acquired organizations merge easily with those of the original organization.

3. \_\_\_\_\_ Credible management is provided for new ventures in an acquired business.

4. \_\_\_\_\_ Ventures into new businesses are set up as manageable experiments with a commitment to divest early if the signs of successful integration fail to materialize.

\_\_\_\_\_ Total

_____ Divide the total by 4.

Mark your score on the scale below.

| 1 | 2 | 3 | 4 | 5 |
|---|---|---|---|---|
| 1.5 | 2.5 | 3.5 | 4.5 | |

Mergers and acquisitions detract from the original business.

Mergers and acquisitions are handled well.

## VII. Structure Is Simple and Managers Manage
### (Simple Form, Lean Support Staff)

1. _____ Bureaucratic layers are minimal, with little red tape required to get things done.

2. _____ People are provided with a fairly stable organizational structure that makes sense and works for them.

3. _____ Flexibility is fostered by creating small subunits and by designating short-term task forces to address problems and develop innovations.

4. _____ Resources are focused on the action line. The organization is not top heavy.

5. _____ Power, energy, and decision making reside at the logical point of concern for a problem. Problem solving occurs at the lowest possible organizational level.

6. _____ Central office staff size is limited, and traditional head office functions are decentralized.

_____ Total

_____ Divide the total by 6.

Mark your score on the scale below.

| 1 | 2 | 3 | 4 | 5 |
|---|---|---|---|---|
| 1.5 | 2.5 | 3.5 | 4.5 | |

There is a complex structure, with line managers having little responsibility.

The basic structure is simple, and the driving force comes from line management.

## VIII. Liberating Talent Within Parameters
### (Simultaneous Loose-Tight Properties)

1. _____ Stable, well-defined expectations are provided from the top.

2. _____ A meaningful value system is promoted throughout the organization that inherently defines appropriate action.

3. _____ Employee involvement is allowed to function as a powerful productivity force.

4. _____ "Quality versus cost" and "efficiency versus effectiveness" arguments are denied in favor of liberating ordinary people to invent and produce the highest quality product every time.

_____ Total

_____ Divide the total by 4.

Mark your score on the scale below.

| 1 | 2 | 3 | 4 | 5 |
|---|---|---|---|---|
| 1.5 | 2.5 | 3.5 | 4.5 | |

Personal autonomy is low, and central direction is lacking. (People feel personally constrained; at the same time, they feel that there is no organizational direction.)

Firm, central direction coexists with maximum individual autonomy.

## INTERPRETATION

Add the average scores for each of the eight attributes:_____.

| If the Total Equals: | The Evaluation Is: |
|---|---|
| 32–40 | Excellent; outstanding. Conditions reflect those in America's best run companies. |
| 24–31 | Very good; solid. However, more work is needed to attain excellence. |
| 17–23 | Below par; unsatisfactory. Improvement is needed. |
| 8–16 | Poor; failing. Much work is needed to solve basic problems. |

Note that overall organizational effectiveness depends on excellence in each of the eight attributes. Low scores in any area represent flaws to be corrected in order to assure long-term success.

# APPENDIX A

## Background Information, Teaching Suggestions, and Testing and Grading

*The Human Side of Work* is a series of desk books for managers, handbooks for practitioners, and workbooks for students. These are applied books that combine behavior theory with business practice. Each book teaches central concepts and skills in an important area of the world of work. The set of eight books includes stress management, communication skills, employee motivation, leadership principles, quality of work life, managing for excellence, employee participation, and the role of ethics.

Each book combines theory with practice, gives commonsense answers to real-life problems, and is easy to read and fun to use. The series may be used as a set or as stand-alone books. The subject areas are made more forceful and the impact greater by the self-evaluation questionnaires and practical exercises that are used for personal development.

## AUDIENCE

*The Human Side of Work* is written for two audiences. One audience includes managers and professionals interested in personal and professional development on their own or within the context of a management development program. Another audience includes students in human relations, organization behavior, and other management-related courses.

The material is appropriate for use at the four-year college and university level as well as in community colleges, proprietary schools, extension programs, and management training seminars.

## CONTENT AND STYLE

The difference between most organization behavior texts and *The Human Side of Work* can be compared to the difference between a lecture and a seminar. Although both are good educational vehicles, the lecture is better for conveying large amounts of information, while the seminar is better for developing skills. The good lecture is interesting and builds knowledge; the good seminar is stimulating and builds competency. *The Human Side of Work* emphasizes the interactive, seminar approach to learning.

The writing style is personal and conversational, with minimal professional jargon. True-life examples clarify points under consideration. Concepts are supported by stories and anecdotes, which are more meaningful and easy to remember than facts, figures, and lists. Each book includes learning activities to bridge the gap between classroom theory and on-the-job practice.

*The Human Side of Work* is more than a series of textbooks. These are "learning" books that actively involve the reader in the learning process. Our goal has been to include material that is interesting to read, relates to the reader's own concerns, and is practical to use. The following captures the spirit of our effort:

### I Taught Them All

I have taught in high school for ten years. During that time, I have given assignments, among others, to a murderer, an evangelist, a pugilist, a thief, and an imbecile.

The murderer was a quiet little boy who sat on the front seat and regarded me with pale blue eyes; the evangelist, easily the most popular boy in school, had the lead in the junior class play; the pugilist lounged by the window and let loose at intervals with a raucous laugh that startled even the geraniums; the thief was a gay-hearted Lothario with a song on his lips; and the imbecile, a soft-eyed little animal seeking the shadows.

The murderer awaits death in the state penitentiary; the evangelist has lain a year in the village churchyard; the pugilist lost an eye in a brawl in Hong Kong; the thief, by standing on tiptoe, can see the windows of my room from the county jail; and the once gentle-eyed little moron beats his head against a padded wall in the state asylum.

All of these young men once sat in my room, sat and looked at me gravely across worn brown desks. I must have been a great help to those pupils—I taught them the rhyming scheme of the Elizabethan sonnet and how to diagram a complex sentence.

*Naomi John White*

The focus of *The Human Side of Work* is self-discovery and personal development as the reader "learns by doing." The material covered is authoritative and up to date, reflecting current theory and practices. The level of material is appropriate for all levels of expertise (new and experienced managers) and all levels of education (undergraduate and graduate).

## TESTING AND REVIEW PROCESS

*The Human Side of Work* has been tested and refined in our classes at Northern Kentucky University. The information and activities have been used with hundreds of organizations and thousands of employees in business, industry, and government. Users include American Telephone and Telegraph Co., International Business Machines Corp., John Hancock, Marriott Corporation, Sun Oil, and Ford Motor Co. in the private sector and the Department of Transportation, the Environmental Protection Agency, the Internal Revenue Service, the National Institutes of

Health, and state governments in the public sector.
The following are sample evaluations:

Good for student participation. My students like the exercises and learning instruments, and the fact each is a stand-alone book that is bite-size. Their reaction: "Everyone should read them!"

*Joseph F. Ohren, Eastern Michigan University*

A comprehensive series dealing with employee development and job performance. Information is presented in an interesting and easy-to-use style. Case studies and readings help teach the topics, and applications make the material more meaningful. It is an excellent guide for the practicing manager. Ideal as desk books.

*David Duncan, IBM*

I am a non-traditional student. As one who has worked for over twenty years, I thoroughly enjoyed the material. An understanding of the world of work is presented in a way that is usable at any level of an organization. The books present a common sense approach to management.

*Naomi Miller, Northern Kentucky University*

Best I've seen on the people side of work. Helps the person. Helps the company. Good for personal and management development. Popular with participants from all backgrounds.

*Charles Apple, University of Michigan*

This is an easy-to-read, comprehensive series in organization behavior. It puts theory into relevant, usable terminology. Methods for identifying and solving human relations problems are pinpointed. It sets the stage for understanding how people, environment and situations interact in an organization.

*David Sprouse, AT&T*

# TEACHING FORMATS

*The Human Side of Work* is versatile and can be used in many formats:

- for seminars and training programs
- as classroom texts
- as supplemental information and activities

The following is a discussion of each option.

## Seminars and Training Programs

Books used for seminars and training programs should be selected to meet the objectives and needs of the participants — communication, stress, leadership, etc. Material can be mixed and matched for training programs in personal development, professional development, management development, and team building. Material in each book is appropriate for a variety of time periods: one-half day (3 to 4 hours), one full day (6 to 8 hours), and two full days (12 to 16 hours).

The books provide excellent learning activities and questionnaires to encourage participation and personalize the subject. Books then serve as "take-home" material for further reading and personal development. In this format, study quizzes are rarely used for grading, and homework assignments are seldom given. See the following table for appropriate audiences, program focus, and recommended books when using *The Human Side of Work* for seminars and training programs.

## Classroom Texts

The series is appropriate for use as texts in college courses in human relations, organization behavior, and organizational psychology. The following is a sample lesson plan using the set for a one-semester course:

| Week | Focus on the Person | |
|------|------|------|
| 1 | Stress | Part One, Part Two |
| 2 | Stress | Part Three, Part Four |
| 3 | Communication | Part One, Part Two |
| 4 | Communication | Part Three, Part Four |
| 5 | Human Behavior | Part One, Part Two |
| 6 | Human Behavior | Part Three |
| 7 | Ethics | Part One, Part Two |
| 8 | Ethics | Part Three, Part Four |

| Week | Focus on the Organization | |
|------|------|------|
| 9 | Morale | Part One, Part Two |
| 10 | Morale | Part Three |
| 11 | Leadership | Part One, Part Two |
| 12 | Leadership | Part Three, Part Four |

## USING THE HUMAN SIDE OF WORK FOR SEMINARS AND TRAINING PROGRAMS

| Appropriate Audiences | Program Focus | Recommended Books |
|---|---|---|
| Personal and professional development | Focus on the individual | * *Stress Without Distress: Rx for Burnout*<br>* *Communication: The Miracle of Dialogue*<br>* *Human Behavior: Why People Do What They Do*<br>* *Ethics at Work: Fire in a Dark World*<br>* *Morale: Quality of Work Life* (optional)<br>* *Performance: Managing for Excellence* (optional) |
| New and experienced managers | Focus on management | * *Morale: Quality of Work Life*<br>* *Leadership: Nine Keys to Success*<br>* *Performance: Managing for Excellence*<br>* *Groupstrength: Quality Circles at Work*<br>* *Stress Without Distress: Rx for Burnout* (optional)<br>* *Communication: The Miracle of Dialogue* (optional)<br>* *Human Behavior: Why People Do What They Do* (optional)<br>* *Ethics at Work: Fire in a Dark World* (optional) |
| Employee development and team building | Focus on the organization | * *Communication: The Miracle of Dialogue*<br>* *Morale: Quality of Work Life*<br>* *Groupstrength: Quality Circles at Work*<br>* *Stress Without Distress: Rx for Burnout* (optional)<br>* *Human Behavior: Why People Do What They Do* (optional)<br>* *Performance: Managing for Excellence* (optional) |

## Popular seminar and program titles with corresponding books are as follows:

| | |
|---|---|
| Managing Change: Personal and Professional Coping Skills | * *Stress Without Distress: Rx for Burnout* |
| Communication: One to One; One to Many | * *Communication: The Miracle of Dialogue* |
| Human Relations and the Nature of Man | * *Human Behavior: Why People Do What They Do* |
| Business Ethics and Corporate Culture | * *Ethics at Work: Fire in a Dark World* |
| Quality of Work Life | * *Morale: Quality of Work Life* |
| The Human Side of Management | * *Leadership: Nine Keys to Success* |
| Managing for Productivity: People Building Skills | * *Performance: Managing for Excellence* |
| Employee Involvement: If Japan Can Do It, Why Can't We? | * *Groupstrength: Quality Circles at Work* |

| 13 | Performance | Part One, Part Two |
| 14 | Performance | Part Three |
| 15 | Groupstrength | Part One, Part Two |
| 16 | Groupstrength | Part Three |

### Related Activities and Homework Assignments

| Week | Suggested Readings, Cases and Applications |
|---|---|
| 1 | *Anatomy of an Illness as Perceived by the Patient* (reading)<br>*The Price of Success* (case) |
| 2 | *Death of a Salesman* (reading)<br>*Scientific Relaxation* (application) |
| 3 | *Barriers and Gateways to Communications* (reading)<br>*The Power of Vocabulary* (application) |
| 4 | *The Dyadic Encounter* (application)<br>*Attitudes toward Women Working* (application) |
| 5 | *The Human Side of Enterprise* (reading)<br>*Significant People and Critical Events* (application) |
| 6 | *Values Auction* (application)<br>*Personal and Interpersonal Growth* (application) |
| 7 | *If Hitler Asked You to Electrocute a Stranger, Would You?* (reading)<br>*How Could the Jonestown Holocaust Have Occurred?* (reading) |
| 8 | *Values Flag* (application)<br>*The Kidney Machine* (application) |
| 9 | *Work* (reading)<br>*The Joe Bailey Problem* (application) |
| 10 | *The Coffee Break* (case)<br>*In Search of Excellence* (application) |
| 11 | *What Happened When I Gave Up the Good Life and Became President* (case)<br>*Black, Blue, and White* (case) |
| 12 | *The Forklift Fiasco* (case)<br>*Train the Trainers* (application) |
| 13 | *Games Mother Never Taught You* (reading)<br>*How Will You Spend Your Life?* (application) |

| 14 | *How to Manage Your Time: Everybody's No. 1 Problem* (reading) |
| | *Chrysler's Turnaround Strategy* (case) |
| 15 | *Groupthink* (reading) |
| | *The Dean Practices Participative Management* (case) |
| 16 | *Decisions, Decisions, Decisions* (reading) |
| | *The Bottleneck* (application) |

This format for a one-semester course uses selected readings, cases, and applications from all eight books. For a two-semester course, additional readings, cases, and applications are provided.

Another popular format is to use fewer books in a one-semester course, and to use these more thoroughly. The books can be selected by the instructor or the class. For example, stress, communication, morale, and leadership may be best suited for a given group.

## Testing and Grading

When using *The Human Side of Work* as classroom texts, study quizzes in each book can be used to evaluate content knowledge. Although quiz scores can be used to assign formal grades, students learn best when they are also asked to apply the concepts in some personal way. Examples include a term journal, a related research paper, a small-group project, a field assignment, and/or a self-improvement project.

Grades can be assigned on the basis of test scores and term project(s). Projects can be evaluated according to the three C's: clarity, comprehensiveness, and correctness. Half the course grade could be based on study quiz scores, and the other half on the term project(s).

## Supplemental Information and Activities

The books in *The Human Side of Work* can provide supplemental information and activities for various college courses. State-of-the-art questionnaires and user-friendly exercises add variety and increase student involvement. Books matched with appropriate college courses are as follows:

| Recommended Books | College Courses |
| --- | --- |
| *Stress Without Distress: Rx for Burnout* | Personal Development |
| | Personal Health |
| | Human Relations |
| | Organization Behavior |
| | Organizational Psychology |
| | Supervisory Development |

| | |
|---|---|
| *Communication: The Miracle of Dialogue* | Personal Development<br>Communications<br>Human Relations<br>Organization Behavior<br>Organizational Psychology<br>Supervisory Development |
| *Human Behavior: Why People Do What They Do* | Personal Development<br>Human Relations<br>Organization Behavior<br>Organizational Psychology<br>Supervisory Development |
| *Ethics at Work: Fire in a Dark World* | Personal Development<br>Business Ethics<br>Human Relations<br>Organization Behavior<br>Organizational Psychology<br>Supervisory Development |
| *Morale: Quality of Work Life* | Personnel/Human Resources<br>Human Relations<br>Organization Behavior<br>Organizational Psychology<br>Supervisory Development |
| *Leadership: Nine Keys to Success* | Management Principles<br>Human Relations<br>Organization Behavior<br>Organizational Psychology<br>Supervisory Development |
| *Performance: Managing for Excellence* | Management Principles<br>Human Relations<br>Organization Behavior<br>Organizational Psychology<br>Supervisory Development |
| *Groupstrength: Quality Circles at Work* | Personnel/Human Resources<br>Human Relations<br>Organization Behavior<br>Organizational Psychology<br>Supervisory Development |

When used as supplemental material, books are rarely tested for grades. The emphasis is on using the questionnaires, exercises, cases, and applications to increase interest and participation and to personalize the subject.

# APPENDIX B

## Additional References

# ADDITIONAL REFERENCES

The following books are recommended for further reading in the area of employee morale and the quality of work life. Each is included because of its significance in the field, support to this text, and value for further personal development.

Borow, Henry. *Man in a World of Work.* Boston: Houghton Mifflin Company, 1964.

Faulhes, Fred K. *Employee Benefits Handbook.* Boston: Warren, Gorham & Lamont, Inc., 1982.

Gellerman, Saul W. *Motivation and Productivity.* New York: American Management Association, 1963.

Levering, Robert, Milton Moskowitz, and Michael Katz. *The 100 Best Companies to Work For.* Reading, Mass.: Addison-Wesley Publishing Co., Inc., 1984.

Likert, Rensis. *The Human Organization: Its Management and Value.* New York: McGraw-Hill, Inc., 1967.

Likert, Rensis. *New Patterns of Management.* New York: McGraw-Hill, Inc., 1961.

Likert, Rensis. *New Ways of Managing Conflict.* New York: McGraw-Hill, Inc., 1976.

Litwin, George H., and Robert A. Stringer, Jr. *Motivation and Organizational Climate.* Cambridge, Mass: Harvard University, Graduate School of Business Administration, Division of Research, 1968.

Mayo, Elton. *The Human Problems of an Industrial Civilization.* New York: The Viking Press, 1960.

Mayo, Elton. *The Social Problems of an Industrial Civilization.* Cambridge, Mass.: Harvard University, Graduate School of Business Administration, Division of Research, 1945.

McCormick, Ernest J., and Joseph Tiffen. *Industrial Psychology.* 6th ed. Englewood Cliffs, N.J.: Prentice-Hall, Inc., 1974.

McKensie, Robert B. *Pay, Productivity and Collective Bargaining.* London: Macmillan Publishing Company; New York: St. Martin's Press, Inc., 1973.

Ouchi, William G. *Theory Z: How American Business Can Meet the Japanese Challenge*. Reading, Mass.: Addison-Wesley Publishing Co., Inc., 1981.

Peters, Thomas J., and Robert H. Waterman. *In Search of Excellence: Lessons from America's Best-Run Companies*. New York: Harper & Row, Publishers, Inc., 1982.

Roethlisberger, Fritz J. *Management and Morale*. Cambridge, Mass.: Harvard University Press, 1975.

Roethlisberger, Fritz J., William J. Dickson. *Management and the Worker*. Cambridge, Mass.: Harvard University Press, 1939.

Sobel, Robert. *IBM: Colossus in Transition*. New York: Times Books, 1981.

Tilgher, Adriano. *Work: What It Has Meant to Men Through the Ages*. New York: Arno Press, 1977.

Watson, Thomas J., Jr. *A Business and Its Beliefs: The Ideas That Helped Build IBM*. New York: McGraw-Hill, Inc., 1963.

Weitzel, Harry J. *Incentive Compensation: A Management Catalyst*. Boston: Financial Publishing Co., 1972.

# APPENDIX C

## Suggested Films

The following films are excellent learning aids. These are supplementary media that can enrich a class or training program. They are ideal for small-group discussion, panel debates, and question-and-answer periods. Topics are listed in the order in which they appear in the text.

## UNDERSTANDING HUMAN BEHAVIOR IN THE ORGANIZATION
### (Document Associates, 26 min.)

How can knowledge of human behavior help in designing more effective organizations? In recent years, many scientific developments have been applied to organizations. This film examines ways organizations can benefit from new insights into the psychology of the individual, as presented by management author Harry Levinson.

Document Associates, Inc.
211 East 43rd Street
New York, N. Y. 10017

## THE PEOPLE FACTOR: THE HAWTHORNE STUDIES
### (Salenger, 15 min.)

Using original footage from the 1920s, this film shows the actual place, people, and events that led psychologists to advocate a humanistic approach to management. In 1924 the Hawthorne Works of Western Electric conducted a sequence of experiments originally designed to increase productivity by improving the physical environment.

Salenger Educational Media
1635 12th Street
Santa Monica, Calif. 90404

## UNDERSTANDING MOTIVATION
### (BNA, 30 min.)

Management author Saul Gellerman explains the theories of behavioral science. To help us understand better why changes in the environment affect employee motivation, he cites these findings: that nearly everyone regards his or her own behavior as sensible and justifiable; that a person's motivation for action, positive or negative, is a product of the world that person thinks he or she lives in; and, most important, that the rank-and-file employee sees his or her world as a far different world from that of the manager. To illustrate this thesis, a dramatized episode explores workers' reasons for restricting output and examines their rationales for negative behavior.

BNA Films
5615 Fishers Lane
Rockville, Md. 20852

## WILMAR EIGHT
### (California Newsreel, 50 min.)

The true story of eight brave women and their struggle to overcome prejudice and discrimination in the banking industry. This is a powerful docudrama that both male and female viewers will find moving. Award winner. Highest rating.

California Newsreel
630 Natoma Street
San Francisco, Calif. 94103

## THE LIFE AND TIMES OF ROSIE THE RIVETER
### (CLA, 40 min.)

The United States' entry into World War II created an unprecedented demand for new workers. Notions of what was proper work for women changed overnight as woman were called to "do the job he left behind." Rosie the Riveter became the symbol of working women during World War II. Women discovered a new sense of pride in their work, but when the war was over and the men returned, Rosie found prewar views on women's place in society dominating the country once again.

Clarity Educational Products
P.O. Box 315
Franklin Lakes, N.J. 07414

## WITH BABIES AND BANNERS
### (New Day Films, 45 min.)

Layoffs. Speedups. Hazardous working conditions. These were daily realities for auto workers in the 1930s. Women workers suffered the added hardships of lower wages, sexual harassment on the job, and limited opportunities. Job pressures often strained the relationship between a working man and his wife, a father and his children. A working woman found something more in her home—another day's work to do.

New Day Films
P.O. Box 315
Franklin Lakes, N.J. 07414

## STAFFING FOR STRENGTH
### (BNA, 25 min.)

The action shows three managers' dealings with their subordinates. After reviewing their problems, management consultant Peter Drucker advises: don't promote a person into a job for which he or she is not qualified; don't hesitate to pay a capable researcher more than his or her boss if you wish to reward and keep the researcher; and introspect constantly regarding the data to give to others to make them more effective.

BNA Films
5615 Fishers Lane
Rockville, Md. 20852

## MOTIVATION: IT'S NOT JUST THE MONEY
### (Document Associates, 26 min.)

This film takes a look at the Volvo auto plant in Sweden, where an innovative approach to manufacturing has been established to fulfill the human needs of employees. Shown are the plant's efforts to increase employee participation in decision making.

Document Associates, Inc.
211 East 43rd Street
New York, N. Y. 10017

## PAY FOR PERFORMANCE
### (BNA, 30 min.)

Two problems—the behavioral effects of pay and goal setting—are examined by Emanuel Kay, Saul Gellerman's partner and former field director of General Electric's Performance Appraisal Study. Kay grants that an open pay program is harder to administer than one based on secrecy. However, a system having equitability and open communication about pay policies can better use pay as a motivator in support of nonfinancial incentives. In a dramatic domestic scene, a wife tries to learn of the pay policies of her husband's company; he admits he doesn't know, and her nagging him to ask for a raise leaves him more baffled than ever.

Goal setting may replace performance appraisal programs. Instead of acting as a judge with the subordinate as defendant, the supervisor works out with each employee mutually agreed-on work targets and time limits. Kay cites examples of goal setting, including a dramatized episode showing a salesman and his sales manager "feeling their way" through their goal setting sessions.

BNA Films
5615 Fishers Lane
Rockville, Md. 20852

## WORKING WITH TROUBLED EMPLOYEES
(BNA, 30 min.)

Every supervisor probably has at least one employee who causes more difficulty than all of the others put together. The supervisor may have hesitated to tackle the problem because he or she doesn't know how to approach it — or even to identify it.

Harry Levinson illustrates two common types of troubled worker — the depressed employee and the overly aggressive employee — and gives tips on how to distinguish emotional troubles from behavior associated with disciplinary action or low morale. He also outlines the supervisor's role in dealing with troubled employees — warning them especially not to play therapist but also not to procrastinate because of guilt feelings or out of sympathy.

BNA Films
5615 Fishers Lane
Rockville, Md. 20852

## CONTROLLING ABSENTEEISM
(BNA, 30 min.)

Saul Gellerman zeros in on the causes of absenteeism and offers practical measures to curb it. According to Gellerman, absentees fall into five categories: the chronic absentee, the escapist, the immature absentee, the abusive absentee, and the legitimate absentee. Each presents a different problem, and each requires a different approach.

BNA Films
5615 Fisher Lane
Rockville, Md. 20852

## THE MANAGEMENT OF HUMAN ASSETS
(BNA, 30 min.)

Rensis Likert explains how to rate an organization to describe its prevailing management system. The scale runs from System I, an arbitrary, highly authoritarian management style (rare today in its "pure" form) through System IV, a highly participative system. System IV firms are most likely to have a record of sustained high productivity, good labor relations, and high profitability. A dramatized sequence demonstrates that an organization, in an effort to cut costs, may lean toward System I, but in doing so sacrifices employee loyalty and operating efficiency.

BNA Films
5615 Fishers Lane
Rockville, Md. 20852

## ORGANIZATIONAL CLIMATE
(CRM, 27 min.)

Managers play an important role in creating a work environment that motivates and satisfies employees. Steps are presented to help employees be more productive. Award winner.

CRM Educational Films
Del Mar, Calif. 92014

## IN SEARCH OF EXCELLENCE: LESSONS FROM AMERICA'S BEST-RUN COMPANIES
(PBS, 90 min.)

This is an award-winning film about America's best run companies and the eight attributes that make them great. It is based on the best-selling book by the same title and is ideal for people of all ages. Especially recommended for business audiences. Highest rating.

Public Broadcasting System Video
475 L'Enfant Plaza, S.W.
Washington, D.C. 20024

# APPENDIX D

## Parts One, Two, and Three
## Study Quiz Answers

# STUDY QUIZ ANSWERS

| Part One | Part Two | Part Three |
|----------|----------|------------|
| 1. d | 1. a | 1. c |
| 2. b | 2. d | 2. a |
| 3. c | 3. b | 3. a |
| 4. a | 4. c | 4. c |
| 5. i | 5. c | 5. d |
| 6. c | 6. a | 6. b |
| 7. a | 7. d | 7. b |
| 8. c | 8. a | 8. c |
| 9. a | 9. a | 9. a |
| 10. c | 10. a | 10. a |
| 11. d | 11. b | 11. d |
| 12. a | 12. b | 12. d |
| 13. d | 13. b | 13. e |
| 14. c | 14. b | 14. a |
| 15. d | 15. c | 15. d |
| 16. c | 16. d | 16. c |
| 17. c | 17. b | |
| 18. b | 18. b | |
| 19. a | 19. c | |
| 20. a | 20. a | |
| 21. a | 21. d | |
| | 22. a | |
| | 23. a | |
| | 24. e | |

# APPENDIX E

## The Relationship of the Quiz Questions and the Discussion and Activities to the Part Objectives

The following chart shows the relationship of the Quiz Questions and the Discussion and Activities to the Part Objectives:

## PART ONE

| Objective Number | Quiz (Q), Discussion and Activities (D & A) | Objective Number | Quiz (Q), Discussion and Activities (D & A) |
|---|---|---|---|
| 1 | Q: 4,14<br>D & A: 1 | 4 | Q: 1, 3, 8, 12, 16<br>D & A: 3, 4, 5 |
| 2 | Q: 2, 6, 9, 10, 11, 20<br>D & A: 1, 5 | 5 | Q: 7, 13, 19<br>D & A: 1 |
| 3 | Q: 17, 18, 21<br>D & A: 2, 6 | 6 | Q: 5, 15<br>D & A: 3, 4 |

## PART TWO

| Objective Number | Quiz (Q), Discussion and Activities (D & A) | Objective Number | Quiz (Q), Discussion and Activities (D & A) |
|---|---|---|---|
| 1 | Q: 2, 3, 4, 6, 14, 19, 20, 24<br>D & A: 1 | 3 | Q: 4, 5, 7, 8, 11, 14, 15, 16, 17, 18, 22<br>D & A: 3, 4 |
| 2 | Q: 1, 23<br>D & A: 2 | 4 | Q: 9, 10, 12, 13, 21<br>D & A: 5 |

## PART THREE

| Objective Number | Quiz (Q), Discussion and Activities (D & A) | Objective Number | Quiz (Q), Discussion and Activities (D & A) |
|---|---|---|---|
| 1 | Q: 7, 8, 11<br>D & A: 1, 4 | 4 | Q: 4, 5, 12, 13<br>D & A: 4, 5 |
| 2 | Q: 6, 15<br>D & A: 2 | 5 | Q: 16<br>D & A: 4, 5 |
| 3 | Q: 1, 2, 3, 9, 10, 14, 15<br>D & A: 1, 3, 5 | | |